Between Grief and Nothing

ALSO BY LISA C. HICKMAN
AND FROM McFARLAND

*William Faulkner and Joan Williams:
The Romance of Two Writers* (2006)

Between Grief and Nothing

The Passions, Addictions and Tragic End of William Faulkner

LISA C. HICKMAN

McFarland & Company, Inc., Publishers
Jefferson, North Carolina

LIBRARY OF CONGRESS CATALOGING-IN-PUBLICATION DATA

Names: Hickman, Lisa C., 1959– author.
Title: Between grief and nothing : the passions, addictions and tragic end of William Faulkner / Lisa C. Hickman.
Description: Jefferson, North Carolina : McFarland & Company, Inc., 2025 | Includes bibliographical references and index.
Identifiers: LCCN 2024044950 | ISBN 9781476696058 (paperback : acid free paper) ∞ ISBN 9781476654287 (ebook)
Subjects: LCSH: Faulkner, William, 1897-1962. | Faulkner, William, 1897-1962—Mental health. | Novelists, American—20th century—Biography. | Alcoholics—United States—Biography. | Mental health services—United States—History—20th century.
Classification: LCC PS3511.A86 Z7872 2024 | DDC 813/.52 [B]—dc23/eng/20241122
LC record available at https://lccn.loc.gov/2024044950

ISBN (print) 978-1-4766-9605-8
ISBN (ebook) 978-1-4766-5428-7

© 2025 Lisa C. Hickman. All rights reserved

No part of this book may be reproduced or transmitted in any form or by any means, electronic or mechanical, including photocopying or recording, or by any information storage and retrieval system, without permission in writing from the publisher.

Front cover image: William Faulkner and Victoria Fielden Johnson at Rowan Oak, spring 1962. Faulkner dedicated his final novel, *The Reivers*, to his and Estelle's grandchildren. A few months before his death, he said to Vicki, the eldest, "'Vic-Pic, the best part it's that it's dedicated to you and my other grandchildren, and you head the list...' And he was just smiling all over himself," Vicki said, "and he was happy, and you could see that Grandmama was happy; she was sharing it with him right there" (Martin J. Dain Collection, Archives and Special Collections, J.D. Williams Library, The University of Mississippi).

Printed in the United States of America

McFarland & Company, Inc., Publishers
   Box 611, Jefferson, North Carolina 28640
       www.mcfarlandpub.com

For my dad,
Jerome Carl Jacobs
"Motivator Extraordinaire"

∼

And for James, Catherine, Claire, Taryn—keep going!

"It's—well, he [the writer] has a, as we all do, an awareness of death, that he will not be here forever, that—that the end can be for him tomorrow."
—William Faulkner, May 15, 1958
Washington and Lee University

"Biography lends to death a fresh horror."
—Oscar Wilde

Acknowledgments

First and foremost, thanks to my husband, Jess Bunn, for his unfailing help and support. It's a lot!

Much appreciation to Jack D. Elliott, Jr., for introducing me to the Castleberrys and expanding my knowledge of Wright's Sanatorium. Special recognition to James C. Castleberry and Karen S. Castleberry (1943–2021) for identifying and sharing valuable information. Also in Byhalia, Mississippi, and with great thanks—Elizabeth and William D. Fitts III; Adolphus and JoAnn Shipp.

Our children, James in spirit, Jeffrey and Jordan are always a source of inspiration. Nothing happens without encouragement from family and friends, particularly early readers Susan Davis, Susannah Northart, and Karen Wright; and to my good fortune, the positivity of an enduring ballet class. Thanks to Maria Thomas for her interest and helping us hold down the home front. Invaluable also were the ongoing assistance and good wishes of Tom Epperson, Ezra D. Bowen, and Matthew W. Bowen, PhD.

The *Los Angeles Review of Books* for featuring a chapter from the manuscript, "The Road to Glory: Faulkner's Hollywood Years, 1932–1936" (27 February 2020). Irish film director Sarah Share and singer and songwriter John Murry for their belief in this book and including me in Sarah's wonderful documentary, *The Graceless Age: The Ballad of John Murry*.

Special Collections at the University of Mississippi—Leigh McWhite, Lauren Rogers, Michelle Emanuel, and Jennifer Ford—for their assistance with images from the Martin J. Dain collection.

With gratitude to all!

Table of Contents

Acknowledgments viii
Preface 1
Introduction 3

ONE. Stonewall Road: 1962   11
TWO. The Old Country Club: Circa 1948   19
THREE. Estelle   34
FOUR. The Road to Glory: 1932–1936   48
FIVE. The Past Is Past: 1936–1937   65
SIX. Southern Danger: 1940–1947   75
SEVEN. Enter Joan Williams: 1949   91
EIGHT. New York and Trouble Follows: 1948–1949   102
NINE. Per Aspera ad Astra: 1950   113
TEN. Spooked: 1951   131
ELEVEN. Superlative: 1952   138
TWELVE. I Wont Stop In: 1953   155
THIRTEEN. Mississippi Ghosts: 1962   182

Chapter Notes 195
Bibliography 203
Index 207

Preface

Stories originate in unusual ways, and once they materialize, insist on being told. On a drive from Oxford, Mississippi, to Memphis, Tennessee, with novelist Joan Williams—I can't remember why we'd been in Oxford—she insisted we pull over. We were on Highway 78 near Byhalia, Mississippi. She said that's the place William Faulkner died! Joan and Faulkner had a long friendship and for several years a searing romance. We made our way to the former site of Wright's Sanatorium. It was a nice day and we walked around exploring the vacant structures with peeling white paint and remnants of green-trim shutters. Joan pointed out what was left of the small cabins that offered more privacy to the couples who were drying out together. We both marveled at that concept. She also related a chilling story a nurse told her about the night Faulkner died.

Some years later when I heard from Mississippi State scholar Jack Elliott about Karen and James Castleberry's discovery at the old Wright's location I was intrigued. The biographies I'd read shed little light on the sanatorium, Faulkner's death, or his hasty funeral. When I met the Castleberrys at their home in Byhalia, Karen still had a *Memphis Magazine* piece I'd written about Faulkner's two treating psychiatrists and the Gartly-Ramsay Hospital in Memphis. She believed Wright's Sanatorium likewise would be a fascinating feature. She'd been a careful guardian of the recovered records and shared much of the material with Jack Elliott and me. In addition to the Castleberrys' preservation and Jack Elliott's expertise, I was fortunate to meet two individuals with a close association to Wright's, William D. Fitts III and Adolphus Shipp; what's more, they were willing to share their recollections. Their memories and the documents helped me envision the need Dr. Wright was trying to meet and the sanatorium's atmosphere.

Originally I envisioned a magazine article but it soon was evident there was more to explore. The context expanded. It wasn't simply the intriguing history of Wright's, with the moniker, "The Old Country Club," but how Faulkner's life intersected not only with Wright's but also with many other hospitals and sanatoria. What personality traits, demons, and life events led him to such places? Was it the unfortunate but frequent overlap of genius and mental instability? Faulkner evidenced a highly addictive personality: rotating love affairs that fed his rich interior world; unrestrained episodes of alcohol abuse mixed with the barbiturate Seconal; and horsemanship that bordered on the maniacal. The book took shape as a targeted look at those forces and ultimately Faulkner's death.

The confluence of a sanatorium tucked away in rural Mississippi and the state's most famous author, a Nobel Prize laureate no less, promised to be a first-class tale. Southern Gothicism, extreme behavior, and human vulnerability all find expression in this book.

Introduction

William Faulkner's broad strokes on writing—that it was the only way to say "no" to death and the only way to alleviate the boredom of living—gained more relevancy with age. His soaring highs and intense periods of dejection were not unlike those of other authors whose creative impulses dominated their day-to-day existence. But Faulkner, a novelist known for his eccentricities and dramatic flairs, was always treading carefully between his work and his domestic sphere. A volatile marriage, roiling love affairs, and increased evidence of addictions dominated the tenor of his mature years. Faulkner's passions fervently guided his life and his art—passions that led to an enthusiastic and elaborate dream world from which his brilliance and madness both erupted. Work was his steadying force; should that fail him, Faulkner was vulnerable to dangerous pastimes and the ever-present culture of alcohol abuse.

Faulkner's excesses—the purchase of Rowan Oak, a dilapidated antebellum home in need of vast repairs, on a struggling writer's income with a wife and small children; the subsequent purchase of a farm and airplane; the roving from one love affair to another with much younger women; fabricating a distinguished military background only to have to walk the story back; the debilitating drinking bouts; the long and stressful Hollywood stints as a script writer; the social whirl of New York and the expectations of his agents, editors and publishers; the world travel that taxed him physically and emotionally—led to inevitable breakdowns. The overspending, rampant romancing, and the intensity of his often-manic writing ended all too frequently in a fog of drugs, alcohol, hallucinations, and hospitalizations.

Still, weakness was not a trait he wished others to see in him: he preferred to present himself as moneyed, handsome, desired, and esteemed, though the reality was often quite different. An admirer of the military, he hoped to contribute to his country's effort in World War I. Those hopes were dashed when the U.S. Army Air Force ruled him ineligible due to his short stature. He then managed in 1918 to enlist in the Royal Air Force in Canada by assuming a British identity and feigning a British accent. While he did receive some pilot training as a cadet, the war ended before he saw any combat, and he was granted an honorable discharge. That was hardly the story he wanted to tell. Instead, he purchased an RAF uniform—lieutenant's rank—complete with a pair of wings on the left breast from the Royal Flying Corps, the RAF's more glamorous and storied predecessor. Upon his return to Oxford, he ceremoniously strolled the square in uniform with a rattan swagger stick. For those willing to listen, he shared stories of his military valor and fabricated injuries including a silver plate in his skull.

Clearly he was grasping for machismo. His slight frame and height were impediments to the period's concepts of masculinity. He needed something besides the classic southern traditions of hunting and hard drinking to bolster his brief RAF experience. He appeared to settle on horses and reckless riding, purposefully choosing headstrong steeds he could claim to have mastered. His back and head injuries from being thrown or falling from the saddle accumulated as did inebriated tumbles down the stairs at Rowan Oak. All these mishaps battered his body—at one point tests revealed a broken back—but the injuries offered another form of boastful bravado.

By 1935, Faulkner's anxieties were mounting. He was married to childhood sweetheart Estelle Oldham and father to a young daughter, Jill, as well as Estelle's two children from her first marriage. From the outset, the couple faced a series of tragedies. Their firstborn, Alabama, died a few days after her birth in 1931; a year later, Faulkner's father suddenly died of a heart attack; and in November 1935, Faulkner's youngest brother, Dean, was killed in a plane crash. Not only were they exhausted emotionally, but also the family was in dire need of cash. When Hollywood came knocking in December, proffering a financial lifeline, Faulkner was in no position to turn the offer down.

But he struggled with the Hollywood assignments and his own work. He already was an acclaimed literary talent, and the scriptwriters he met in Hollywood took note of his achievements. Numerous short stories had appeared in popular magazines; and his novels *The Sound and the Fury*, *As I Lay Dying* and *Light in August* were recognized masterpieces. His current effort, *Absalom, Absalom!*, promised to be no less remarkable. Yet the creator of Yoknapatawpha County, Faulkner's fictional kingdom, was careening between euphoria and despair. His youthful genius and talent was matched by an early proclivity to alcohol abuse fueled by anxiety and depression. Physical maladies compounded his emotional disturbances. His answer to chronic back pain was alcohol and Seconal. For years his drinking episodes rarely merited much attention. Such behavior was often considered the purview of men, especially southern men.

But in January 1936 what had been ordinary became unordinary. Upon his return from Hollywood and after completing the manuscript for *Absalom, Absalom!*, Faulkner found himself hospitalized for drinking. That dynamic changed his trajectory. The forward momentum was now circular. The cycle of addiction seized control.

These chemical addictions were particularly dangerous for Faulkner: his brain was considered hypersensitive to alcohol and near the borderline of abnormality.[1] Worse, any form of mental unease produced even less resistance to alcohol, and Faulkner's home life was rife with emotional disequilibrium—and liquor. His wife, Estelle, faced her own alcoholism, mental instability, and poor health, and the couple's battles raged with more frequency than the occasional truce. For Faulkner, they often devolved into madness and misery. A 1936 hospitalization was followed by another episode eight months later; another the next year, April 1937; and then again in 1948, 1949, 1950, and 1951. But the final descending spiral began in earnest in 1952, when Faulkner wrote often of his despair, "Never in my life have I ever been so unhappy and depressed."[2]

* * *

In a way, the Nobel Prize–winning novelist became his own fictional creation, and no one understood better the complexity of such an undertaking. He mirrored the intricate and nearly unfathomable characters he conceived in stories and novels. During class sessions at the University of Virginia when he was writer-in-residence in 1957 and 1958, students asked about these puzzling characters. Speaking about *Absalom, Absalom!*, Faulkner succinctly summarized the novel as "The story of a man [Thomas Sutpen] who wanted a son and got too many, got so many that they destroyed him."[3] A second question proved more troublesome. Did anyone in the novel who spoke of Sutpen actually know Sutpen? Faulkner addressed narrative reliability: "Every time any character gets into a book, no matter how minor, he's actually telling his biography—that's all anyone ever does, he tells his own biography, talking about himself, in a thousand different terms, but himself."[4] And he acknowledged the inherent difficulty of truth and perception:

> I think that—that no one individual can—can look at truth. It—it—it blinds you. You look at it, and—and you—you see one phase of it. Someone else looks at it and sees a slightly awry phase of it, but taken all together, the truth is— is in what they saw, though nobody saw the truth intact.... It is, as you say, thirteen ways [of] looking at a blackbird. But the truth, I would like to think, comes out, that when the reader has read all these thirteen different ways of looking at the blackbird, the reader has his own fourteenth image of that blackbird, which I would like to think is the true one.[5]

Discovering Faulkner's elusive fourteenth image may rest with exploring the darker and more difficult years. The euphoric and triumphant early publications, when it seemed like one success miraculously and effortlessly followed another, naturally have garnered the spotlight. The publications that came toward the end, with the exception of *The Reivers*, were dutifully if doggedly composed. Faulkner would write letters describing the labored process. Complicating this trying creative period was *A Fable*, his "magnum o" as he sometimes called it, or the big book. Faulkner's books generally had a significant gestation period and *A Fable* must have been near the top in longevity. No one will know exactly when the novel's idea first presented itself, but he talks about the composition as early as 1943, though it would not be published until 1954.

Some speculated that part of the difficulty was the book's European setting. It had been many years since Faulkner set a piece outside of the customary southern milieu. Another contributor to the torpor may have been the author's lofty and philosophical motives. This early outline that Faulkner shared with his agent Harold Ober in 1943 might well have been a harbinger—"It is *A Fable*, an indictment of war perhaps ... it continues on, through the Three Temptations, the Crucifixion, the Resurrection. The Epilogue is an Armistice Day ceremony at the tomb of the Unknown Soldier."[6] Faulkner's feelings toward *A Fable* mirrored the emotional roller coaster of his life—fatigue, frustration, anticipation, and sometimes, tenderness. Reading his various letters, the novel appears an albatross: he was in too deep to discard the book but writing it brought him little pleasure.

* * *

A telling anecdote: Faulkner's psychosis came to the fore in 1951. He and Estelle and their daughter, Jill, were driving to Wellesley, Massachusetts, so Jill could begin her first year at Pine Manor Junior College. One of Faulkner's Random House editors, Robert Linscott, thought he had a real treat in store for the family: He arranged for an overnight stay in South Sudbury at the Wayside Inn, the home of Henry Wadsworth Longfellow. Though the inn was by then primarily a museum, Linscott made sure Faulkner and Estelle would have Longfellow's largely untouched former bedchamber. When the travelers arrived, the idea so upset Faulkner that they drove on, hoping to find another hotel. Unsuccessful, they returned to South Sudbury and asked for different accommodations. Instead of enjoying drinks with Linscott by the fire in the old barroom—the setting for Longfellow's collection of poems, *Tales of a Wayside Inn*—Faulkner bolted. He spent the evening wandering unfamiliar backroads, walking in a panicked daze. In the morning, he told Linscott that Longfellow's ghost had thoroughly unnerved him. The harrowing and sleepless night signaled an imminent mental breakdown.

Of the various hospitals and sanitoria where Faulkner was treated, the Leonard Wright Sanatorium in Byhalia, Mississippi, 46 miles northwest of Oxford, had for years held a unique marker. In his double biography published in 1974, Joseph Blotner listed Wright's as the site of Faulkner's first hospitalization for drinking and the site of his death. It has taken fifty years to correct the notion that Wright's bookmarked both those events. When new owners, James and Karen Castleberry, purchased the property in 1989 they discovered records under a stairwell at the abandoned sanatorium.[7] That discovery led to communications with Jack Elliott. Elliott's research confirmed that Wright's was built and operating circa 1948.[8] These recovered documents, including Faulkner's final bill sent to Mrs. Faulkner, provide a heretofore unknown window into Faulkner's care and condition.[9]

Wright's storied history goes well beyond Faulkner's involvement. The fascinating institution and others like it were part and parcel of southern culture at the time. It was a sheltering and, some would say, pampering environment to recover from excessive drinking and drug use. As it was a private facility, patient expenses were out of pocket. (Faulkner complained about the price of such recovery, even more so when it was his wife who needed the care.) The sanatorium went above and beyond to ensure privacy and restore health to their clientele.

* * *

When Faulkner would go off the cliff it generally involved the end of a love affair. A borrowed line from a character in his novel *The Wild Palms* became a near mantra. "Between grief and nothing, I will take grief," he would tell his love interests or write the same in letters.[10] These affairs seemingly were another form of addiction. He wrote literary scholar Malcolm Cowley in 1946 that "It's a dull life here. I need some new people, above all probably a new young woman."[11] His obsessive fantasies kept his mind active and distracted. Letters served as another outlet when distance separated him from a romantic interest. He constructed elaborate plans to meet, sending bus, plane, and train schedules. Telegrams were another favorite form of communicating travel itineraries (more times than not the rendezvous failed to occur). Sometimes he even suggested appropriate attire for the various clandestine dates. Stranger yet, he involved Estelle in his intrigues—Faulkner at times would orchestrate social events involving the young women and his wife, inviting a furor.

His ascending literary fame also spelled trouble. A shy nature such as his was hardly suited to the spotlight, and along with recognition came unwelcome attention. Feeling pressured and uncomfortable in many social situations—the seemingly endless round of New York cocktail parties, Hollywood dinners and events, interviews with the press—his response was to drink. It might stay under control, or it might initiate a bender. As his world expanded far beyond Oxford, a host of luminaries entered his orbit.

Colorful exploits began to circulate: his appearance in the Beverly Hills Hotel lobby with a deer rifle following a wild boar hunting expedition with Nathanael West or passing out on the shoulder of Mrs. James Thurber after the Rose Bowl. Suddenly, he was socializing with such celebrated and creative artists as Clark Gable, Humphrey Bogart, Lauren Bacall, Claudette Colbert, Juana Hernández, Ernest Hemingway, Albert Camus, Truman Capote, Dorothy Parker, Dylan Thomas, and John O'Hara. Life was much more interesting but also brimming with temptations.

In December of 1935 while working in Hollywood, he became involved with fellow southerner Meta Dougherty Carpenter, soon to be Meta Rebner. Meta was an assistant to movie director Howard Hawks with whom Faulkner became acquainted in 1932. This burgeoning affair coincided with completing *Absalom, Absalom!*, and when he returned to Rowan Oak in January 1936 the stress of the novel, Hollywood, and trying to hide the love affair landed him in the Gartly-Ramsay Hospital in Memphis, Tennessee, more than seventy-five miles from Oxford. Disturbances within the Faulkner household escalated rapidly when Estelle discovered the true nature of her husband's involvement with Meta. After Meta told Faulkner in the fall of 1936 that she intended to marry Austrian pianist Wolfgang Rebner, another hospitalization occurred, this time at the Cedars of Lebanon Hospital in Los Angeles; and when Meta and Wolfgang's actual wedding took place in April 1937, a third hospitalization was arranged, in Los Angeles at the Good Samaritan Hospital. Meta and Wolfgang twice married and divorced. In between breakups and reunions, Meta and Faulkner rekindled their relationship. The tremendous strife provoked by these dalliances coursed through his marriage to Estelle and accelerated her alcoholism. Estelle, likewise, was treated at Wright's Sanatorium.[12]

* * *

For the years between 1936 and 1948, there were a handful of acknowledged alcoholic episodes troublesome enough to require professional care; but at the age of 55, with more success and financial security than he previously had known, Faulkner's life was in free fall. This last decade of his life involved 17 reported hospital, sanatorium, or sanitarium stays. The troubles of that decade—a virtual roller coaster of medical interventions—began in earnest when his friendship and mentorship with aspiring Memphis writer Joan Williams metamorphosed into a love affair. At the same time, he was pursuing Else Jonsson, a widow whom he met in Stockholm while receiving the Nobel Prize. Faulkner was a household name in the Jonsson residence. Else's husband had been a journalist and traveled to Oxford to meet Faulkner, announcing in 1946, four years before it occurred, that Faulkner would one day receive the Nobel.

Else and Faulkner's friendship advanced rapidly but intermittently due to sheer distance. Ruth Ford, a young actress from Oxford who had dated Faulkner's brother, Dean, was in his sights as well. They worked in Hollywood together and she asked him to write a play for her. Thus, at the behest of Ruth, he tackled playwriting. Ironically, he seemed ill-suited for the genre even with his screenwriting experience. The challenges *Requiem for a Nun* presented, while minor in relation to *A Fable*, nonetheless troubled him.

Faulkner was insecure in the romance with Joan, thirty years his junior, that began in 1949 and ended the winter of 1953. He was serious enough about Joan to follow her to New York and to discuss marriage, although his clumsy proposal left her speechless: Should he tell Estelle that he and Joan wanted to marry? Joan couldn't reconcile his mentioning his wife along with a so-called proposal. Their ups and downs contributed to his drinking bouts. There was something powerful about Joan and their relationship that was more meaningful and consequential than the others. Faulkner's physical, mental, and emotional health spiraled when it ended.

His last reported involvement was with Jean Stein, a 19-year-old American student studying at the Sorbonne in Paris. Faulkner met her at a 1953 Christmas Eve party in St. Moritz, Switzerland, hosted by Howard Hawks, just one month after he and Joan parted ways. When Jean moved on without him in the spring of 1957, Faulkner seemed almost resigned to such endings.

Perhaps "philandering author" was yet another aspect of his fictional persona. Ever resourceful, he even found a way to use *A Fable*'s slow evolution as part of this particular identity; Joan would be his muse, someone to write, not to, but for. In truth, these affairs often appeared to bring him more torment than satisfaction. All along he may have been fighting against his true nature—a domestic, monogamous man—and this internal conflict propelled some of the legendary drinking episodes. In 1959, two years after Faulkner's break with Jean, Jill found her father a changed man. He had settled. She noted his contentment and satisfaction. "He became so much easier for everyone to live with—not just family, but everybody ... he was a different man.... He was enjoying life."[13] Likewise, Estelle was a changed woman, having in 1955 gained sobriety through Alcoholics Anonymous.

The peacefulness his daughter observed did not influence his behavior on horseback. Faulkner's reckless riding was unabated by the passing years. In the summer of 1962, he was thrown from a favored iron-gray mount. Stonewall had a peevish and unpredictable nature; a contrarian like his rider. The pain from the fall had Faulkner self-medicating and the old, destructive cycle of addiction necessitated a trip to Byhalia. After a stay of mere hours at Wright's Sanatorium on a searing night, William Faulkner was dead in the predawn hours of July 6. His life ended so eerily that it could have been conjured by Faulkner himself, a great fan of mysteries and ghost stories. What led up to that night—and the falsehoods that abounded after his death—bears telling.

ONE

Stonewall Road: 1962

Reaching the intersection of Highway 309 and Stonewall Road, Jimmy Faulkner eased on to the sanatorium's private drive. The trip from Oxford to Byhalia had been mostly quiet and unremarkable, thereby making it remarkable. A parsimonious wind passed through the station wagon's open windows begrudging what little comfort it might bring the woeful passengers. Late summer afternoon in Mississippi is a formidable force when blazing sun unites with unremitting humidity. The temperature on July 5, 1962, registered 95 degrees.

His uncle, William Faulkner, "Brother Will" to Jimmy, normally resisted a trip like this that meant professional help, but he'd readily agreed to go to Wright's only three days into the episode. He'd been drinking Beefeater's gin without restraint. When his aunt Estelle called Jimmy to suggest they go to Byhalia, he'd come right over. To his surprise, Faulkner said, "I don't want to start this again."[1]

Jimmy promised to make the trip later in the day. He wondered if his uncle's age was catching up with him. Faulkner would turn 65 in September. He'd said some peculiar things during their annual bird hunting trip that January. They had passed the cold nights relaxing near the fire with some black label Jack Daniels. Despite an enjoyable day in the fields—Faulkner's marksmanship hadn't let him down—the conversation took a somber turn. "There are some things I want you to do after I'm gone," he'd said. And he was in no mood for Jimmy's assurances that death was in the far offing. "Now you listen to me. I'm about ready to die, and I'm just not ready yet."[2]

Jimmy recognized his uncle's confusion when he asked him where he'd like to go and Faulkner said home even though he was at home. Regardless, the family pressed on with their plans for Byhalia. Around 4:30 that afternoon, Jimmy helped him out of the single bed Faulkner kept in his office; guided and steadied him as they made their way to Jimmy's car; and positioned him in the backseat where he could stretch out for the 46-mile drive.

When Faulkner complained of his back and chest, there wasn't much Jimmy could do to alleviate his uncle's misery. Before the drinking started in earnest, he had offered Faulkner some of his Darvon capsules. After recently having an impacted wisdom tooth removed, Jimmy sympathized when he talked about being in pain. Faulkner declined the Darvon, and when he'd suggested trying aspirin, Brother Will's ironic response would have been humorous if it hadn't been delivered with such solemnity. "No," he had said, "I don't want to get addicted to aspirin."[3] Now he looked static reclining there on the seat with his eyes closed.

Not that many days before uncle and nephew enjoyed an idle visit, chatting with no great purpose. Jimmy [James Murry Faulkner] bore a strong likeness to Faulkner. Their facial features were uncannily similar. Jimmy, however, was a large man and a former Marine pilot who served during World War II and the Korean conflict. He was a decorated veteran who received the Distinguished Flying Cross, the World War II Victory Ribbon, and the Pacific Theatre Ribbon. Those details might have evoked a little jealousy in his uncle, whose failed attempt at the military due to his small stature was a well-recognized sore spot.

Faulkner was enamored of his great-grandfather, William Clark Falkner, "The Old Colonel," and had long aspired to military service. But he was very proud of Jimmy, who had attained the rank of lieutenant colonel, and he even referred to him as Colonel Faulkner whenever possible. As was their custom, Jimmy sat in a lawn chair Faulkner kept in his study near the hearth. Faulkner himself preferred to sit on the side of the small, single bed. Before Jimmy left, Faulkner inscribed his new book, *The Reivers*, to Jimmy and his wife, Nan. It was perhaps one of the last signed copies.

Estelle sat motionless beside him in the car's passenger seat. She was like a helpless sparrow, her tiny frame accentuated by age—she was now 66 years old—and exhaustion. Her sharp features had intensified rather than softened with the passing years. All the way from Oxford, she'd gripped a drink in her hands. She and Jimmy were prepared should Faulkner ask for it; surprised when he didn't. He complained of back and chest pain and murmured incoherently—something about "sergeants and captains"[4]—but was otherwise docile. The trips to hospitals, sanitariums, and sanatoriums were well-oiled machines in Faulkner's personal history. In the last decade of his life, he had at least 16 documented admissions. But he also exhibited amazing restorative powers. Estelle had been to Wright's many times, either checking in herself or visiting her husband, but Faulkner's resignation this time had her on edge. It was out of character and troubling.

* * *

The Stonewall Road sign didn't escape Jimmy's notice. Stonewall was the name of the iron-gray horse his uncle favored; an unpredictable, peevish mount who threw his uncle a month ago. That spring Faulkner had purchased Stonewall and another horse, Beauregard, in Oklahoma. (He would later joke after Stonewall tossed him that "I know now why I got him so cheap."[5]) Faulkner loved a challenge and Stonewall accommodated. Stonewall lived up to his reputation by putting this trip to Byhalia in motion.

On the morning of June 17, Faulkner left his home, Rowan Oak, for a solitary ride on Stonewall through Bailey's Woods and the bypass that crossed Old Taylor Road. A while later, Chrissie, the family cook, looked up to see Stonewall calmly heading toward the barn without his rider. Alarms went off in the household, and Estelle set off in the family's Rambler. When she spotted Faulkner angrily making his way home, he was in poorer shape than Stonewall. He was limping and holding his back, already a source of chronic pain from numerous riding-related injuries.

Faulkner was not one to spare the crop, whip or reins. This might go some way in explaining why frequently he found himself on the ground instead of the saddle. Moments later belligerent horse and belligerent rider met again in the paddock. Faulkner remounted Stonewall and took him over the jumps, saying later to his friend, Felix Linder, a retired orthopedist, "You don't think I'd let that damned horse conquer me, do you? I had to conquer him."[6]

As tough as he sounded, Faulkner couldn't shake the injury and pain from the forceful fall. Two days later he was in bed. His physician, Chester McLarty, visited him at Rowan Oak and, as he had many times over the years, told Faulkner he needed to go to the Campbell Clinic in Memphis, an orthopedic group. He refused as usual. When the injection in his back did little to help, he turned to his stash of Demerol, tranquilizers, and gin.

McLarty saw Faulkner at the post office a week after the accident. Faulkner was pale, spoke of the nagging back pain, and his physician noticed his pallor. In the week following McLarty's post-office sighting, Faulkner ambled the half-mile distance to the Linder home where he found Felix on the front porch. Faulkner blurted out that he didn't want to die and Felix responded saying he could keep him from suffering. "That ain't what I want," Faulkner retorted, and retraced his steps to Rowan Oak, leaving Linder to puzzle the intent of Faulkner's outburst.[7]

In the 18 days after the fall, but before he entered Wright's, Faulkner would have good and bad days with varying degrees of pain. His habit of walking to the Oxford Square occurred less often. "If I sit down I'm not comfortable. If I lie down, I can't stand it," he told a friend who asked how he was feeling.[8] Occasionally there would be bursts of energy when he would accomplish some correspondence. One of those intervening days involved a visit from Joan Williams, a former love interest of Faulkner's, now married to Ezra Drinker Bowen. Joan was in Oxford to see her cousin Regina Moore Holley, who, along with her husband, John Reed Holley, had first introduced

Joan to Faulkner in 1949. Estelle answered the phone when Joan called and encouraged her to come over. Joan thought Faulkner looked very pale and they sat on the front porch and talked for a half hour or so.

"He had some—I don't know—fragility about him that was more than for a man his age," she said. "He talked about himself as being older than he was and maybe he had some sense that he wasn't going to live a long time. I just think he always had the feeling that he wasn't going to be an old man somehow."[9] He told her he wasn't writing another book, that he never wrote in the summer. Joan had received a signed first-edition of *The Reivers* as she had all his books since she met him, and they had seen each other only two months earlier in New York when Joan received a grant from the National Institute of Arts and Letters for her first novel.

During that same May ceremony, Faulkner was recognized with the Gold Medal for Fiction. It was presented to him by Eudora Welty. Joan thought he appeared uninterested in the event, and she was pretty sure that when she walked past Faulkner on the stage he was asleep. What Faulkner wanted to know that summer afternoon on his porch was if there was any money in the envelope presented to Joan. She said no, they sent the money later.

* * *

Few would dispute that *The Reivers'* June 4 publication was the apex of the year; a booming success after a number of underwhelming books, especially the disappointment of *A Fable*. Faulkner himself said *The Reivers* (a Scottish word for "the thieves") was "the funniest story I've ever read."[10] The novel follows 11-year-old Lucius Priest's journey from Jefferson to Memphis with an affable but daft family friend and a stowaway stable hand. The trio travels in Lucius's grandfather's 1905 Winton Flyer, a town marvel and one of the first automobiles in the county. Exploits include staying in a Memphis brothel and other shenanigans that are capped off by swapping the car for a race horse. (Steve McQueen starred in the 1969 film adaptation.)

Besides being a delightful book, it was dedicated to all of Faulkner and Estelle's grandchildren. Victoria Fielden, "Vicki," the Faulkners' eldest grandchild, remembered how pleased her grandfather was with the novel. It was a light-hearted spring day in 1962 when he and Estelle shared the news of the book's dedication, "Vic-Pic, the best part is that it's dedicated to you and my other grandchildren, and you head the list.... And he was just smiling all over himself," Vicki said, "and he was happy, and you could see that Grandmama was happy; she was sharing it with him right there. They didn't hold hands or touch or anything like that, but they were together in his happiness, their happiness."[11]

Vicki was thrilled to see her grandparents growing close again, "They became very close friends again. At times they even looked and seemed like they were a newly married couple."[12] She knew he was proud of Estelle's sobriety and enjoying the domestic calm that had settled the normally turbulent waters. Since early 1957, the Faulkners had been living back and forth between Oxford and Charlottesville, Virginia, where Faulkner had a writer-in-residence position. They had rented two homes and eventually purchased the second rental property. Now he was fixated on purchasing a large century-old home in Virginia, Red Acres, a sprawling estate with various smaller houses, buildings, and a nine-stall stable. He wrote his friend, Linton Massey, a wealthy Virginian who collected Faulkner's works, for a loan of $50,000 to realize his dream.

Vicky was the primary reason the Faulkners were in Oxford that summer rather than Virginia. She had graduated from the University of Mississippi and they were in attendance. Afterward, Faulkner and Estelle hosted her graduation party at Rowan Oak. She was not as fortunate with her copy of *The Reivers*. When she eventually received the book, it was inscribed by Faulkner's daughter Jill rather than her grandfather, "For Vicki, because Pappy would have—if he'd had the time before July."[13]

Faulkner was religious about getting copies of his new works to those near and dear. A few days before Faulkner delivered an inscribed copy— "To Emily and Phil/from Bill"—to Phil Stone's office on June 12, Stone saw Faulkner in passing. In a postscript to a letter he wrote June 8 to a Faulkner scholar, Stone expressed his concern over his friend's appearance. "Don't repeat this to anyone, but Bill has been home for a few days and I saw him on the street the other day. I have never seen him look so old before. It is not his eyes, but the skin around his eyes; looks like that of an old man, and he looks to me like he has aged about five years since I saw him a few months ago."[14]

On the morning of July 3, Faulkner walked to the square to mail a copy to long-time friend and love interest, Else Jonsson, in Sweden. He apologetically asked for help addressing the package; his aching back had him distracted and he'd left his glasses behind. Later that same evening, the Faulkners had dinner at their usual haunt, the Mansion (also the title of Faulkner's 1959 novel which concluded the Snopes trilogy). Their customary waiter knew to cut off the jukebox as soon as he arrived and to escort Faulkner, Estelle, and whoever else might be dining with them to the best available table. The Mansion's owner was well acquainted with Faulkner's dislike of what he considered "noise," a distraction Faulkner believed "kept you from thinking about the things you should remember."[15] That evening Faulkner complained that his filet mignon tasted the same as the bread. Food hadn't been tasting right.

Sometime after dinner, a cousin and hunting buddy called to alert Jimmy that Faulkner had started drinking. Upon his arrival, Jimmy found Faulkner lying down on the bed in the study. He had a fifth of gin on the table near him and talked a good bit while Jimmy listened. Their routine, however, was slightly off. Usually Faulkner would ask him for a drink, saying "dink," and his nephew would oblige by pouring it for him, or even, need be, assisting him further by getting the glass to his lips.[16] That night he didn't ask for a drink. When he circled around the next day to check on him, Jimmy noticed Faulkner had dispatched about half a second fifth of gin—below normal in terms of a "regular" bout—and put up no resistance when he raised the trip to Byhalia. Faulkner was ready.

* * *

The long, private road to the back door of Wright's Sanatorium where patients entered was oddly reassuring. "Help awaited" it seemed to promise. The large oak tree with its welcoming canopy served as a greeter of sorts. As usual a few individuals lingered under the tree absorbed in idle conversation. A beautiful rose garden was in view from a large porch enclosed by windows. The sanatorium's main structure was just the beginning; Wright's was a compound of sorts. The road behind the circular drive for debarking patients continued past numerous small cabins, and ended with Dr. Wright's private residence and a separate building where he hosted card games. Dr. Leonard Wright, Sr., had a vision for the place which he had realized—simplicity and comfort in a verdant, rural setting.

Jimmy parked the car and Willie Jamison, a 22-year-old attendant at Wright's, carried Faulkner inside, undressed him, put his pajamas on and helped him into bed. "Shorty," Faulkner said, presumably to Jamison, "I need a pair of carpet slippers."[17] Forty-one years later Jamison clearly remembered the celebrity patient, "He passed the same night he came in. He was a good friend of mine. I took care of him."[18] Faulkner's condition evidently caused heightened concern. An attendant was assigned to stay with him for some time for which Faulkner was charged an additional $7.50 fee. Faulkner's room 8d was one of two on the sanatorium's main floor. It was located near the nurse's station.[19]

Dr. Wright was proud to advertise the facility as air conditioned. What a relief that was for the threesome after their drive in the hot car. In contrast to the abundant exterior landscape, the sanatorium's interior décor was plain and functional, some might say stark. Wood chairs and tables; rocking chairs in some of the bedrooms. Faulkner's room was near a small lounge with a TV set and to the right was a dining room, adequately but certainly not enthusiastically furnished.

The record noted Faulkner was admitted at 5:50 p.m. Jimmy and Estelle stayed in the room while Dr. Wright examined Faulkner. His examination showed Faulkner's heart, blood pressure, and chest to be normal. The patient complained of significant chest and back pain which Dr. Wright noted could have been a symptom of heart pain yet there was no direct indication of such.[20] Faulkner remained quite agreeable throughout, even cracking jokes.

Twenty minutes after his admission, Faulkner's examination was complete. Nourishment and medications were ordered. Dr. Wright's method of gradually diminishing drinks of alcohol as a detox method was a standard approach at the time though some doctors were instead favoring tranquilizers. Dr. Wright also administered various opioids. The first orders that night for Faulkner included an injection of one cc of vitamin B-1, pure thiamine, and another injection of one cc of Betalin, a multi-vitamin injection, both scheduled for 6:10 p.m. Dr. Wright then ordered ½ ounce of alcohol every hour with the first doses being given at 6:15 and 6:45 p.m. Doses of alcohol continued at 7:45 p.m. and then every hour through 10:45 p.m., after which the patient hopefully would be asleep. Another tried and true remedy was provided at 6:15 p.m., the classic egg flip, offered in beverage form as a protein boost.[21] Dr. Wright's regimen for Faulkner—carefully measured alcohol drinks, egg flips, and vitamin injections—was consistent with his method of providing vitamins, nutrients, and waning doses of alcohol.

Along with the setting sun at Wright's, the staff's night orders went into effect. At 9:00 and 9:40, Faulkner drank egg flips, and at 9:45 p.m., the allocated liquor. To ward off nausea, he received 200 milligrams of Tigan at 9:55 p.m. Orders included nourishment to be provided again at 1:30 and 3:00 a.m., and the patient's sleeping position needed to be changed every two hours to prevent bed sores. Significantly, and another sign that Faulkner's condition merited a somewhat heightened alert, was a notation in the left margin of the order book: "Call Dr if no sleep by 12:00."[22] Though Estelle must have been drained with the travails of the day and the two previous days, she wasn't saying a hasty goodbye. Her health was almost always perilous. She'd long been a heavy smoker and was rail thin. Sober six years now, she rejoiced at the newfound freedom it afforded. She might have said another silent prayer, that when this latest episode passed, her husband would make the same decision.

It seemed Dr. Wright had worked his magic again. Jimmy noticed Faulkner finally had relaxed and might be ready for sleep. The room he occupied had two double beds positioned along opposite walls. Jimmy sat on the other bed and talked with him awhile. Somewhere between 10 and 10:30 p.m. he indicated to Estelle that perhaps it was time to set out for Oxford. Her goodbyes, whispered in her husband's ear, were known only to him. She then waited in the hall for her nephew. Jimmy took his turn by the bed. "Brother Will," he said, "When you're ready to come home, let me know and I'll come for you." What a surprise when Faulkner looked at him with bright, sharp eyes, and answered in a clear, resonate voice. "Yes, Jim, I will."[23] What would have otherwise been a tranquil parting was disrupted at 10:15 p.m. by the boisterous arrival of a new patient from Greenville, Mississippi, who was assigned room 9d across the hall. She was known to the staff from other visits and, like many, diagnosed as an acute alcoholic. During this four-day stay she required twice daily doses of Dilaudid, an opioid analgesic. With her arrival, the patient count for the night settled at 10.[24]

Nurse Jean Burrow helped Faulkner prepare for sleep at 10:45 with his prescribed medications: Compazine Spansule [anti-nausea], Benadryl [sedative], Analexin [muscle spasms], and alcohol. As always, records only tell so much. Burrow, who worked with Dr. Wright for twenty years, believed Faulkner knew his condition was dire. "I think he knew he was dying," she said. "Dr. Wright insisted he go to the hospital in Memphis but Faulkner refused. He said he did not want to be made a spectacle." When she said goodnight at 11 p.m., not even an hour after Estelle and Jimmy's leave taking, Faulkner's response was alarmingly different from the one Jimmy received, "I told him, 'I'll see you in the morning.' He said, 'I don't think so.'"[25]

While accounts varied as to what transpired between Estelle and Jimmy's departure and Faulkner's death at 1:30 a.m., there was no denying the finality. One of America's greatest authors was gone. Faulkner's death on July 6 fell on the Old Colonel's birthday, a poignant detail that wouldn't have eluded the novelist.

Two

The Old Country Club: Circa 1948

Situated on the outskirts of the small Mississippi town of Byhalia, the Leonard Wright Sanatorium occupied twenty acres of rolling countryside. Abundant mature trees, flower beds, and other eye-catching landscape features distinguished the property. The sanatorium's dominant structure—once the home of a sprawling family—included a significant wing addition. Several small cottages reserved for couples were scattered behind the primary facility, and at the farthest recess was the private residence of Dr. Leonard Davidson Wright, Sr., physician and proprietor.

Years after Wright's ceased to exist as a sanatorium, or "drying out" place, the house and cottages remained intact. The vacant structures, with peeling white paint and the remnants of green-trim shutters, and especially what was left of the tiny cabins, fascinated passersby. Folks traveling from Oxford or other locations en route to Memphis, Tennessee, were known to make an abrupt stop to tour the abandoned property. Those who knew a bit of the history—that Wright's most famous inhabitant was Nobel Prize–winning author William Faulkner—would wander around the grounds peering inside the dilapidated house and cottage windows wondering about the lives and situations of those who found themselves, albeit briefly, residents of Wright's. And for those who knew more of the folklore, their concentration would shift to what occurred the night of July 5, 1962, when, after a mere six hours as a patient, William Faulkner was dead shortly after midnight on July 6.

* * *

Wright's story is a southern story, a story William Faulkner himself would have appreciated. But it is also a story of time and place. The individuals treated there referred to the sanatorium as "The Old Country Club." The main structure, located on the slope of a hillside, had been the Burrow family home. Thomas "Tom" D. Burrow, a Byhalia merchant, purchased the property in 1898 and later built the two-story home. In 1922, Burrow's first wife, Myra Herring Burrow, was killed by a bull charging their children in a pasture. His second wife, Lillian, was the rosarian. Dr. Wright bought the Burrow homestead in 1947.

Approximately two years passed between the purchase of the Burrow place and the sanatorium's opening, most likely in 1948. (Contrary to long-standing belief, Faulkner's first hospitalization was not at Wright's—which didn't exist in 1936—but at the Gartly-Ramsay Hospital in Memphis, Tennessee.) Renovations occupied some of that time, including enclosing the front porch. Folks relaxing there could gaze at the closely guarded rose garden. A stipulation of the sale was that Lillian Burrow, who was known for her green thumb, would continue to maintain the garden and her permission was required before a single rose was cut. A circular drive ran in front of the house though the significant comings and goings occurred at the back door where patients arrived and departed.

A rather notorious tree grew parallel to the porch but a good distance from the main house. The huge, old oak—the Byhalia name comes from the Chickasaw words for white oak standing—offered considerable shade for a gathering spot. Metal, sling-back lawn chairs clustered about. At times, there would be eight or ten patients under the tree at the same time. The staff knew to closely monitor new arrivals. If they kept trying to slip away to the oak, chances were they had stashed a bottle nearby before checking in. Sometimes the bottles were found in the prized rose bushes.

Far from evoking any kind of social stigma, staying at Wright's was a status symbol of sorts. Individuals recovering at Wright's were considered well-off financially. They convalesced with a similar class of people in a quiet, bucolic retreat. Wright's ads included aerial photographs of the sweeping grounds stressing "reservations necessary." The sanatorium specialized "in the treatment of Alcoholic and Drug Addiction and Mild Nervous Disorders. Experienced in all methods of treatment and the use of modern drugs." It was located on "twenty acres of beautifully landscaped grounds sufficiently removed to provide restful surroundings and capacity limited to insure individual treatment" and "the building is Air Conditioned."

For more reassurance, the ad stressed the facility's medical credentials. "The Sanatorium is a Member of the American Hospital Association, the National Association of Private Psychiatric Hospitals, and the Mississippi Hospital Association."[1] Family members could rest assured their spouse, parent, or friend would have excellent and comfortable care. It is easy to see the appeal of such a facility when the situation was unmanageable for family members.

Two. The Old Country Club: Circa 1948

That was the scenario after Jill Faulkner's August wedding in 1954. Once the wedding party and most of the guests departed, the drinking, or the "chemistry of craving"[2] as Faulkner called it, began in earnest. Estelle led the way and Faulkner joined her, switching from champagne to whiskey. When Faulkner's Random House editor Saxe Commins and his wife, Dorothy, sought out their hosts the next day to say goodbye, they found Faulkner in bed. The Comminses' departure for New York left 16-year-old Vicki alone with her grandparents.

First her grandmother had succumbed, then Pappy. Vicki imagined Faulkner thinking, "'Stelle's gone and done it, I might as well too.' He went on a binge of binges," she recalled. "Finally, after two days or so of my trying to keep at least the beds clean of vomit and excrement and everything else, Pappy somehow, in his drunken stupor, realized I couldn't take it anymore, couldn't handle it, I was too immature. I really couldn't drive, I couldn't go to the bootlegger for them or do anything, really." Faulkner began to call for Estelle's son, Malcolm Franklin. "'Get Malcolm! Get Malcolm to take me to Byhalia.'" A few days later when Vicki returned from an errand she found Faulkner sitting on the front porch in his favorite rocking chair, "'Yessum, I knew you were in trouble,' he told her. He realized I couldn't cope with the situation and he'd gone to 'dry out.' Grandmama took a while longer."[3]

* * *

Retired Marine Lieutenant Colonel William "Bill" D. Fitts III, a stocky man with generous volubility and expressive features, was born August 3, 1934. Many years after his service, Fitts retains his military bearing. As a child, young man, and adult, his life intersected with the Dr. Wright and his family. He was friends with Leonard Wright, Jr., and his father and mother were close friends of Leonard Wright, Sr., and his wife, Ida. More particularly, his father was often a patient at Wright's. As a young man, the sanatorium served as a place of employment. Fitts would drive patients to and from the airport or rail stations. The word "patients" itself is a bit cloying as they were treated more as clients or visitors. Fitts described them as "guests."[4]

"It was probably more of a master-servant thing," Fitts said. "They, Wright's staff, were the servants, and the guests were the masters. I think the staff was very respectful to them and they expected that." Fitts' father, William D. Fitts, Jr., checked into Wright's three or four times a year; some years more if he had the money, some years less. One year, sometime between 1946 and 1948, prior to Wright's opening, his father went to a facility in Kankakee, Illinois, for four weeks. "They kept trying to find a way to fix him. The grave was the only thing that would fix him. Most of them, I believe, were self-centered and seeking self-gratification; and if they were worried, it was about the money they'd spent. You can become a millionaire, you can drink yourself rich in your mind, but when you sobered up, you still owed the money."

Dr. Wright "saw a niche that no one in the area was fulfilling. There were people who could afford it and wanted it and he provided a service," Fitts said. He also thought the area was attractive to Dr. Wright because he and his wife were "comfortable with small, southern communities."[5] Leonard Wright, Sr., grew up in Covington, Tennessee, and his wife in Hernando, Mississippi. Behind the family's living quarters on the sanatorium property, Dr. Wright built a clubhouse where he had a group of five or six friends who would play poker one night a week.

The choice of a rural area accentuated the private nature of Wright's; and with a new paved highway system, his clientele was not limited to locals. Far from it. Patients came from a number of nearby states, and Byhalia's proximity to Memphis offered several travel options. Besides being discerning in location selection, Fitts credited Dr. Wright with carefully vetting his staff. "They always had one or two male attendants. Quality people like Adolphus Shipp. The staff had to be honest and trustworthy. They could have used information to blackmail the patients." The staff also had to fend off bribes. It was not out of the question for a patient to try and offer cash for liquor. Discretion was expected. And even though Leonard Wright, Jr., and Fitts were friends, they never discussed his father's stays.

The residents of Byhalia were aware of the sanatorium but not excessively interested, except perhaps in the liquor bottles planted along the road. According to Fitts and his wife, Elizabeth "Lis" Fitts, "Wright's was just kind of there. It operated quietly and off the skyline." Lis, a native of Denmark, married Fitts in 1962, and the couple eventually settled in Byhalia. Fitts said:

> There were several people who picked up Wright's patients at the train station and airport. And it was not uncommon for them to want to stop in Memphis and buy five or six pints. As they were coming out here, they would ask the driver to slow down and stop, and they would go hide them in a ditch. They were stashing it on their way out there so they could slip off and go out and get it. Just like children. You have twenty grown men there. They slip out of prisoner of war camps. They were the same age group. It was a game for them. Then, some of the people around the area realized what was going on, and they'd go up and down the ditches and harvest the bottles![6]

* * *

Dr. Wright's appreciation of his staff extended to providing transportation. Because the sanatorium was located outside Byhalia's city limits—the population census in 1960 was 674—he ordered cab service to collect and return the nurses to their homes. The grounds included a separate living facility—a few rooms at the end of the Wright family's private residence—where nurses could spend the night. The nursing staff numbered five or six. In turn, the staff reciprocated, and were described as dedicated to the doctor, some even regarding him as a father figure.

By and large, the individuals recovering were successful and high-achieving bankers, doctors, lawyers, farmers, and businessmen. Word-of-mouth referrals played a large role in the sanatorium's popularity. Wright's clientele came from Mississippi, Tennessee, Arkansas, Alabama, Missouri, Texas, and Chicago. Many were sportsmen—hunters and fishermen—who enjoyed traveling to Alaska. Fitts remembers picking up one gentleman and his wife at the Memphis airport. He was the president of a bank in Pine Bluff, Arkansas. His wife apparently eschewed the sanatorium cabins and instead checked into the Peabody Hotel in downtown Memphis while Fitts continued on to Mississippi with her husband.

The Peabody, built in 1869, boasted of being "The South's Grand Hotel." Author David Cohn said "The Mississippi Delta begins in the lobby of the Peabody Hotel and ends on Catfish Row in Vicksburg." (Ironically, his quotation is often attributed to Faulkner.) Guests included United States presidents Andrew Johnson and William McKinley as well as Confederate generals Robert E. Lee and Nathan Bedford Forrest. Prior to becoming president of the Confederacy, Jefferson Davis lived there. A new, opulent hotel with an Italian Renaissance structure replaced the original Peabody in 1925. Lobby features included a travertine marble fountain from Italy circled by five pampered Mallard ducks, enormous fresh flower arrangements, a grand piano and pianist, bars, restaurants, salons, and shops.[7] For the banker's wife, it would have been an easy choice between those luxurious accommodations and a cabin at Wright's.

To Fitts, for its purposes, Wright's was also a featherbed of sorts. "Wright's was a thousand dollars per week," he said. "It was a featherbed. But most of them could afford it." Women stayed there as well, though not as frequently as men. The ratio was approximately 75 percent male to 25 percent female. And while they didn't have a sign that said "whites only," Fitts does not think they ever had an African American patient.[8]

The expense was not lost on Faulkner, who complained about the cost, not only for himself but also his wife. During one of her stays in 1955, Estelle required around-the-clock special nurses. Wright's charged an additional "special nurse fee" for Essie Campbell, who was special nurse to Estelle for eight nights, and Mae Moran for five days.[9] Estelle's problems with alcohol were severe and often provoked by Faulkner's philandering. "My grandmother," Vicki said, "was the classic alcoholic—a glass of wine at dinner was enough to set her off. Once she started, she couldn't stop and wouldn't until she passed out. That was it. I mean, she was a *real* alcoholic. It had an allergic effect on her."[10]

Jill Faulkner noted the same about her mother, qualifying that "while she drank 'as an escape' and 'to relieve tension,' her ultimate goal was 'oblivion—just to get away from things. She drank to get drunk, as a means for coping with her everyday life. Living as she did was more than she could face.... My mother was not a happy person; she was a lot more sophisticated and intelligent than anyone gave her credit for and I think that's why she was unhappy."[11]

For Vicki, a distinction existed between Faulkner's and Estelle's drinking: "'Pappy was not the same kind of alcoholic Grandmama was. He could control his drinking if he wanted to, and I guess he couldn't understand why Grandmama couldn't do the same thing.... Pappy could drink socially and not get drunk. He could have a few drinks, wine at dinner, and that would be that. But when he was under a great deal of stress, he might decide, 'I'm going on a binge,' and he would make the decision consciously and soberly."[12]

An intercepted letter from Joan Williams in 1952 triggered heavy drinking and arguing between Faulkner and Estelle. Faulkner feared that Malcolm, seeing his mother in such a state, would take her to Wright's, about which Faulkner wrote Saxe Commins,

> Hell's to pay here. While I was hors de combat, E. opened and read Joan Williams' letter to me. Now E. is drunk, and I am trying to nurse her before Malcolm sends her to a hospital which costs like fury and does no good unless you make an effort yourself. I can't really blame her, certainly I can't criticize her, I am even sorry for her, even if people who will open and read another's private and personal letters, do deserve exactly what they get....[13]

* * *

Yet the high cost of staying at Wright's didn't serve to deter many. Dr. Wright had wonderful instincts about the environment he cultivated. "It was just calm," Fitts said, "Just a comfortable feeling. Low key." Wright's provided healthy but appetizing meals, employed four or five cooks, and allowed as much freedom as possible. "Dr. Wright," Fitts said, "didn't want any belligerent patients. He didn't do lockdowns." His patients' needs were met quickly and courteously. If necessary they had help with grooming, especially shaving, and Dr. Wright, after making his medical rounds, would collect the daily cigarette list and go into town and buy the preferred brands. Fitts recalled the patients lounging about in pajamas and bath robes, smoking and drinking coffee, or ambling around the grounds. He believed some actually scheduled their stays together based on the way they greeted each other and interacted. "They would be happy to see each other and exclamatory. They were good old boys who liked to get drunk."

Fitts' home became a destination for some of his father's "drunk buddies" who made their way to town from Wright's. The family would wake up in the middle of the night to loud knocking at the front door. One man asked Bill Junior to take him out in the country where he could buy some moonshine. He bought a quart of white whisky and Fitts returned him to the sanatorium. Mission accomplished it seemed, until Fitts' passenger opened his door and fell out. He didn't appear to be in any pain and made his way inside. Fitts learned later he'd broken his hip.

Another delivery Fitts made was a good friend of his father who lived in Oxford. "I don't know how I wound up with him but he was drunk. I took him home—and I don't know what I expected—but I didn't expect to be dumped on by his wife when I propped him up in the door. I thought why the hell didn't I leave the SOB down in the Tallahatchie bottom? I don't need this!"[14]

* * *

The Leonard Wright Sanatorium's main structure had 17 rooms—two of which were on the main floor—with 22 available beds (some rooms were doubles), plus the cabins out back. The large upstairs rooms had high ceilings and nice windows and were cooled by a pull-down attic fan.

Adolphus Shipp, who is in real estate development and property management, was an attendant and trusted confidante of Dr. Wright's. Shipp's striking brick home sits on a hill with sweeping views not only of his property but also the neighboring acreages. Shipp, who was born January 3, 1943, is an imposing and confident figure who easily inhabits his accomplishments. It's not hard to imagine—with his ready laugh and smile—that he would have been a staff favorite. He recalled that upon arrival most of the patients—indeed, repeat business was key to Wright's success—asked for "their room." "See one one time, you're just about going to see them again," he added. Although the upstairs was without air conditioning for a long time, many requested rooms there. "A lot of patients wanted to go upstairs," Shipp said. "Every room had a great big rocking chair they liked. Some of the big rooms had two beds and two rocking chairs. At times, two people would be in one room."[15]

In a January 1960 letter to Estelle, Faulkner recounted a humorous story about Wright's accommodations and his visit there with his brother Johncy [John Wesley Thompson III]. Faulkner was ill with pleurisy, and started, according to Blotner, "his own course of bourbon therapy." The situation—soon out of control—spanned six days. Friends in Oxford recall seeing an ambulance traveling up South Lamar, a dominant city street, and spotting William Faulkner inside. Faulkner had little memory of the escapade's first few days, but he did remember waking up at Wright's.

> Dear Estelle: Keep this letter; it's one of the funniest tales of good intent and human foolishness I know.... John drove into the yard in an ambulance, came up to my bedside and said, "I'm going to save you." I probably said, "Fine, I'd like a nice ride this morning." Now this, Wednesday is built up from evidence not mine. When we got there, John demanded a single room with two beds in it, and wanted a rate. So he gave them his check for one. I evidently knew where I was; I just didn't remember until sometime Thursday, because I asked for a drink at once. They brought it to me. John, in the other bed, said he would have one too. They told him he had only paid for me and they couldn't give him one. He said, By God, he would go back to Oxford then. They said, 'But the ambulance has already gone, Mr. Faulkner.' 'Then call me a cab,' John says. So they did, and he left. The first thing he did was to stop in Holly Springs [Mississippi] and buy two cases of beer.

After more medicine and "a jug of that stuff they hang on a thing like a hatrack," Faulkner left Wright's sooner than the usual recommendation, "If I had stayed the full week, I would have got all of John's money back, since in a poker game Saturday night another patient and I won thirty-five dollars from the young doctor on duty; maybe that's why he discharged me so readily Sunday."[16]

Others shared the experience of finding themselves at Wright's without much knowledge of when or how they came to be there. In November 1966, Blotner paid a visit to Dr. Wright at the sanatorium. He described Dr. Wright, who would have been 56 years old, as

> ...about 5'8", ruddy complexion, short brown hair—almost a crew cut—a bit of grey in it, blue eyes, a snub nose, pleasant-looking man. His father was a country doctor in Tennessee and his two sons are physicians in Tennessee. There is a hall immediately beyond the Dutch door, and beyond that is WF's room that time. Beyond this is a little lounge with a TV set and to the right a dining room, simply furnished with a table, chairs, and a large glass-doored cupboard at the lift with glasses, etc., in it. I sat there and had coffee with three men who were obviously patients (flushed complexions) getting over drinking bouts.
> Dr. Wright is pleasant and obviously competent, no-nonsense sort of man, very quiet, soft-spoken, not a particularly pronounced accent. His staff is composed of some registered nurses—I saw perhaps two—and two Negro boys, one in his twenties, the other in his teens, who I suppose act as busboys and help with the patients. The men were in pajamas or pajamas and robes, or in street clothes, depending I suppose upon the extent of their recovery. One of them (the day is Thursday) had come in apparently last weekend. He'd started drinking after the Mississippi–Tennessee football game and had

wound up in Byhalia. And all of them spoke very freely about whiskey and what time their pills were due. They talked about another man who apparently was still having something like dt's—talking to trees, talking to himself—the kind of camaraderie of the afflicted that appears in the [Faulkner] story "Dr. Acarius."[17]

* * *

Blotner's observation of Adolphus Shipp as "a Negro boy" who, he surmised, worked as a "busboy" was far off the mark. Shipp began working for Dr. Wright in 1960 while still in high school and worked for him a total of 17 years. The last five years were at the Holly Springs facility Wright opened after closing down Byhalia. Wright's staff referred to patients by their surname. "If I needed to discuss a patient with Dr. Wright, I said, 'I need to talk with you about Mr. So-and-So or Mrs. So-and-So.'" It was important to the protocol to quickly learn names. When Dr. Wright discovered Shipp was so adept at it, he relied on him. "A lot of times—years later—after he and I got closer working together, he would say, 'Adolph, So-and-So called me and wants to bring in her husband. 'What do you think?' And I'd remember what kind of patient they made. And I'd say, 'Yes, tell them to bring him on.'"

While the nurses enjoyed cab service back and forth to work—"that cab would be full!" Shipp recalled—he usually walked.

> I lived in town and I walked a good many of those years. That was after my wife and I first got married. [The Shipps have been married over fifty years.] She taught school down in the Delta and she'd take the car and I'd be without. At the time, being young, you didn't think much about it.
>
> JoAnn, my wife, she had a toothache one night and it was giving her fits. So, I went up to Dr. Wright's about one or two a.m. and he gave her a couple of pills and she didn't have any more trouble with that tooth. He met me at the back door, gave me the pills, and said, "Now both of us can go get some sleep."[18]

The Byhalia facility closed in 1972, and for about a year Dr. Wright "retired," and Shipp found other employment. But Dr. Wright wasn't quite finished. "He came by my house one Saturday morning and said, 'I have a chance to open on the third floor at Marshall County Hospital [Holly Springs, Mississippi]—providing you go with me.' And I had a job I didn't particularly care for, so I said, 'Sure, I'll go with you.'"

Shipp recognized the original sanatorium's charm. He explained:

> Everybody liked the way Dr. Wright treated patients. It was a lot different from the way other sanitariums treated patients. When we went to Holly Springs, it was a totally different atmosphere, and we tried to accommodate them as much as we could, but it was never the same. Wright's used the method of gradual withdrawal. By starting them off on—first twelve to twenty-four hours—a little

shot of alcohol every hour. And then the next day, you went to an hour and fifteen, hour and a half. Then cut them off and start them on medication.[19]

Dr. Wright described his method to Blotner during their 1966 meeting:

> Dr. Wright said that his methods do not involve the administration of paraldehyde, which he said is a very powerful, quick-acting sedative, and everybody, including the staff is glad that he does not, because apparently it's a foul-smelling drug. He indicated also that their method was one of gradual withdrawal of alcohol, that is, making the drinks weaker, probably, and certainly giving them at more spaced intervals as time goes on until it is completely withdrawn. At the same time apparently he continues with the vitamin therapy and mild sedation as needed.[20]

Sanatorium records show dilaudid as frequently administered as well as other drugs, primarily opioids: morphine, demerol, dromoran, nalline, percodan, nisentil, codeine, pantopon, and dolophine.[21] Speculation easily suggests that a certain number of Wright's repeat patients were drug seeking. Shipp understood that

> they wanted to get straight but didn't want to go through the initial stage. They might call a friend to come and visit and ask them to slip them something. When they first came in, they were feeling good, on the spirit. Just having a bunch of fun, joking. Then after the first day they began to start going through withdrawals and settling down. Some of them would be on edge. Not so much violent but using a lot of profanity, behavior like that.

Patients at this point required more care. "We helped them with their bath and some of them wouldn't be able to shave themselves," Shipp said. "They would be nervous. A lot of times we just stayed with them, talked with them. Some would decide to go home. Once they decided to go—no talking them out of it—we didn't keep them against their will, though usually they'd be back in a couple of days."

Even though Dr. Wright's procedure was generous with alcohol, they were seeking more—and asking for it—"all the time. When they were close to their scheduled drink, they sat on a couch close to the nurse's station. Waiting. After about four or five days they were pretty much back," Shipp recalled. "Then they started talking business with one another. I learned a lot from them. If one of them liked to talk a business I was interested in, I would sort of cling to them. I made lot of friends and kept relationships with some of them for years. If there was anything they could do to help me, they did it."

Another remedy for patients at the outset of their stay was an egg flip. "Take two eggs, put them in a bowl, sugar, vanilla extract, nutmeg, and put it in blender and mix it," Shipp instructed.

> Then, we'd take it by the nurse's station and they'd add a little alcohol. We'd give them to patients to drink because they wouldn't eat anything for a while

Two. The Old Country Club: Circa 1948

and that was a way to get nourishment in them. It had a good taste to it. And then some of them would say, "Adolph, would you fix me an egg flip?" There wouldn't be any alcohol in those but they'd [the patient] be kind of coming around and they knew they needed nourishment.[22]

Indeed, on the night of his last stay at Wright's, doctor's orders for Faulkner included "egg flips" at 6:15, 9:00 and 9:40 p.m.[23]

There were more people battling their alcohol addiction than drugs at Wright's. Dr. Wright required a full week's stay for alcohol—that was about 80 percent of the patients—and a month for drugs. Shipp recalled that most of the drug issues involved morphine addiction. It was commonplace for such an addiction to follow an injury.[24] "One fellow," Fitts said, "a big farmer from Sardis [Mississippi] was thrown from his horse and broke his back. And if I'm not mistaken, virtually the same thing happened twice. They got him hooked on morphine at the hospital and he came here [to Wright's] to get off it."[25]

The Leonard Wright Sanatorium
BYHALIA, MISSISSIPPI
● For the treatment of Mental and Nervous Disorders, Alcoholics and Drug Addictions.
● Located 24 miles S.E. of Memphis on highway 78 and the Frisco R.R. Twenty acres of beautiful grounds sufficiently removed to provide restful surroundings and with a capacity limited to insure individual treatment.
● Equipped for and experienced in the use of all types of SHOCK and SLEEP THERAPY.

Wright's—colloquially referred to as the Old Country Club and "drying out place"—and other facilities like it were part and parcel of Southern culture at the time—a sheltering and, some would say, pampering environment to recover from excessive drinking and drug use (courtesy James C. Castleberry).

* * *

The irony of Wright's location—where Highway 309 and Stonewall Road intersected—could not be denied, considering Stonewall also was the name of the horse that threw and seriously injured Faulkner, who was taken to Wright's for treatment and very soon would die (courtesy James C. Castleberry).

"Beautifully landscaped grounds sufficiently removed to provide restful surroundings and capacity limited to insure individual treatment," read the description of Wright's in a medical journal. Newly arriving patients were known to strategically stash bottles in bushes and other foliage on the grounds. Staff kept an eye out for too many outside excursions (courtesy James C. Castleberry).

Two. The Old Country Club: Circa 1948   31

Several small cottages were reserved for couples and scattered on the grounds of Wright's and, although vacant, remained until 2015. The abandoned buildings often attracted passersby, who would wander freely around the property peering into the dilapidated cabins through dusty window panes (courtesy James C. Castleberry).

Estelle had been to Wright's many times, either checking in herself—facing her own alcoholism, mental instability and poor health—or visiting her husband. An August 1952 record shows her condition upon discharge after a single night as "poor" (courtesy James C. Castleberry).

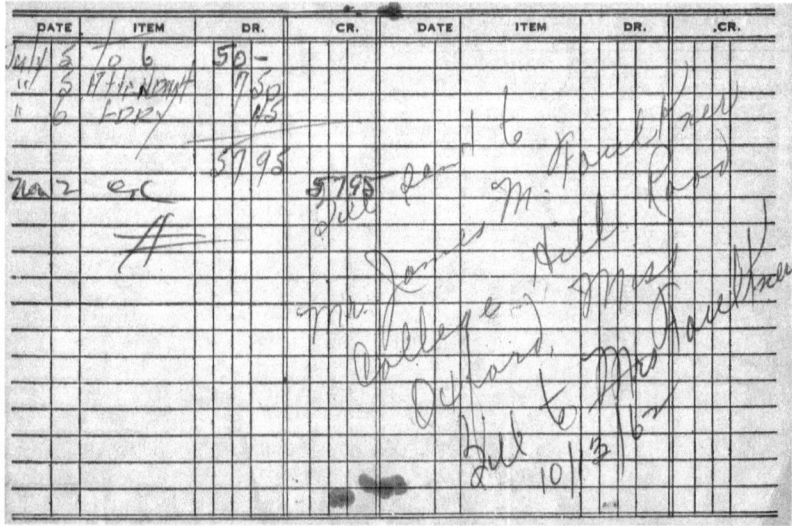

For what turned out to be Faulkner's final hours, records note he was admitted at 5:50 p.m., July 5, 1962. Jimmy and Estelle stayed in his room, and Dr. Wright examined him. Heart, blood pressure, and chest appeared normal. Faulkner complained of chest and back pain which Dr. Wright noted "could have been heart pain but there was no direct indication" of such. Faulkner remained quite agreeable throughout, even cracking jokes (courtesy James C. Castleberry).

Records, including Faulkner's final bill for treatment, were discovered at the abandoned sanatorium and provided a heretofore unknown window into Faulkner's care and condition (courtesy James C. Castleberry).

However comfortable the sanatorium may have been, it was still occupied by people with no real purpose except to wait for their next drink or round of medication. The staff realized activity was important, and walking around the grounds was encouraged, though monitored. "If one patient just came in and wanted to get out in the lawn pretty bad, you kept your eye on him. A lot of time they'd be trying to find their stash," Shipp said. The enclosed porch became the hub for recreation. "It was glassed and done right." There was a large table where patients would take their meals. One end of the porch had a large pool table and the other a poker table. The patients played with chips and kept records, and "there was enough money involved to keep it interesting. They'd start a poker game midmorning and it would go into night. Ragging each other and having fun."[26]

Fitts and Shipp agreed the stays at Wright's were almost factored into the lives of some individuals. Shipp said many of them were "workaholics as much as alcoholics. A lot of them had the mentality that they just wanted to have fun for a while—drink and have fun—and they knew they were going to run into trouble. So, I'm going to do this for a week and then I'm going to go over and get sober. Take a week out to get sober. And then I'm going to tend to my business."[27] Fitts concurred, "They were fraternity brothers come home to nest for a while."[28]

* * *

No doubt there were other patients besides Faulkner and Estelle who did not fit the fraternity mold. Nurse Jean Burrow, an employee of Dr. Wright's for 20 years, characterized Faulkner as "a gentleman and a scholar" who was "totally likeable. He was just a delightful person." She confirmed that while staying at Wright's Faulkner "took the door knobs off when he wrote ... so he could be undisturbed." When her shift ended the night of July 5, 1962, Nurse Burrow assured Faulkner she would see him in the morning.[29]

Three

Estelle

Her garden was where Estelle felt most at ease. Naturally tense and anxiety ridden, she could feel utter calm descend when she started working outside regardless of the task. The yellow, prolific beds of goldenrod always lifted her spirits. They stood in stark relief to her needy roses. Bill admired her magical green thumb. He said when pioneer women were making the treacherous journey to the unknown and unyielding land they carried flower seeds with them. The men worried about food and the women flowers. She knew it surprised many, this slight, middle-aged woman vigorously turning the soil and targeting the endless weeds. Maintaining the flower beds was only the beginning. The vegetable garden was known to be abundant and harvesting time meant canning. She didn't stop there but also made jams and jellies. If anyone thought she was a lady of leisure she had a lot to tell them.

The heat and humidity were persistent companions—Bill wouldn't allow air conditioning in the house. He said people were trying to change the climate—and often the yard provided more relief than the house's stifling air. He also wouldn't tolerate a radio despite Estelle's campaign. On many fronts he was intractable, and over the years she chose her battles more sparingly. When Bill was home it seemed like he was a million miles away—thinking, writing, reading—and other times he was in New York or another remote destination. After 20 years of marriage, companionship was what she most desired.

* * *

Originally her husband's dream, Rowan Oak became her albatross. She'd poured so much of herself into the antebellum home that she couldn't imagine life elsewhere. Even after all the projects and remodeling, there was always a needed repair that Estelle tried to handle as inexpensively as possible. She dreaded having to bring that kind of news to her husband. Though he had done most of the original work on the house himself, Bill didn't understand the resources the place required, especially when he was gone and the work had to be hired. Instead, he preferred to blame Estelle for poor management or overspending.

English architect William Turner built the Greek Revival–style house around 1848 for Robert B. Sheegog, a wealthy Irish planter. By 1860, Sheegog's property included over six thousand acres with a labor force of close to ninety enslaved African Americans. Large front and back halls dominated the L-shaped structure's ground floor. The front hall was flanked by a parlor to the right and the library to the left. Faulkner's original writing space was the library, though he was known to travel around the house as he worked, sometimes in the middle bedroom upstairs or downstairs in the dining room. Later, off the library, he would add an office complete with a closet, cot, and bathroom. The walls would be famously decorated with an outline for his 1954 novel, *A Fable*. It was a small space with one window but it kept him stationary when working. His writing table and chair were gifts from his mother: a frail spindle-legged table and a stiff occasional chair he modified by sawing the back off and adding a seat cushion.

The dining room, butler's pantry, and kitchen flowed off the back hall. There originally were three bedrooms upstairs though they would add a fourth and a sewing room. The upstairs balcony—supported by two sets of paired columns—was positioned over the front doors. Combined, the portico and Georgian doors made for an elegant entrance, and the upstairs balcony offered a pleasant place to pass a summer night.

The day Estelle realized they were actually going to live at Rowan Oak was one she would never forget. She'd embraced Bill's romantic vision of living in the beautiful, secluded area. They were both seeking more privacy and had wonderful childhood memories of the woods there. But on moving day, a year later in June 1930, the house looked like it was literally sinking into the soil—and if it didn't drown first, a windstorm might take it away.

It was quite a transition from her other living spaces. Since her divorce in April 1929, and her remarriage to Bill two months later, they'd lived comfortably in the downstairs floor of Miss Elma Meek's home on University Avenue. (Miss Meek was the first person to call the University of Mississippi "Ole Miss," a title conferred upon the mistress of a plantation.[1]) The high ceilings and generous space made the accommodations quite pleasant. And her parents had a lovely Oxford home on South Lamar. Estelle's father was former U.S. District Attorney Judge Lemuel E. Oldham, and her mother, Lida, a gracious homemaker and hostess.

And then there were the lavish homes she'd shared with her first husband, Cornell Franklin, in Hawaii and Shanghai. She'd had an abundance of household help and, especially in Shanghai, no obligations except shopping and socializing. There, her life was a whirlwind of fashionable lunches, teas, cocktail parties, and receptions, only to end with a late-night dinner party. Both Cornell and Estelle enjoyed gambling. Her cigarette smoking went from moderate to heavy; and all these years later, she hadn't been able to stop.

Over time she became fairly accustomed to the city's character which careened between sophistication—with a lively arts and culture scene— and decadence. The customary and prolific drinking was accompanied by drug use—opiates mostly. She'd eventually found the endless drinking and parties exhausting and unfulfilling. Rowan Oak promised a different kind of exhaustion.

* * *

The house was not yet called Rowan Oak nor was it the old Sheegog house. In 1872, when John M. Bailey and his wife, Ellen C. Bailey, bought the property from Robert Sheegog's son, the house became known as Bailey Place, and the wooded land between the University of Mississippi campus and the house, Bailey's Woods. After John's death in 1877, his widow continued to live there with their nieces Sallie and Ellen, whom they had reared. The younger Ellen resided there until her death in 1922 at which time her sister, Sallie, who had married W.C. Bryant of Coffeeville, Mississippi, inherited the place. Sallie and W.C. remained in Coffeeville and became absentee landlords with the house receiving little if anything in the way of refurbishment.

Estelle and Bill agreed that once they took ownership the place needed a new, distinct identity. Who but Bill could come up with Rowan Oak? It would be named for a tree that was not an oak but instead a mountain ash indigenous to Scotland! His vast reading trove included Sir James George Frazer's *The Golden Bough*. From that volume he learned about Scottish folklore and the farmers' belief that placing rowan twigs above the doors of barns kept witches from stealing milk, casting spells, and other mischief. The rowan tree came to symbolize protection, stability and peace— virtues any family would treasure, the Faulkners being no exception.

There was already an element of the supernatural about the place. Rowan Oak came complete with its own ghost: Judith Sheegog, and according to the oft-told story, her grave was on the property beneath a magnolia tree in the formal garden. (Did Faulkner create the lovely but doomed young woman who embellished Rowan Oak's lore? Some believe that is indeed the case since "Judith Sheegog" failed to appear in the 1850 or 1860 census.)

When Union troops occupied Oxford, the story went, Judith fell in love with a Yankee soldier. Their attempted elopement involved Judith climbing out her upstairs window to avoid her parents' knowledge. When the rope broke halfway on her descent, she fell to her death. The Faulkners and their children would become familiar with Judith's presence. Sometimes the piano played when no one was in the parlor or an apparition of a dark-haired, slender figure with lovely features glided through the house and down to the magnolia tree. Faulkner loved to include Judith's story as part of his Halloween ghost stories.

The tale of the ill-fated romance between Judith and her Yankee lover spread among Union soldiers. Houses in Oxford were being burnt to the ground by Union troops, including the Jacob Thompson house, a 20-room mansion known as "Home Place," across the road from the Sheegogs. Thompson was in Canada on a secret mission for the Confederacy when Union forces arrived and his home was a particular target for destruction.[2] While the Sheegog place was spared in honor of Judith and her gravesite, "Home Place" was reduced to brick remnants of the kitchen.

Thompson, an original board of trustee member of the University of Mississippi,[3] was a colorful and controversial landowner and Confederate activist. He and others in 1864 hatched a retaliation plan—the burning of New York City—for the burning and pillaging of the South by Union General William Sherman and others. He was rumored to have met with John Wilkes Booth,[4] and after the Civil War, he fled the country. He later returned and spent the rest of his life in Memphis, Tennessee.

* * *

Why, she wondered, hadn't they listened to her father and Bill's father, Murry? It was the only thing the two men had ever agreed upon. Together they tried to talk Bill out of what they considered a foolish and reckless purchase. Reaching the main road from the house required a wagon and mule since it was impossible by car. To start with, besides the years of neglect and deterioration, the house was without electricity and plumbing. Faulkner's father and father-in-law knew that expensive repairs and improvements were likely beyond Bill's means. The house needed virtually everything from a new foundation to a new roof. The exterior hadn't been painted in countless years, making for a dire first impression, and it would be more than twenty years before fresh paint would revive the home's appearance.

Regardless of Lem and Murry's efforts, on April 12, 1930, for the sum of $6,000, Bill and Estelle took ownership of the dilapidated house on four acres with a barn and what was once the outdoor kitchen made from hand-fired bricks (Bill would use it as a smokehouse for smoking meats). The reddish-orange bricks were formed from a clay ditch on the property. Sallie and W.C. Bryant fully financed the sale with a deed of trust and no down payment. Faulkner was to make monthly payments of $75. Bill and

W.C. hit it off from the outset and the Bryants liked Bill's commitment to restoring the house and the landscaping.

In its original splendor, the Sheegogs had employed a landscape architect responsible for the curved driveway, cedar-lined brick walk, and the gardens near the front entrance. Unfortunately, much of that landscaping had been forfeited for a vegetable garden. The Bryants' last tenants in 1928, the Claude Anderson family, plowed under much of the landscaped areas. They raised chickens, cows, and produce which they sold in the area. Their concern was not the once lovely beds or the deteriorating house, it was securing a livelihood.

Somehow, the Anderson family learned to live with the leaking roof, rotting beams, and an attic full of mice and squirrels. House snakes even occupied one of the closets, leaving behind skins they'd shed. Removing the discarded snake skins was just part of the staggering cleaning labor—dusting, knocking down spider webs, plugging old rat holes—required before Bill and Estelle would be able to move furniture into the home. Estelle realized later that as hard as those days leading up to the move had been, they had not prepared her for the day-to-day labor of living there.

Estelle scolded herself for being too much the romantic. She shared that and her artistic temperament with Bill, or Billy as she sometimes called him, lapsing into their childhood vernacular. She was an accomplished seamstress, a pianist who wrote her own music and lyrics; she wrote fiction, including a novel, *White Beaches*, and painted. Yet even she couldn't romanticize the house that stood before her. Her tiny frame would hardly stand a chance against the rigors of this new life! Bill admired her petiteness and how her small size matched his own. Even if she tried to gain, her weight by and large held steady at around ninety pounds.

How would she cope without basic necessities? A rickety outhouse surrounded by high weeds and grass on the property with oil lamps to use at night were one answer. How she dreaded those terrifying evening trips! Would she encounter a snake, spiders, or some horrifying rodent? The relentless Mississippi summer was upon them and a month passed before they even had screens on the windows. Water—for which there seemed to be an endless need—was drawn and carried to the house from the cistern. Bathing in warm weather also occurred at the cistern with drawn buckets for washing and rinsing. What an onerous ordeal!

Even as a small child, she'd never cared for camping and rustic conditions, rough and tumble play, getting dirty and mussed. She liked her clothes and hair just so. Bill, who was often remiss in his hygiene—a source of friction between them—would find outdoor bathing of little or no concern.

At night, all she wanted was to collapse from exhaustion but Bill had other ideas. He was a newlywed for the first time, she for the second. She was 32 years old when they married, seven months older than Bill, and a divorcée with two children as evidence. She couldn't help but feel his enthusiasm for her would have been even greater if the specter of that first marriage didn't hover. Even though Bill understood the situation better than anyone, her marriage to Cornell was a betrayal of sorts. It was a simmering source of unrest for her husband. She sometimes wondered if that didn't account for his unexpected outbursts of anger or long periods of silence. Estelle thought again of how much more resilient women are. She hardly looked back or thought much at all about Cornell. If she thought about anything, it was how the pace of that life was too much for her. She didn't have the stamina or emotional strength for the endless social whirl they had inhabited.

* * *

Cornell Sidney Franklin epitomized the ambitions of Estelle's parents. A successful young lawyer from an old Mississippi family, Cornell relocated to the Hawaiian Territory three years before his marriage to Estelle in 1918. There, he moved up quickly, from lawyer to deputy attorney general, and, one year after their marriage, to a circuit judgeship. Their courtship had been long distance and of no real sustained depth. It was reminiscent of an arranged marriage—more so because the Oldhams put their foot down to the prospect of Estelle marrying Billy Faulkner. They, like others, referred to him as Count No 'Count, and would in no way entertain the notion of their daughter in that match. Likewise, Bill's own family didn't think he was ready for the responsibilities of marriage. Bill wanted approval from both families, even for an elopement. That effectively ended their chance to marry.

Yet the torch continued. For eleven years, Estelle pined for Bill, as he pined for her. During one of her visits home from Honolulu, Estelle, always on the verge of exotic and the quintessential belle, created quite a splash. She hadn't lost any of her youthful appeal when she was known as the best dressed girl in Mississippi. Lively and popular, she thrived on conversation and social interaction. Her parents hosted nonstop gatherings with friends and admirers. Her young daughter, Victoria Franklin, had a Japanese nurse who called the child Cho-Cho, an endearment meaning butterfly. The nurse wore the traditional Japanese dress including the obi with the large bow in back. For many people in Oxford, including Faulkner's college friend and early agent, Ben Wasson, she was the first Japanese person they had ever met (though according to Wasson she spoke very little English).

Wasson, a frequent guest at the Oldhams' home during Estelle's 1921 visit, was entranced by the spectacle of the Japanese nurse and Estelle as fashion muse. In fact, Wasson seemed quite smitten with Estelle, who he felt captured and exuded extreme femininity, not only in her attire but also in her flirtatious behavior. Her eyes were animated with a bewildering charm, particularly in conversation with men. She appeared completely absorbed in any such exchange however trivial.

Whatever the state of her marriage at the time, Estelle made the most of this visit home, even surprising Wasson with a passionate and spontaneous kiss, interrupted, according to Wasson, by Cho-Cho's appearance in the room. Faulkner, in his manner, pursued Estelle with his verse, presenting her with a book of poems, *Vision in Spring*. He listened to Wasson's tale of the stolen kiss with seemingly mild interest, "Watch out," he finally said, "and remember, Bud, that Eve wasn't the only woman who handed out an apple, just the first one."[5]

* * *

Estelle's parents were still unconvinced that Faulkner was a real option when she returned from Shanghai in 1926. Cornell had asked her to leave their Shanghai home; she chose to keep the details of their separation to herself. In 1920s southern society, "divorcée" was an awkward title for Estelle and her family. Her reception from the townspeople contrasted starkly with her exuberant welcome when she was still Mrs. Cornell Franklin. Once back in Oxford, she and Bill picked up where they left off. The prolonged divorce proceedings between Shanghai and Oxford allowed for a long courtship, though some might argue the courtship already had consumed much of Bill and Estelle's life. Their wedding—with only her sister Dorothy Oldham in attendance—occurred slightly outside of Oxford in an old Presbyterian church (the Episcopal Church wouldn't accommodate them because of Estelle's divorce). Nothing seemed to assuage her parents' assessment of Bill as a wastrel. Bill, for his part, refused to ever step foot in their home.

The rather unceremonious wedding was followed by a casual honeymoon on the Gulf Coast in Pascagoula, Mississippi, where Bill's brooding silences sometimes dampened their first married days together. There was much during those weeks in a rundown beach house to give her pause about her decision to remarry. The rental was long past its prime with little evident maintenance. The newlyweds' household help was a gift from Cornell's mother, Mrs. Hairston. Estelle's former mother-in-law insisted her own housekeeper accompany them as well as some of her silver.

By the time she and Bill reached their beach destination, it seemed the only remnant of Estelle's once comfortable life was her extensive wardrobe. Like her tendency to overcharm and overtalk, she was often overdressed for a place like Pascagoula. Other vacationing couples noted the Faulkners' elaborate dinner outfits (though sometimes Bill went barefoot and skipped shaving for days) and that husband and wife would drink with equal enthusiasm.

Estelle was grappling with Bill's quiet streaks, sporadic grooming habits, and intense periods of concentration, and wondering if life with a creative genius was really for her. She also was feeling neglected. Shouldn't she have been the recipient of his attention on their honeymoon? Instead he was absorbed in reading proofs of his new novel, *The Sound and the Fury*, and corresponding with his agent. It soon felt like a calamitous error in judgment, this hasty second marriage. Old feelings of wishing to escape started to pull at her—feelings she'd had on occasion with Cornell. One night after admittedly too much liquor, she simply walked into the water in a silk gown. Had Bill not called out and a neighbor rushed in to rescue her, she might have quietly slipped away, the warm Gulf waves welcoming her in a manner that had eluded her most of her life.

* * *

Besides her own discomfort with the primitive conditions at Rowan Oak, she worried about her daughter, 11-year-old Victoria, who was still often called Cho-Cho, and her 7-year-old son, Malcolm. Cho-Cho let her mother know how much she disliked the idea of living at Rowan Oak. On moving day, she sat down on the house's front steps and cried. How would she ever invite her friends to such a place? She petitioned to stay at her grandparents' home on South Lamar. They even had a radio!

Malcolm, for his part, was more agreeable, seeing it perhaps as an extended adventure. Estelle and the children had picnicked in Bailey's Woods with Faulkner, outings which often included exploring on the part of Malcolm and Bill. Her son came to really appreciate all Bill taught him about nature. Later Malcolm wrote that "fundamentally the house was beautiful. I suppose Billy was the only one who could see the fine, clean structure of its lines, which showed the delicate simplicity of the Southern Colonial period during the 1840's when it was built."[6]

None of Malcolm's enthusiasm alleviated Estelle's worries about her son, who wasn't a very healthy child. How would he handle the rigors of such challenging conditions? There wasn't any kind of heat in the winter besides the various fireplaces. With the urgings of her parents, Estelle came to believe the comforts of their home would be better for Malcolm. As time unfolded, he would spend a good deal of his childhood and adolescence with his maternal grandparents. The Oldhams had lost a young son, Estelle's brother, Ned, and they more than welcomed having their grandson live with them. (Bill felt they also welcomed taking Cornell Franklin's child support checks of which Estelle saw little.) Only later did the pangs of regret strike for those lost years. Why did she allow the separation to occur?

Bill almost fervently embraced the project of restoring Rowan Oak. She had to admit she was shocked by his industry. With money so scare he was committed to doing as much of the work himself as possible. Fortunately, there also were friends and family to call on when necessary. And, last resort, he hired reasonable local labor. They sometimes relied on credit for necessary supplies, and if he sold a story, those funds would already be appropriated tenfold!

When "Red Leaves" did sell in July 1930 to the *Saturday Evening Post*, they were able to wire the house for electricity. Bill did this with the help of a family friend who had been a boy scout under Bill's reign as scout master. It was a tedious and time consuming job. The tight space in the attic required crawling and there was a constant fear of disrupting hibernating snakes. It was hard for Estelle to remember which caused more rejoicing, electricity or the plumbing and upstairs bathroom. The house was still cold, freezing at times, and heated by open fireplaces. There was scant insulation and 14-foot ceilings. It would be 1933 before they were able to install central heat.

As her fatigue intensified that summer, Estelle tried to tell herself it was the countless tasks that consumed her day, but soon she had to accept the telltale signs of pregnancy. Her doctor took note of her spent condition and cautioned her to rest and care for herself. She knew his advice would be hard to follow with her current living situation. Plus, she had a history of difficult pregnancies and this one most likely would be as well. The timing wasn't good but they had done nothing to prevent it. All that aside, Bill seemed thrilled at the thought of being a father and she was happy they would at last have a child together.

Given her precarious health, Estelle was especially thankful for the presence of Ned Barnett, "Uncle Ned," and Caroline Barr, "Mammy Callie," who had appeared at Rowan Oak without any sort of summons to help out around the place. Both had long relationships with the Faulkners—it was Bill who changed the spelling to include the "u"—and were beloved members of the family. Uncle Ned's service dated back to Bill's great-grandfather, William Clark Falkner, "The Old Colonel." A very distinguished looking gentleman, Uncle Ned, who was a runaway slave when he met the Old Colonel, sometimes wore a tie around the place while performing menial tasks; at dinner, he might show up in a frock coat he'd inherited from Bill's grandfather, John Wesley Thompson Falkner, "The Young Colonel."

Three. Estelle

Mammy Callie reigned supreme at Rowan Oak, and everyone, adults and children alike, accepted her authority. She had been born into slavery in South Carolina and married a Barr slave. Somehow, she met Bill's family and her long tenure commenced. She helped Bill's mother, Miss Maud, rear her four sons. Now, at Rowan Oak, she lent a hand with the children and also helped in the kitchen. Besides serving at dinner, Uncle Ned handled a variety of chores in the yard and with the livestock. Estelle and Bill couldn't afford wages but they provided food and housing and other possible necessities.

Remembering Uncle Ned's cedar chest still brought tears to Estelle. After his passing in Ripley, Mississippi, a place he considered home and where he had returned toward the end of his days, he was buried in the Ripley cemetery, resting place of the Old Colonel and other Falkner relatives. It fell to Estelle to sort his belongings. Inside the chest, carefully wrapped, she found the birthday cake she had baked for him four years earlier. There were even remnants of the Old Colonel's Confederate uniform. Uncle Ned was the dearest man, she often thought, and Mammy Callie, whose funeral service took place in the parlor at Rowan Oak with Bill delivering the eulogy, one of the most capable people she'd ever met.

* * *

Their first Christmas at Rowan Oak was a beautiful and special time with their carefully selected cedar Christmas tree and greenery coming from their own property. Family and friends dropped by and complimented all the improvements. Christmas morning meant gift opening—first at Rowan Oak, then at the Oldham home. Faulkner skipped the later, visiting his mother instead, but Estelle's parents were invited to Christmas dinner at Rowan Oak. As much as she enjoyed the festivities, Estelle, now quite pregnant, tired quickly from the entertaining and increased activity. They kept the gift-giving simple—pipe cleaners were the only gift Bill would accept from family and these small bundles were cleverly wrapped and hung from the Christmas tree—as she knew Bill was very concerned about the stagnant cash flow. The family's basic needs were far outpacing their income.

When Bill told her he made more money from one story sold to the *Saturday Evening Post* than his first four novels—*Soldiers' Pay, Mosquitoes, Sartoris,* and *The Sound and the Fury*—combined, it was hard to believe. During the past year, they basically had lived off of the four magazine stories he was able to place. She loved his work and believed in him, always telling him that his critical reputation soared with each new novel. In October of 1930, just four months after they moved into Rowan

Oak, he published *As I Lay Dying*. Still, work and worry were persistent companions.

The January night in 1931 when she went into labor, two months early, was as cold as she ever remembered being. She was actually relieved when Bill came around with the car to leave the frigid house and head to the hospital, despite the ordeal of labor she knew awaited her. When her baby girl was born the next day, Estelle's recovery was so involved that she didn't even have them bring the baby to her room. She and Bill had decided on her name though, Alabama, after Bill's favorite great-aunt, Alabama Leroy Falkner, the Old Colonel's youngest child. Days went by, and as she convalesced, Alabama's condition deteriorated. It didn't help that the hospital lacked an incubator.

Desperate for a way to help the baby, Bill and his brother, Dean, drove to Memphis to get an incubator, but their efforts were too late. When he returned, she knew the worst the moment he walked in her room. His grief-stricken face said it all. And, until that moment, she'd never known such heartache. In all the years she'd known him, since she was seven years old, it was the first time she saw Bill cry. She even encouraged him to go have a drink. His reaction startled her. He refused the idea, saying this was one time he wasn't going to give in to that.

Estelle never held or even saw the tiny infant. That loss of her baby plagued her. While she was recovering, Bill had been with Alabama, watching her brave struggle for life that ended after nine days. And she didn't go with Bill to the St. Peter's cemetery in Oxford. She had never greeted her baby in life and had missed the formal goodbye. There was little in the way of a service except Bill's father who offered a prayer at the gravesite. Faulkner rode stoically in one of the three cars which made up the small procession. He held Alabama's slight coffin in his lap the entire way.

Estelle said to Bill what everyone expected of her: that they would have another baby. Yet her recovery remained prolonged. Physically, she was weak and anemic and often depressed. It seemed her depression matched his and made for trying, cheerless days. Bill's drinking was on the uptick. He was angry at her obstetrician, angry at the hospital, and generally despondent. Even the publication of *Sanctuary* in February—a scandalous rendering of rape and voyeurism; a novel with the promise of generating income regardless of outrage—and a record number of published stories—16 in 1931—did little to lift his spirits. When the story collection *These 13* appeared in September, dedicated to "Estelle and Alabama," she felt herself soften toward Bill and also the familiar pang of grief.

Thankfully in October he had business trips—a writers' conference in Charlottesville, Virginia, and a visit to his publishers in New York. She embraced his absence knowing it would be a relief to shift his fog of sadness. But along with relief came guilt. She recognized his vulnerability left him susceptible to overdrinking. That was indeed the case from his arrival at the southern writers' assembly until he departed New York for Oxford. His first order of business after checking into a hotel on Court Square was procuring a bottle of whiskey. And so it went. His contribution to the discussions with 34 writers ranged from "I agree, I agree" to "I dare say" to softly humming "Carry Me Back to Old Virginia."[7] Sherwood Anderson noted, "From time to time he appeared, got drunk again immediately, and disappeared."[8]

During an afternoon tea at Castle Hill, the storied mansion of Amelie Rivers, a femme fatale in her day and author of a rather racy novel, Faulkner wandered off to explore the famous residence on his own. The proprietress was very particular about her settings when she met with guests—the room had to be lit by mere candlelight or fireplace. "Mr. Faulkner," she said, "I have seen how you have walked through my house and looked through my rooms, but I have forgiven you because you were accompanied by genius."[9]

While Faulkner was a focal point of interest to many participants and the press—*Sanctuary* was an attention grabber—his interest flagged at best. Lewis Mattison, a Charlottesville reporter, believed the conference was meaningless to Faulkner, and that "He didn't give a damn about Ellen Glasgow or any of them."[10]

* * *

Bill's letters—he was a prolific letter writer—were pouring in with greetings for Cho-Cho and Malcolm as well. Once in New York his tone became even more ebullient and heightened; Estelle worried about his mental state. Various publishers were courting him and he heard rumors of Hollywood deals. "I have the assurance of a movie agent that I can go to California, to Hollywood and make 500.00 or 750.00 a week in the movies," he wrote her. "I think the trip would do you a lot of good. We could live like counts at least on that, and you could dance and go about."[11] Stranger yet was a letter boasting of his importance:

> I have created quite a sensation. I have had luncheons in my honor by magazine editors every day for a week now, besides evening parties.... In fact, I have learned with astonishment that I am now the most important figure in American letters. That is, I have the best future. Even Sinclair Lewis and [Theodore] Dreiser make engagements to see me, and Mencken is coming all the way up from Baltimore to see me on Wednesday. I'm glad I'm level-headed, not very vain.[12]

Was he headed for a breakdown? She registered little surprise when the telegram came from Wasson, who was now living in the Manhattan and acting as Bill's agent, asking her to come to the city and care for her husband. What a taxing trip that turned out to be! First there was the train ride from Memphis to New York, then there was Bill. He was in a full, alcoholic episode, and she was hardly up to the ordeal. They were both consumed with their loss of Alabama and diverting themselves in destructive ways.

Once in New York, it was evident the rescuer was in need of rescuing. Estelle was exhausted, and at the hotel, longing for bed, she discovered instead a host of invitations. Seeing Bill confirmed what she'd suspected; he confided that the stress had been too much for him. She scaled back their social obligations as best she could. She began to understand why Bill favored the Algonquin. The staff made such an effort, even moving a piano into their room for her. It was a comfortable but also fascinating place with celebrities as guests and lobby regulars.

Despite her efforts the parties continued. Meeting new people—like the author and personality Dorothy Parker—and others—especially those consumed with impressing Bill—frayed her nerves. Dorothy lived at the Algonquin and was very much in Bill's circle. She arranged a shopping trip that apparently heightened Estelle's anxiety. On their return to the hotel, Estelle became extremely agitated, tore her dress, and threatened to jump out the window. Too much alcohol heightened her volatile condition. Her wide eyes in her thin face made a haunting impression.

At a party at his Central Park apartment, Random House publisher Bennett Cerf gave her a curious look. She remarked on the loveliness of the stunning city view, telling Cerf such beauty made her want to throw herself out the window. Cerf took her at her word and guided her away from the window. (Cerf evolved into an ally who would divert her with records and dancing. On her return home, she displayed his photograph in her bedroom.) Her unsteady mental state was rivaling—if not outpacing—her husband's. Bill's veneration was new to them and they responded badly: one drink after another.

Both were emotionally unhinged. During an evening of drinking, Bill, in some misguided attempt to calm Estelle, forcefully slapped her face, and then without any explanation resumed his conversation with others. Rather than continue the spectacle in front of his new entourage, she feigned submission. How unfortunate it was that their private woes unfolded for display. There was one last stop en route to Mississippi. They stopped in Baltimore for dinner with Mencken. Estelle retired early, correctly anticipating that the two men would make quite a night of it.

Their two weeks in New York evoked unpleasant memories of her time in Shanghai and she was thankful to see Mississippi. They were home before Christmas and a sense of calmness descended. Christmas at Rowan

Oak was a decorous event. Faulkner donned an "elegant and ornate silk Chinese robe" and Estelle a "lovely Chinese wrapper in soft, muted pastel shades." The family moved through various rooms in a predetermined sequence. First, stocking contents were explored in Estelle's bedroom; then a move to the parlor to gather by the tree. This group included the domestic help as well.

After he offered a prayer, Bill distributed the presents in an orderly fashion. With the gift opening behind them, the family dressed and reappeared for breakfast at a festively decorated dining room table and a glass of Bill's famous Christmas punch. Malcolm recalled the recipe as "apples, bourbon, dry burgundy and soda water, chilled by a generous portion of ice chunks. During the morning and through the day frequent knocks at the kitchen door were followed by shouts of 'Christmas Gift!' and various folks that had worked for us during the year received in return a Christmas drink and cheerful word."[13]

The tradition and goodwill of the holidays carried over into the new year. Bill's writing was going well and he was in good spirits. That spring the family needed a revenue stream and he took a screen-writing stint in Hollywood. By the fall of 1932, *Light in August*, his seventh novel, was published. There also was talk of a movie deal for *Sanctuary*. Along with Bill's success came happiness of a different nature. Estelle's promise of another child was fulfilled.

On June 23, 1933, Jill Faulkner, a small but healthy baby, made her appearance. Her parents, in their mid-thirties, were a little older than average for the day. Estelle couldn't suppress a laugh when Bill showed up at the hospital in his RAF uniform with nine-year-old Malcolm, who had been dismissed from school for the occasion. It was big brother's first chance to meet his new sister. A few days later Jill came home with both a nurse and a wet nurse. Not long after her arrival at Rowan Oak, Bill summoned Estelle, family members, and household help for a toast in the tiny baby's honor. Estelle felt immensely gratified. It was wonderful to witness his happiness.

Four

The Road to Glory: 1932–1936

Life in the 1930s for Faulkner and Estelle was a piling on of complex and blistering life events. The slow recovery after their daughter's death and the plodding improvements at Rowan Oak continued. It seemed the couple inched toward stability only to have it evaporate. Faulkner's work in Hollywood introduced the temptation of a lovely young script girl from the South. And there was yet another shattering family tragedy. Meanwhile, Faulkner's creative output went unchecked. Every year more stories appeared in national publications: eight in 1932; three in 1933; eleven in 1934, the same year the genesis of *Absalom, Absalom!* came to him; and five in 1935.

The publication of *Absalom* in the fall of 1936 was a triumph. An American tragedy in a southern setting, the novel features Thomas Sutpen, an unlikely anti-hero whose merciless quest for a dynasty—driven by a decades-old insult—proves his ruin. The Virginia mountain boy whose hardscrabble upbringing depended on his father finding piecework on various plantations helped his family as needed. Sent to yet another plantation manor on an errand for his father, Sutpen is rebuked. A Black butler in fine livery bars the youth from entering, telling him to use the back door, not the front. Stunned by the servant's hostility and disdain, Sutpen loses his naïveté at that moment; and, though he is only 13 or so years old, the encounter sets his course, "design," in motion. He would acquire a grand house, plantation, and a respectable wife, and father sons. He travels to Haiti, works on a sugar plantation as the overseer, quells a rebellion, and earns the owner's respect and gratitude. Marriage to the planter's daughter follows, and soon after, a son. Upon discovering his wife was part Black, Sutpen repudiates her and the child. "I found," Sutpen said, "that she was not and could never be, through no fault of her own, adjunctive or incremental to the design which I had in mind, so I provided for her and put her aside."[1]

While his first wife was no longer "adjunctive to the design," the twenty Haitian slaves Sutpen had acquired were. He relocates with them to

Four. The Road to Glory: 1932–1936

Jefferson, Mississippi, where they supply the labor the kidnapped French architect needs to build the largest home in Northern Mississippi. Sutpen's Hundred is his answer to the butler who refused to let him deliver his message. A second marriage follows (her race was not in question) and two children. Though Sutpen's design is realized, it is far from secure. It is haunted and destroyed by denying his first family: the discarded wife and unacknowledged son. Miraculously, this complicated novel emerged despite marital difficulties and personal loss, a masterpiece conceived and completed while bouncing between Oxford and Hollywood.

* * *

Navigating the contrast between his life in Hollywood—with a room at a trendy hotel—and the quiet retreat of Rowan Oak tucked deep in the woods proved challenging. While in Hollywood, Faulkner frequented restaurants and supper clubs popular with actors, movie industry deal makers, and writers: Schwab's Pharmacy, Lucy's, LaRue's, Pig-'n-Whistle, Musso and Frank's (a haven for screenwriters), and The Players. The Players especially achieved Hollywood notoriety with its assignation tunnel leading to the nearby Chateau Marmont and its convenient location across from the Garden of Allah Hotel, an extended stay place with a legendary guest book including Humphrey Bogart, Lauren Bacall, Greta Garbo, Dorothy Parker, Ernest Hemingway, and F. Scott Fitzgerald.

Little of this glitz and glamour extended to Mississippi. Apparently his inclination to socialize was not exercised much in Oxford, where he and Estelle, to her displeasure, were mostly homebodies. Faulkner embraced the solitude and would remain silent for unnerving periods of time. His frustrating wall of silence wasn't easily pierced. Estelle, who had been instructed by her mother as a young girl to be charming since she wasn't particularly beautiful, enjoyed people, parties, and dinners. She wanted to go out and resented his stubborn streak. It was lost on Faulkner that Estelle didn't have an alternative to her isolating existence at Rowan Oak.

Hollywood soon became synonymous with increased income and long absences from home. The manna from Faulkner's work on screenplays and the movie options on his novels was very welcome indeed, but it did not come without cost to his marriage. When Metro-Goldwyn-Mayer offered six weeks at $500 a week in May 1932, the couple was significantly overdrawn and without credit for even a few groceries. Faulkner literally spent his last few dollars wiring MGM that he would accept their offer. He then asked his uncle for a five-dollar loan. John Faulkner instead offered a $500 loan to cover his nephew's overdraft, but Faulkner declined and held out for a studio advance.

Meanwhile, Faulkner's own father was incredulous that his son's writing could fetch $500 a week. Murry's displeasure with Faulkner's vocation was never resolved. Even when his son found success, Murry remained dismissive and unsupportive. But at this particular juncture, Faulkner remained independent. Luck intervened and the advance money arrived along with a train ticket to the MGM studio located on the outskirts of Los Angeles.

Faulkner made quite an impression with his late arrival at the studio on May 7, 1932—disheveled, his head bleeding, and clearly inebriated. Faulkner brushed off the idea of seeing a doctor and said he preferred to get right to work so they asked him to view a film in the projection room. After a few moments, a fidgety and excessively voluble Faulkner sought the exit, saying he already knew how the film would end. Nine days passed before he reappeared, with the far-fetched story that he had been wandering in Death Valley. Quite a shocking story, as it was 150 miles away and he didn't seem to know how he got there. This inaugural Hollywood stint with a string of days lost to drinking became more the norm than not. It eventually led to his tarnished and unreliable reputation as a screenwriter. The strain of the past months no doubt contributed to his mental disorder. Shortly before leaving Oxford, Faulkner completed *Light in August*, a 527-page manuscript, that Estelle, in a pique of anger, threw out the car window. That left Faulkner scrambling through the weeds and ditches for manuscript pages. He had hoped a magazine would serialize the novel—an epic tale of race and retribution—but as usual, Faulkner was years ahead of public readership.

Good fortune struck again in July 1932 when Faulkner met movie director Howard Hawks. Hawks was a year older than Faulkner and a fan of his novels and stories. He soon took a liking to Faulkner and bestowed more tolerance than others in Hollywood were wont to do. Hawks was not terribly unlike Faulkner in temperament. Reserved with a British affectation, he didn't let many people into his personal orbit. A tall, imposing figure, with great reserves of charm, Hawks was aware of the clout he exerted in Hollywood, his ability to help make or break careers. Like many of the agents and editors in New York who admired Faulkner, Hawks proved a loyal supporter and an ongoing source of sustenance.

It seemed Faulkner had scarcely settled into a somewhat productive routine in Hollywood when, on August 7, his father, who was just shy of 62 years old, suffered a fatal heart attack. Faulkner must have felt a thunderous conflict of emotions. His relationship with Murry had always been an uneasy one. It was nothing like the close bond he shared with his mother, Maud. While Murry would indulge his youngest son, Dean, who embraced a volitionless path and c'est la vie attitude, Murry didn't find similar traits attractive in his eldest. Bill's choice of an occupation perplexed him, and he believed if his son was determined to write books, they should be westerns.

When *Sanctuary* (1931) was published and Faulkner actually realized some financial gain, Murry took issue with the novel's sexual theme and tried to have it suppressed and withdrawn from the market. He even stopped an Ole Miss coed one day who was walking on campus with a copy, telling her, "It isn't fit for a nice girl to read."[2] Faulkner's father wasn't alone in his outrage. His cousin, Sallie Murry, asked Faulkner if he thought up that material when he was drunk. "Sallie Murry," he replied, "I get a lot of it when I'm drunk."[3] About the novel himself, Faulkner commented, "When I finished it I went to look at myself in a mirror. And I thought, did that ugly, ratty-looking face, that mixture of childishness and unreliability and sublime vanity, imagine that? But I did... I listen to the voices, and when I put down what the voices say, it's right. Sometimes I don't like what the voices say, but I don't change it."[4]

After he returned to Oxford for the funeral, Faulkner, like it or not, assumed responsibility for his father's affairs. His time in Oxford also was devoted to reading the galleys of *Light in August*. The plan was for Estelle to go back to California with him in September, but she was pregnant; instead, his mother and Dean accompanied him on the long drive west. They stayed only two months but Dean and Faulkner enjoyed themselves. Faulkner felt more at home when Hawks invited him dove hunting along with another friend, Clark Gable.

When Hawks began talking books, Gable asked Faulkner whom he considered the best modern writers. He replied, "Ernest Hemingway, Willa Cather, Thomas Mann, John Dos Passos, and myself." To Gable's surprised response, "Oh, do you write?" Faulkner quipped, "Yes, Mr. Gable. What do you do?"[5] That entertaining repartee—and the fact that Faulkner greatly admired Gable's .410 over-and-under shotgun—led to a friendship between author and actor.

Though Hawks offered him an extension, Faulkner had much to occupy him in Oxford and money wasn't so pressing. Paramount had optioned *Sanctuary* for $6,000 and *Light in August* was newly released. But the real driving force was Maud, who was eager to return to Oxford. Over the next twenty-two years a pattern was thus established: Faulkner would live between Hollywood and Oxford as needs dictated.

* * *

In 1933, with more money than they'd ever had thanks to MGM, Faulkner installed central heat and bought three adjoining lots to Rowan Oak, plus his own airplane, a red Cabin Waco Biplane with the number 13413 which Maud pronounced bad luck. Flying seemed to be in the Faulkner brothers' blood. Faulkner received his pilot's wings that year; his brothers Murry Charles, Jr., "Jack" and Johncy were already pilots; and Faulkner was financing Dean's flying lessons. By the fall of 1935, the brothers, now all pilots, even staged an air show in Oxford billed as "The Flying Faulkners."[6]

Yet the money went out as fast as it came in, and by the summer of 1935 he wrote his agent, Morton Goldman, of a pressing need for cash. On mutually agreed upon terms, his brother, Dean, would acquire Faulkner's plane, and Faulkner considered selling the manuscripts of *Sartoris*, *The Sound and the Fury*, *As I Lay Dying*, *Sanctuary*, and *Light in August*. Fortunately, an advance from his publisher and a new contract in Hollywood prevented such a drastic measure. Howard Hawks' offer of $1,000 a week starting mid-December was readily though not happily accepted. Faulkner would rather be home concentrating on his novel. The importance of *Absalom* was increasingly evident as he advanced the narrative threads of miscegenation in the still deeply divided South and the central character's towering ego. Later, when he shared the sole manuscript copy with Dave Hempstead, a Twentieth Century–Fox colleague, Faulkner declared it the greatest novel yet written by an American. (James Campbell would write 87 years later in the *Wall Street Journal* that "*Absalom, Absalom!* [is] one of the most astonishing novels in the English language."[7]) Hempstead, who knew Faulkner was drinking when he handed him the manuscript, was terrified of keeping it overnight. Such brilliance often ushered in manic spells and set a debilitating cycle in motion.

* * *

Four years after Faulkner and Estelle lost their baby girl Alabama, tragedy struck again. Faulkner's youngest brother, Dean, was killed November 10, 1935, in a plane crash along with his three passengers. Dean, born August 15, 1907, was just 28 years old, and his wife, Louise, was four months pregnant with their first child. Dean was ten years Faulkner's junior and that might have played a role in the love and protectiveness Faulkner felt for him. Already a duo, the youngest and eldest Faulkner boys formed an even deeper bond in 1922 when the two middle brothers both married and established careers. Dean quite openly took to mimicking many of his eldest brother's eccentricities—going barefoot, wearing shabby clothes, even moving into Bill's empty tower room at the Delta Psi House.

Temperamentally, the two were quite different, Bill quiet and reserved; Dean good natured and light hearted. Dean was a natural athlete, quite an accomplished baseball player and an avid outdoorsman. His efforts in college were negligible, cycling in and out of semesters and classes. An indulged youngest child, he would promptly lose jobs his father would find him and suffer no repercussions. After Murry died in the summer of 1932, Dean, still unemployed at 25 years, moved in with his mother.

Faulkner detected a despondency about Dean. His pattern of drifting through life seemed to be catching up with him. Realizing his brother needed a purpose, Faulkner encouraged him to take up flying, and it seemed like providence—Dean was a natural and soon a talented pilot. His life took off in his late twenties—a job he liked, a happy marriage, and a child on the way—only to end abruptly when his plane came down near Pontotoc, Mississippi. On the day of Dean's accident, Faulkner, who knew the worst, called the Oxford central switchboard and asked that they hold all calls to his mother's house. He needed to tell her himself and he feared for her. Her attachment to her youngest son was profound.

There were rampant speculations about the cause of the crash, though most agreed Dean had allowed a young passenger who was taking flying lessons to take the controls. The Waco, which had been shooting straight up, suddenly shot straight down and drilled five or six feet into the hard earth. Likewise, various accounts of the condition of Dean's body circulated, from an unbroken face to a flattened body. The Pontotoc undertaker couldn't manage the necessary repairs; so another, more experienced undertaker came from Grenada, Mississippi. Faulkner, again fearing for his mother, spent the night at Carr's funeral home.

Dean's shattered body was placed in a bathtub while Faulkner and the undertaker, with a nearby bottle of whiskey, did their best. The result was less than Faulkner had hoped, and at the family home on South Lamar, relatives managed to convince Maud and Louise to remember Dean as they last saw him. They agreed to a closed casket and a small, family service followed in the living room. This formal, emotional goodbye portended years of prolonged mourning. On November 11, 1935, for the third time in five years, the Faulkners made their way to St. Peter's Cemetery in Oxford.

* * *

Sadness compounded by searing guilt consumed Faulkner. He believed he was unwittingly the cause of his brother's death since he instigated Dean's career as a pilot and Dean lost his life in Faulkner's Waco. Faulkner, along with Dean's pregnant widow, moved into his mother's South Lamar home in Oxford. He vowed to financially care for Dean and Louise's baby as if she or he was his own. When Dean Faulkner was born March 22, 1936, Faulkner made good on his promise. Faulkner was there for his niece's milestones and Dean grew up close to her uncle, aunt, and cousins. Dean decided to attend the University of Mississippi and, as pledged, Faulkner covered her tuition and expenses, even a senior year of study in Europe. Stepping in for his deceased brother, Faulkner walked Dean down the aisle at her November 1958 wedding and hosted, along with Estelle, the wedding reception at Rowan Oak.

* * *

Maud Falkner's home was a place of sustained mourning. Together, Maud, Faulkner and Louise gradually found their way through the sorrow. For three weeks, Faulkner looked after the women and worked on *Absalom* at the dining room table. Like *Light in August* and Alabama's death, it was another novel intricately bound to loss. Maud kept her sleeping pill supply close at hand, sometimes threatening to take them all to end her suffering. Faulkner's drinking accelerated and Maud explained to Louise that he couldn't help himself. Even though Maud was strongly averse to alcohol, having witnessed the toll it took on her family, an exception was granted.

She had been prescient in declaring the numbers on the Waco unlucky, and she made her son, John, promise to quit flying over her house as had been their ritual when he or Dean flew to Oxford. They would buzz their mother's house and she'd know to drive to a field outside of Oxford and pick them up. Years passed before she told John it was okay to buzz her house again. She knew John, Bill, and Jack were not going to give up flying. Jack made a career of the FBI and flew around the country in a Monocoupe. Better that she knew they had arrived home safely.

* * *

His grief compelled Faulkner to hold even tighter to his evolving novel. The work migrated from his mother's dining room table in Oxford to his living quarters in Hollywood. The manuscript's journey was duly noted by the author, who inserted notations on the last page of *Absalom*—Rowan Oak, Mississippi 1935; California 1936; and Mississippi 1936. During the editing process, Faulkner added a map to *Absalom* with the legend: "Jefferson, Yoknapatawpha Co., Mississippi. Area, 2400 sq. mi. Population, Whites 6298 Negroes 9313. William Faulkner, Sole Owner and Proprietor."[8] Printed in red and black, the map appeared in the final volume folded among the endpapers.

* * *

Faulkner's new month-long contract with Hawks and 20th Century–Fox began December 16, 1935. He lodged at the Knickerbocker Hotel. Built in 1929, the hotel was gaining popularity among those in the film industry. Guests could rent apartments as well as rooms. Like many hotels that catered to directors, producers, scriptwriters, and actors, the Knickerbocker garnered Hollywood folklore. Its mysterious aura—haunted to some—originated at Halloween 1936 when Bess Houdini, Harry Houdini's widow, organized her tenth séance on the roof. The séance coincided with the third annual convention of the Pacific Coast Association of Magicians. Hotel guests might have seen a magician escaping from a straitjacket while hanging upside down outside the entrance or a Hollywood Boulevard car race featuring blindfolded drivers.

The actress Frances Farmer lived at the hotel, drank to excess, and was arrested there in 1943 for a pile of unpaid DUI fines. Not anticipating company, Farmer was drunk and nude when the police arrived. After a prolonged scuffle—she fiercely resisted—she was carried through the lobby wrapped in a shower curtain. Death came to the hotel in 1948 when famed director D.W. Griffith, an obscure, solitary figure later in life, had a heart attack in his room. He was one of several discarded Hollywood remnants who called the Knickerbocker home. The Knickerbocker was losing luster in the 1950s as Los Angeles's popularity surged. It transitioned into an intimate, niche destination. Marilyn Monroe and Joe DiMaggio frequented the bar and were said to have honeymooned there in 1954. Following an extensive renovation by a prominent architect, Elvis Presley was a guest during the filming of *Love Me Tender* (1956).

In decline by the 1960s, the hotel was no longer even a faded beauty. Irene Gibbons, a renowned costume designer who was troubled and discouraged by 1962, jumped to her death, landing on the hotel's roof. William Frawley, affectionately remembered as Fred Mertz from *I Love Lucy*, was a Knickerbocker fixture. When he had a stroke in the street, Frawley was pulled into the lobby only to die later at a hospital. Eventually the Knickerbocker became low-income housing for seniors though stories of stars and hauntings continued. Residents cited unexplainable sounds, slammed doors, and glimpses of Marilyn Monroe in the powder-room vanity mirror.

* * *

For Faulkner, even an empty room in the eerie hotel would be welcome after grappling with the difficult script Hawks assigned. It was a war story based on *Les Croix de Bois*, a 1919 novel by Roland Dorgelès, that was adapted into a French film in 1932. Hawks' developing script—first called "Wooden Crosses" and finally *The Road to Glory*—depicted trench life for a French regiment during World War I. The working draft concluded with a procession of the dead. Coming on the heels of Dean's death, the gloomy script was particularly funereal. Yet even if he felt mired in darkness, Faulkner continued the heavy lifting. Without neglecting *Absalom*, he might show up at the studio with 35 script pages he'd written the night before.

When the movie was released nine months later on September 4, 1936, Faulkner shared the screenplay credit with Joel Sayre. As would be the case with his subsequent screenplays, *The Road to Glory* went through a number of incarnations: various writers cycled in and out of scripts, actors interjected new lines, movie titles changed, and the director reimagined the story as well. Fortunately for him, Faulkner was rarely overly invested in any of his Hollywood assignments. They seemed pesky tasks to complete before he could get back to his own work. The city continued to annoy him and he was far from starstruck, turning down invitations to parties and dinners others would rejoice to receive. At one event, not wanting to appear a discourteous guest, he climbed out a second-story window and down a trellis.

He veered from his standoffishness to accept a lunch invitation at the home of French-born actress Claudette Colbert. Colbert told Ben Wasson, Faulkner's Oxford friend and early agent, to arrange a meeting. Colbert and Faulkner shared mutual admiration. He had enjoyed *It Happened One Night*, Colbert's movie with Clark Gable, and she was a fan of his books. No one was drinking that afternoon. Faulkner requested sweet milk which confused the hostess until Wasson explained it was just plain milk. Perhaps looking to enliven the visit, Colbert suggested a game of tennis at the home of her neighbor, actress ZaSu Pitts. Pitts and Faulkner played singles as the other two looked on. The two men agreed on one thing during the drive back from the pleasant outing: Colbert's legs were even more beautiful in person than onscreen.

* * *

Like other serious authors in Hollywood, he was thankful to discover Stanley Rose's Bookshop on Hollywood Boulevard, a real bookstore frequented by book lovers. Authors, whether they were short on cash or otherwise in need of encouragement, would find a friend in Rose. Many would simply while away the time there, knowing they were likely to meet kindred spirits. It was genuine shelter from what many—especially Faulkner—considered the foolishness of Hollywood. Here Faulkner met John O'Hara and reunited with Nathanael West and Dashiell Hammett, both of whom he knew from New York.

Faulkner also enjoyed spending time with Dorothy Parker, another New York friend and drinking companion. But making friends in Hollywood did not come easily to him. (Some would say he had difficulty keeping them as well. He exhibited a strange pattern in life of "dismissing" friends, as Wasson would discover, leaving them stunned and bewildered by the sudden cold shoulder after many years of friendship.) Except for a select few, like Sayre and Albert "Buzz" Bezzerides (another close friend

Faulkner would suddenly shun), most screenwriters found Faulkner remote. Worse, if someone should try and engage him in a conversation about his novels or stories, he usually would not say a word. The unfortunate person would be left prattling on as he walked away in disgust.

* * *

Even gems like Musso and Frank's and Stanley Rose's shop couldn't banish Faulkner's mournful, homesick mood. That December in Hollywood offered little relief until he met Hawks' secretary and script girl, Meta Carpenter. Positioned professionally at her desk outside of Hawks' inner office, Meta might well have been an apparition. The 28-year-old's beauty, coupled with her quiet composure, arrested Faulkner from the outset. And when she addressed him in her Mississippi accent, the vision was complete. Meta, he discovered, was from the Delta—Tunica, Mississippi—and educated in Memphis, Tennessee. He quickly found reasons to stop by her desk.

The southern provincialism Faulkner later found so maddening in his love affair with Joan Williams afflicted Meta—albeit briefly—as well. Meta had married young and moved to California in the early 1930s with her husband, Billy Carpenter, hoping to pursue a career as a concert pianist. Neither the career nor the marriage went as planned. When she and Billy divorced, having never achieved a fulfilling sexual relationship, Meta moved into a chaperoned female dormitory, the Hollywood Studio Club. Under the umbrella of the YWCA, the Studio Club offered social opportunities and performing arts classes. Teas, dinners, dances and other organized events—as well as frequent outings to popular spots like the Cocoanut Grove—led some to classify the Studio Club as a sorority. In reality, it was a safe and affordable choice for many single women working in the motion picture business.

Meta's single accommodation was $9 a week, while those willing to have a roommate could pay as little as $7. Faulkner wasted no time asking Meta out to dinner, though it would take several invitations before she agreed. She knew he was married, and for a while, that stopped her cold. Then there was the afternoon he showed up drunk and began pressing her again for a dinner date. Meta was shocked and relieved when Faulkner was whisked away to the Knickerbocker. Her good sense and upbringing cautioned against a heavy-drinking, married man.

It was Faulkner's illegible handwriting that finally cracked her armor. She was transcribing his contributions to *The Road to Glory* script, and Hawks advised her to seek Faulkner's help deciphering the pages. Soon they were working side-by-side, with Faulkner putting as little physical distance between them as possible, and staring at her with scant regard to politeness. At 38 years, he was eager for an intimate relationship that he lacked with Estelle. He told Meta his wife had rebuffed him since the birth of their second daughter, Jill, three years earlier (a difficult, if not impossible, claim to substantiate).

The loneliness he felt in his marriage deepened Meta's affection for him, and their southern kindredship proved a building block. Meta recalls being drawn to Faulkner's calm strength and strong masculinity. Both had been disappointed in marriage, though Meta sought her freedom after a brief union. Living in a hotel and facing dinner alone hardly suited Faulkner, especially not when a lovely young woman was within reach. Meta was used to catching men's eyes—she had a slight figure, blonde hair, and pleasant features—but Faulkner's appreciation was more than she'd ever known. Looking at her with wonder and worship, he "pedestaled"[9] her. Night after night he asked for her company. As their dinner dates increased—their first outing was at one of Faulkner's favorite haunts, Musso and Frank's—it soon became a ritual for them to end their days together.

Faulkner poured on the southern charm, presenting her one night with a single gardenia and stopping by a bookstore on another to buy a copy of his poetry collection. Without revealing his identity, he asked the store clerk if they had any other Faulkner books, only to be told no. If he was dashed when the clerk added that Faulkner didn't sell well, he didn't show it. He was nonetheless delighted to present the lovely edition of *A Green Bough* to Meta.

Their affair advanced rapidly. Faulkner was charged with sexual urgency and Meta found herself responding and discovering her own desire. The couple enjoyed a sustained and enthusiastic love affair. Faulkner wrote poems for her laced with sexual references and imagery. He could be ribald and shocking. He gave himself the sexual persona of Mr. Bowen, often signing his poems and letters as such, and casting Meta as Mrs. Bowen. (Some of these explicit letters and erotic drawings remain sealed until 2039 in the Berg Collection at the New York Public Library.) He considered Meta his Hollywood salvation, assuring her that she had rescued him from loneliness and despair. His gratitude was profound. Meta brought him out of a deep and bottomless pit. Even as he relentlessly pursued Meta, Faulkner continued to send homesick letters to Estelle describing himself as an orphan in Hollywood. His letters were often tender and filled with details of their family rituals he missed. At one point, he suggested she meet him in New Orleans for a two-week vacation though nothing came of it. Estelle might have wondered if he was dissembling.

* * *

At LaRue's on Sunset Strip, Faulkner ordered an expensive bottle of wine. Meta realized it was quite a splurge just as she knew Faulkner's

Hollywood paycheck was the only thing keeping Rowan Oak and his family afloat. He revealed another painful, domestic secret: Estelle's excessive drinking caused him great concern for Jill's safety. Money woes and missing his daughter were never far from his mind. His somber, silent moods usually meant he was absorbed in thoughts of Rowan Oak.

Meta wasn't without conflicts of her own. She was being diligently courted by Austrian pianist Wolfgang Rebner, who was not encumbered by a wife. He professed his love for Meta and hoped they would marry. Rebner, unlike Faulkner, shared Meta's passion for music. Music could be a source of tension between Meta and Faulkner. He felt slighted by her deep concentration and immersion, and he openly admitted to Meta he couldn't appreciate music. It was an odd assertion as Wasson credits Faulkner with introducing him to classical music. They would have music sessions in the home of another Oxford friend, Phil Stone. Faulkner and Wasson, both University of Mississippi college students in 1919, would relax at the Stones' residence when the family was away. Faulkner felt comfortable letting himself in the house, appraising their library, and even lighting a fire as the two friends played Beethoven and other composers on the family's Victrola. The pleasure Faulkner took in music as a young man escaped him now, even if it meant disappointing Meta.

* * *

Faulkner was content spending every available moment with Meta but she grew restless. A social person, she missed her friends and finally prodded Faulkner into meeting a few of them. They started to enjoy outings with a friend of Meta's from Memphis, Sally Richards, and her boyfriend, John Crown. (Crown was also a friend of Rebner's.) Both John and Sally were classically trained pianists and deeply involved with the music scene. He pursued a concert career while she performed as a jazz musician for necessary income. They lived the uncertain life of artists, a common theme in Hollywood. The foursome's blossoming friendship took a new turn when Faulkner rented a bungalow at the Miramar Hotel in Santa Monica.

The Miramar already was a favorite getaway for Sally and John. This soon became the weekend outing of choice for both couples when it was within their means. Faulkner was rapturous about Meta's pale complexion. He described her skin as a shade of white with ivory and alabaster. It was a sight he had never before seen and he discouraged any sunbathing. On the beach, he would hustle her under the cabana, and Meta kept her light color to please him.

Perhaps it was registering as Mr. and Mrs., or the more upscale accommodations than his hotel room—whatever the reason, Faulkner's amorous impulses reached new heights when he covered the bungalow's bed with gardenia and jasmine petals. Meta was completely enamored of his gesture and bewildered as to how he'd obtained and concealed the flowers. If this display pleased her, an earlier effort was less successful. One day he had presented her with a box containing a hair ribbon. Even as she wore it on occasion, she was uncomfortable with his odd idealization of her as a young girl, a fantasy he cultivated.

* * *

Despite his obvious delight in this whirlwind affair, Faulkner began drinking heavily during his last few days in Hollywood. Until this point, Faulkner's drinking hadn't been an issue for the couple. He had shown remarkable restraint around Meta, having a drink or two with dinner and wine. He'd been so responsible that it angered her when she overheard a lunch conversation in the studio commissary between two people she didn't know. One man quite loudly declared Faulkner an alcoholic who would mess things up with the script and Hawks. Worse, at the Studio Club, an actress and fellow resident warned her against Faulkner because of his drinking.

Upset but loyal, Meta had brushed both incidents aside. She attributed this recent episode to his internal conflict. He was torn between his desire for home and his daughter—of Estelle he said next to nothing—and his reluctance to leave her. This was a difficult farewell for both of them. His parting gift was as uncharacteristic as the expensive wine or weekends at the Miramar. Faulkner gave her a full-length brocade evening coat. It would serve her well in the coming years when she lived in New York with Rebner, her second husband. Cold and broke, Meta found the coat to be not only a source of warmth but also comfort.

In early January, Hawks temporarily released Faulkner, citing illness as the cause. It seemed the drinking that was underway when Faulkner attended the Rose Bowl Game in Pasadena and took the chartered bus back—barefoot, having lost his shoes in the stadium, and sleeping on the shoulder of Mrs. James Thurber—never settled down. Hawks and Meta were said to have seen him though a ten-day drinking episode until he could safely return to Oxford. Hawks also had intervened on Faulkner's behalf with Louis B. Mayer, co-founder of Metro-Goldwyn-Mayer, and movie producer Darryl Zanuck. The wording of Faulkner's release served as quite as favor. It would allow him to return on salary and resume his affair with Meta.

* * *

His unsteady and anxious mental state accompanied him back to Mississippi. The love affair in Hollywood meant a double-life and secrets from Estelle. Meta would write him letters in care of Phil Stone at the law office of James Stone and Sons. The longtime and loyal friend understood Faulkner's unhappiness in his marriage. Stone and Faulkner's friendship began in the summer of 1914. Stone, 21 years old, was back in Oxford after graduating from Yale with a second B.A., having earned his first at the University of Mississippi. He was intrigued by Faulkner's writing aspirations—Faulkner at the time was only 16 years old—and the two young men soon discovered a shared love of literary heavy hitters: Balzac, T.S. Eliot, Swinburne, Keats, A.E. Housman, Yeats and others. Though Stone realized a law degree was on the horizon—he was expected to join his father's firm—his real passion resided with books and writing. He was curious and brilliant with a somewhat uneven personality (sadly, four months after Faulkner's death, at the age of 69, he was committed to Whitfield, Mississippi's state mental hospital, where he died in 1967). Besides acting as Faulkner's earliest advocate and mentor, Stone personally financed *The Marble Faun*, Faulkner's first book, and his patronage extended in many ways. Sometimes he was the sole source of Faulkner's living expenses. His presence in Faulkner's life was indisputable even at the very end when he headed Faulkner's interment procession.

But the one person Stone did not believe would advance Faulkner's writing career was Estelle Oldham. He felt she and Faulkner loved each other from childhood, and her marriage to Cornell Franklin convinced him she was duplicitous. Upon hearing of Estelle's engagement, Stone unleashed strong words to Katrina Carter, his one-time romantic interest and mutual friend of Faulkner's. "[Estelle] was not worth a damn to anybody and never would be, but ... she always lived off the fat of the land and always would."[10] Fearing Faulkner might reunite with her when she and Franklin divorced, he cautioned his friend that marrying Estelle would be the end of William Faulkner the author. That breach may have been too much.

After Estelle and Faulkner married, Estelle and Stone seemed to settle for a polite but aloof arrangement, and the men's friendship became a little more testy. Nevertheless, Stone, with a law degree from the University of Mississippi and Yale, handled Faulkner's legal matters such as his will, its many revisions, and other estate affairs. Stone eventually would say Faulkner was "at times and in some small ways ... the sanest and most wholesome person I have ever known ... [and] the most aggravating damned human being the Lord ever put on this earth."[11] By 1956, Stone proclaimed Faulkner "insufferable."[12]

* * *

So scattered was Faulkner's mental state that on a visit to Helen and Guy Lyman's hunting camp in Picayune, Mississippi, not far from

New Orleans, he left *Absalom*'s handwritten manuscript. His drinking now was beyond the family's common ministrations—slowly reducing his liquor supply, cajoling him into drinking eggnog, and slipping him tea he thought was whisky—and Estelle for the first known time sought professional help—not at Wright's Sanatorium in Byhalia, Mississippi, which would not exist for another twelve years, but most likely at the Gartly-Ramsay Hospital in Memphis. Faulkner's Oxford physician would have been familiar with the Gartly-Ramsay, which opened in 1910, and was the only psychiatric hospital in Memphis at the time. Presumably, as was the future pattern, his physician would have assisted with a referral. Days later, home again, he returned to his novel—faithfully recovered by the Lymans. *Absalom, Absalom!* had been the one consistent thread through his sorrow and displacement; and by the end of January, he had finished the heartbreaking work and officially noted on the last page, "31 Jany 1936."[13]

* * *

There was little rest after the troublesome and tide-turning January (the 1936 hospital stay would be one of many). Faulkner was back in Hollywood the next month for work on *Banjo on My Knee* and *Gunga Din*. This time he lodged at the relatively tranquil Beverly Hills Hotel. Though he was still very much involved with Meta, he showed less discretion with his conduct. Unflattering stories about him circulated.

After a wild boar hunting trip with West, Faulkner entered the lobby of his quiet hotel in great disarray. Dirty and unkempt from crawling through the brush on Santa Cruz Island, Faulkner walked through the lobby in hunting clothes carrying a deer rifle. That spectacle would have been alarming enough, but in his absence during the hunting trip, the Beverly Hills Hotel had been robbed and most in the lobby believed the wild looking man with the rifle was the criminal back for seconds. Reports of such antics along with his unpredictable nature—curt and prickly or hospitable and charming—damaged his reputation. Studios sensed that he was unreliable, and future contracts would be more difficult to land and less generous.

* * *

Four months later he was at Rowan Oak in time to see *Absalom*'s production process through. The hard-fought manuscript now had to be typed and revised. There were editors in New York to appease who struggled with the book's complexity and knotty southernisms. The anticipated reunion with his family, including his and Estelle's June 20 wedding anniversary, was tarnished by a domestic brouhaha, instigated by Faulkner.

News of the upheaval reached Meta in Hollywood through a friend brandishing a *Time* magazine.

Faulkner had placed an ad in *The [Memphis] Commercial Appeal* and *The Oxford Eagle* (June 22, 1936) that he would not be responsible for his wife's debts, bills, notes or checks. It was such a curiosity that *Time* magazine carried a short article about it. Faulkner had threatened such an action but Meta believed he would think better of it, given the damage it would do to the Faulkner and Oldham family names. His homecoming tirade included removing the purchased radio—a forbidden source of entertainment at Rowan Oak—and the new sofa and other pieces from the sparsely furnished home. As Meta correctly anticipated, Estelle's father, Major Lemuel Oldham, was furious. Faulkner met with him as requested in Oldham's Oxford office overlooking the town square. There, also as predicted, Oldham unleashed his anger and proceeded to upbraid his son-in-law.

* * *

By all appearances, Faulkner and Estelle, working harmoniously on their daughter's party, had tried to pick up the pieces in time for Jill's third birthday on June 24. They then settled on a new Hollywood arrangement. Estelle and Jill, along with Jack Oliver and Narcissus McEwen as domestic help, would accompany him back to Hollywood in July. It was a bold move as he intended to keep his affair with Meta active even with his wife on the scene. They rented a two-story house—only a half-mile downhill walk to the ocean—in Pacific Palisades north of Santa Monica. Faulkner enjoyed taking Jill to the beach and Estelle appreciated a more active social life. Clark Gable would stop by for drinks, and they had dinners with some of Faulkner's fellow scriptwriters and their wives. Estelle, attired in a floor-length gown, sometimes played the piano for guests.

The good times ushered in by the change in locale didn't last long. Estelle's drinking problems were also very pronounced and the dysfunction of the couple resulted in eruptions and embarrassing displays. It wasn't long before Estelle detected the transparent arrangement between her husband and Meta. Epic fights ensued—one involving Estelle wielding a croquet mallet, and another time, Faulkner's face was badly scratched.

When he received a dinner invitation to the Faulkner home not long after Estelle's arrival, Wasson naturally accepted. It was then Faulkner convinced him to bring Meta to dinner with him. She was to pose as Wasson's girlfriend. Faulkner's motive in this charade was a mystery, unless it was an attempt to assure Estelle that Meta was a mere studio acquaintance. Meta's youth stood in stark contrast to Estelle, whose pale, thin appearance at forty years confirmed her trials—a dismal marriage, a lost child, and a battle with alcohol. The group conversed pleasantly enough but the dinner was an excruciating exercise in subterfuge. Estelle had a reputation for being a charming and gracious hostess, but this meal seemed to try even her inordinate skills. One pitcher of martinis followed another.

Wasson recalled of the awkward evening, "[Estelle] and Meta, when I introduced them, gave one another that femininely characteristic once-over, and I was reminded of Bill's comment so many years before that even small girls, when they meet for the first time, looked one another over, and knew everything about each other."[14] With more maturity, Meta recognized her participation as an immoral and unthinkable intrusion.

Wasson felt terrible about his role in trying to deceive Estelle, and worse when she had finished with him. He woke early the next day to a livid phone call. "You didn't fool me for a second, you and Billy. I know that person you brought to my house last night is Billy's girl out here and not your girl at all! I know about that movie actress you're so crazy about. I don't appreciate it one bit your flinging his mistress right in my face, and all these years you've been like a member of our family!"[15] With those final stinging words, she slammed down the receiver, leaving Wasson to believe Faulkner's latest hijinks would be the end of the marriage.

* * *

Estelle insisted Faulkner end it with Meta. She hadn't uprooted her family and traveled across the country to Hollywood to be displaced by a script girl.

FIVE

The Past Is Past: 1936–1937

The snowballing stress and exhaustion of late 1935 ushered in a watershed moment in Faulkner's life: his first documented collapse and admittance to a hospital or sanitarium. The dislocation and turbulence of the previous year left him unmoored and unhinged. He surrendered his profound attachment to his home and family for the necessary Hollywood income; his brother died; he was deeply involved in an extramarital affair; and he wrestled with a demanding novel.

Resources some individuals might summon to deal with personal trauma and difficulties eluded him. Faulkner's habitual fallback plan was drinking which began in adolescence and continued unabated. There were periods when it was under control, and at times he could drink socially without difficulty, but when he was well into his cycle and lost interest in food, it inevitably ran its destructive course.

Seeking professional help changed Faulkner's life. He was 38 years old and a reliance on this form of treatment became habitual. It is possible that prior to his first local stay in January, Faulkner had already experienced professional treatment in California. Sources note that an extended drinking spree preceded his return to Oxford in January 1936. Hawks, who would have been familiar with drying out places in Hollywood considering his work with actors and others in the movie business, would have been more likely to suggest professional help than to nurse Faulkner through a ten-day episode. It may have been the Cedars of Lebanon Hospital in Los Angeles at 4833 Fountain Avenue that came to Faulkner's rescue. Much more likely is that Hollywood or Los Angeles was the site of his first treatment. (Later, his friend and fellow scriptwriter "Buzz" Bezzerides confirmed checking him in to Hollywood sanitariums five or six times between 1942 and 1945.)

* * *

The options Estelle faced in Oxford—once it was clear she had to take action—would have been nothing like the accessible care Hollywood offered. Getting Faulkner to a hospital meant a 75-mile drive to Memphis. Neither the roads nor the vehicles in 1936 suggest comfort, especially in the cold January weather. Malcolm, 12 years old then, would have tried to help his mom. Perhaps he rode to Memphis with her. In April 1968—32 years having passed—Blotner asked Estelle about Faulkner's first hospitalization. She said it was around 1935 to 1936: "E [Estelle] 29apr1968. WF first hospitalized for drinking c. 1935–1936 when worried about Hollywood. Byhalia in early 1940s."[1] Blotner's two-sentence interview entry engendered the longstanding erroneous impression that Faulkner's first and last hospitalization occurred at Wright's Sanatorium. Rather, records indicate September 1950 for Faulkner's first stay at Wright's which opened circa 1948. Presumably in 1936, and for several stays in the late 1940s and 1950s, it was the Gartly-Ramsay Hospital in Memphis that offered the help he needed. By 1927, Gartly-Ramsay had fifty beds, and in 1937 advertised such healthcare methods as physical therapy, Swedish massage, hydrotherapy, and electrotherapy.

* * *

Largely because of the University of Mississippi's close proximity to Memphis, the respective residents of the two cities often intersect. Three overlapping Oxford–Memphis medical relationships would become important to Faulkner's care: Dr. John C. Culley, Dr. Chester McLarty, and Dr. D.C. McCool. Dr. Culley and Dr. McLarty guided local medical treatment and when necessary, arranged hospitalization in Memphis, usually under the care of Dr. McCool, who began work as a psychiatrist at the Gartly-Ramsay in 1935.

* * *

Years before their paths would cross as physician and patient, McCool knew Faulkner by sight from the University of Mississippi campus. An Ole Miss freshman in 1924, McCool recalled standing in the university post office chatting with a student assistant. The young man reported to Faulkner who was at the time the university postmaster. There was no one else in the post office and the student looked up and asked McCool if he saw that fellow coming across the campus. McCool said,

> He was dressed in an outfit that you would probably think of as a karate thing, sort of loose fitting short pants, a belted robe that was short above his ankles, open at the chest—a hairy chest. Unshaven, hair uncombed, and wearing sandals. I remember the student said, "Do you know who that is?" And I said, "No." He said that's William Faulkner, he lives over there in that little fraternity house, and they call him Count No 'Count and he will never amount to a damn.[2]

Five. The Past Is Past: 1936–1937

The undergraduate remembered a few other sightings of the eccentric author and postmaster, but McCool primarily was absorbed in his own studies and social life. He distinguished himself on campus when he took his love of music to a new level and organized a college jazz band. Another music enthusiast, Chester McLarty, joined the Mississippians Jazz Band as a trumpet player a few years later. McLarty, who attended Tulane University Medical School after graduating from Ole Miss, joined Dr. Culley's medical group in Oxford after serving four years in the Navy during World War II and achieving the rank of Lt. Commander. In 1948, Dr. McLarty established a solo practice and became Faulkner's longtime Oxford physician. Faulkner respected veterans and often was drawn to conversations about World War I and World War II. No doubt Dr. McLarty's service was a building block of their relationship.

* * *

When Estelle was seeking help for Faulkner 1936, she seemingly would have reached out to Dr. Culley, who was well acquainted with Faulkner's drinking problem, to coordinate his care in Memphis. Dr. Culley's surgical nurse, Mary Jenkins, lived with Estelle's parents and "had for years been almost a member of the family. She had on numerous occasions taken care of Faulkner during serious drinking bouts."[3] Dr. Culley, described by Blotner as good looking and opinionated, cared for Estelle throughout her pregnancy with Alabama and attended to the baby when she was born prematurely. Faulkner wasn't fond of Dr. Culley; but Estelle apparently was, and his wife, Nina Culley, was a close friend of hers.

If anyone had reason for reservations about Dr. Culley, it would have seemed more Estelle than Faulkner. Dr. Culley treated her eight-year-old brother, Ned, for what he believed was malaria. Ned's fever and symptoms came on suddenly after a late November possum hunting trip with Dean Faulkner. By the time Ned made it to a specialist in Memphis, the boy was past saving, his tragic death the result of rheumatic fever. Ned, nicknamed Little Major, would have been nine years old on Christmas day 1916. The Faulkner boys shared the crushing blow since Ned was known to them all.

Faulkner openly blamed Dr. Culley for Alabama's death—a belief not shared by Estelle—and a rumor circulated that Faulkner shot Culley in the shoulder. The origin of the rumor was none other than Faulkner. He said as his daughter's condition worsened, he called Dr. Culley but he didn't come. Faulkner then claimed he went to the doctor's office and shot him. A second version of the story was that Dr. Culley arrived too late and Faulkner fired at him but missed. Eventually the rumor was softened and modified—Faulkner wanted to shoot Culley. As he dealt with his loss, Faulkner prioritized attaining an incubator for the community. A positive pivot occurred when he purchased an incubator and donated it to Oxford physician Eugene Bramlett.

* * *

Who knows what time of day or night, or whom, if anyone accompanied Estelle, as she navigated his transfer to Memphis. If indeed Dr. Culley arranged Faulkner's admittance to Gartly-Ramsay, the only hospital admitting private psychiatric patients in 1936, the staff and physician's immediate task would have been his sobriety. Faulkner's 1936 stay involved several days, and when he returned to Rowan Oak he continued the regimen of nutrition and rest. Faulkner's general treatment at the hospital, according to Dr. McCool, would have involved vitamins, nutrition, medication with his meals, and providing what sedation he required. The sedation would be some sort of barbiturate, maybe Seconal. Dr. McCool's daily visits with him might range from five to thirty minutes, depending on Faulkner's mood. Faulkner was never pressed to talk but Dr. McCool remembered a "wild, hallucinatory nightmare he had. He was in a cemetery in France where at each grave there was a head of a German aviator and they all looked at him and said, 'You and your friends shot me down.'"[4]

Aggressive therapy for depression, often believed to be the underlying cause of alcoholism, also existed at Gartly-Ramsay. Metrazol shock involved an intravenous injection of approximately 5 cc of Metrazol, a preparation chemically related to Camphor. It produced within a few seconds a violent convulsion that lasted about 20 seconds, after which the patient would fall into a deep sleep for anywhere from two to four hours. After a short period of confusion, the patient would feel better. Dr. McCool described it as a drastic but effective treatment for depression that shortened hospital stays considerably.

An even earlier treatment purported to break the cycle of addiction was the Keeley Cure. This was well known to Faulkner as his father and paternal grandfather were patients at a Keeley Institute located 15 miles outside of Memphis. The treatment involved injections of bichloride of gold, the effects of which supposedly made patients uninterested in alcohol. Despite the method lacking any real science to back up the claims, it was for a time a popular if controversial measure, and Keeley Institutes flourished across the country in the late nineteenth century.

Faulkner's tender and revealing story of addiction, "Uncle Willy," features an endearing character who finds himself an unwilling patient at Keeley in Memphis. Uncle Willy, as he's known to children and adults alike, lives quietly just outside of Jefferson with old Job Wylie, his sole household help and only employee in the drug store he inherited from his father. The story's young narrator describes Uncle Willy as weighing "about a hundred and ten pounds and his eyes behind his glasses kind of all run together like broken eggs,"[5] and he declares him "the finest man I ever knew."[6] He is one of the ball players who appreciate the cool, dim refuge of Uncle Willy's store where the teams gather afterwards for ice cream. And though he never attends a single game, Uncle Willy awards a prize to the day's winner, making his place an even more attractive destination. For twelve or fourteen years Uncle Willy goes about his morphine habit, often with a flock of observers:

> And we would eat the ice cream and then we would all go behind the prescription case and watch Uncle Willy light the little alcohol stove and fill the needle and roll his sleeve up over the little blue myriad punctures starting at his elbow and going right on up into his shirt ... and somebody would say, "Don't that hurt?" And he would say, "No, I like it."[7]

A harum-scarum scene erupts when the do-gooders of his small community decide to "save" him. Without any knowledge of withdrawal techniques, Uncle Willy is kidnapped from the Sunday school class he regularly attends with the young ballplayers and held captive—"Uncle Willy still trying to hold back and looking around at us with his run-together eyes blinking and saying plainer than if he had spoke it: 'What's this? What's this, fellows? What are they fixing to do to me?'"[8] The group's intent is to "fix it so he would not have to face his Maker slave body and soul to Morphine."[9]

Through open windows of the house where he's held captive, the young boys hear Uncle Willy "crying and cussing and fighting to get out of the bed." The primitive intervention leaves him so ill people say he is going to die and he's sent to Memphis. On his return from Keeley, he seems to have left his memory behind.

> One day he came home with his skin the color of tallow and weighing about ninety pounds now with his eyes like broken eggs still but dead eggs, eggs that had been broken so long now they didn't even smell dead any more—until you looked at them and saw that they were anything in the world except dead. That was after he got to know us again. I don't mean that he had forgotten us exactly. It was like he still liked us as boys, only he had never seen us before and so he would have to learn our names and which faces the names belong to.[10]

The narrative continues with Uncle Willy practicing the boys' names and rekindling friendships. A number of humorous exploits follow the story's somber beginning. This fascinating depiction of addiction, with its harrowing side effects and the shortfalls of treatment, specifically the

Keely Cure, was published in 1935, presumably a year before Faulkner's first sanatorium stay.

*   *   *

The amnesia Uncle Willy experiences in Faulkner's story is more generally associated with electroshock or electroconvulsive therapy. Physicians began to favor electroshock over Metrazol primarily because it didn't involve finding the patient's vein to induce a seizure. Within five months of its introduction in the United States circa 1940, Gartly-Ramsay had the twelfth or thirteenth electroshock apparatus made. The device operated by attaching two instruments to the patient's head while an electrical current coursed through his or her brain. Dr. McCool said he used electroshock almost routinely for schizophrenia and depression but did not use it on Faulkner.

Faulkner's other treating physician at Gartly-Ramsay, Dr. Justin H. Adler, likewise said he never used electroshock treatment on Faulkner. Dr. Adler vividly remembered caring for Faulkner and the two men conversed easily. Dr. Adler served four years in World War II with the U.S. Medical Corps as a psychiatrist and two of those years were in Europe. His background was of interest to Faulkner and he would likewise relate RAF tales.

One doctor–patient interaction was quite memorable. Faulkner invited Dr. Adler to go to the circus! It was April 14, 1949, a date the psychiatrist could hardly forget; his wife was in the hospital giving birth to their daughter, Susan. The outing included Estelle and Jill, who had driven to Memphis, as well as Dr. Adler's son, Michael. Faulkner was quite fond of the circus, Dr. Adler said, "He got a great kick out of it."[11] The doctor also noted the chilly air between Faulkner and Estelle. That night Faulkner returned to the hospital and he believed Estelle and Jill stayed in Memphis with friends.

Soon enough, the demand for psychiatric care eclipsed general care at Gartly-Ramsay, and by 1950 the hospital focused on mental health. When it closed in 1973, patient records were transferred to microfilm and all existing paper records destroyed. A few weeks or a month later, the microfilm was burned.

*   *   *

The lull from his recovery wouldn't last long as Faulkner's domestic demons followed him to Hollywood six months later. Meta was waiting for him, having to some extent put her life on hold. While she hadn't entirely discouraged Wolfgang Rebner, Meta wasn't operating as a single woman. Her attachment to Faulkner and false belief he might end his marriage kept her from embracing other opportunities. His report on the state of his marriage when he returned in July 1936 was so dire it fed her hope he really would pursue a divorce. He told her his arguments with Estelle skinned him alive.

If she had sought counsel from Buzz, Meta would have been discouraged. Buzz was close to the situation through his friendship and work with Faulkner. He felt sorry for Meta and believed she was being used. He knew that for their affair to advance beyond Hollywood, Faulkner would have to be willing to take her to Oxford, to face all the recriminations and difficulty of divorce. Buzz did not believe Faulkner was capable of permanent relationships. He was at this best when writing letters to his love interests from afar where he was safe—"Live up to what you said. I can't; I'm two thousand miles away."[12] Over and over, with different women, Buzz felt Faulkner failed to respect them as persons.

* * *

As she and Faulkner reestablished their love affair, Meta initially was undeterred. But there was a disturbing change. The earlier restraint Faulkner had shown with his drinking was discarded. Early mornings she would find him on her front porch waiting for her to wake up, drinking from what had been a full bottle of wine. A drink before dinner turned into four or five straight shots of bourbon. None of which prepared her for Faulkner in the throes of delirium tremens, a sight that greeted her one Sunday after she returned from working with Hawks.

Crouched in a corner of her bed, Faulkner waved off the approaching German soldiers who shot at him from airplanes. There was no reasoning with him; in fact, he didn't seem to know Meta, wouldn't let her comfort him, and lashed out at her when she tried; "He looked up, no recognition whatever in his face, and screamed, 'They're going to get me! Oh, Lordy, oh, Jesus!' He covered his head with hands that alternately flailed and supplicated, shouting over and over in a litany of dread, 'They're coming down at me! Help me! Don't let them! They're coming at me! No! No!'"[13] She immediately called a violinist friend who worked as a male nurse. He came to her rescue and carted Faulkner off to Sunset Strip and a drying out place. This scenario—minus the dramatic German enemy—occurred a number of times during their involvement. Still she remained resolute. At least for a while.

* * *

Meta's increasing openness to Rebner's pursuit probably had less to do with Faulkner's accelerated drinking, and more to do with sharing him with Estelle, who was now on her Hollywood turf. When Meta directly asked Faulkner how long she had to wait until Estelle let him go, he gave her a penetrating look, turned abruptly away from her, and got in his car. Their stolen meetings and dates after that went on but that image was seared in her mind. Faulkner began relating to Meta his conversations and battles with Estelle for the divorce he sought. If she wanted assurances that he shared her determination for a real future, Meta had only his word. Not only did his wife promise a marathon fight over Jill, he said, but she also swore to take everything he had. The latter seemed to stun him. Amazingly enough he seemed genuinely surprised by that. When Estelle bought a new dress and Faulkner objected to the price, $125, she shredded it in front of him with scissors.

Finally, Estelle relented some ground—he could keep Meta but she would keep his name. As the reality of that scenario settled around her, the next curtain fell. Faulkner told her he'd given up hope until Jill was old enough to tell a judge which parent she preferred to live with. When an astonished Meta asked for a time line, he guessed ten years or so. And if that wasn't enough, he told her Estelle was threatening to name her a correspondent in divorce proceedings.

It wasn't a lightning bolt but something akin to it. Rebner's proposals of marriage—there were more than one—gained traction and by April 5, 1937, they were married. The couple left for an extended stay in Europe as the Nazis' reach was intensifying and terrorizing. That Rebner came from a prominent Jewish family in Frankfurt eventually put them all in great peril. Meta and Rebner's return to the United States came not a moment too soon, but the financial inheritance and stability that would have been theirs vanished.

* * *

Faulkner had ample time to prepare for Meta's marriage, yet that apparently didn't soften the blow. A milestone birthday—40—was on his near horizon and he had lost hope for a fulfilling union. The compatibility he'd found with Meta—emotionally and physically—left a gaping void. A ray of optimism was the start of a better Hollywood contract. His pay in late February 1937 increased from $750 a month to $1,000, and he and his family had moved into a more modest home in Beverly Hills that was close to the studio. The increase in salary came with a caveat. If he did any drinking on the studio lot, his contract was voided.

Hawks relayed the details to Faulkner's typist, Julie Davies, whom Faulkner had requested because of her excellent work, and Hawks requested she alert him immediately if her suspicions were raised. A quick survey of Faulkner's desk revealed a bottle of cognac. She checked the drawer stash religiously and was relieved to find it unopened. Then one day she heard the cork and opening and closing of the drawer—his way of seeking solace from Meta's April wedding.

Five. The Past Is Past: 1936–1937

Hawks arrived quickly and went in Faulkner's office, closing the door behind. He then summoned Miss Davies and told her to bring her dictation book. Silence enveloped the three as she sat in front of Faulkner, who lounged comfortably in his chair with his feet on the desk, quite a departure from his usual proper demeanor. Finally he spoke: "Hostile," he said. Then he added, "That is all, Miss Davies."[14]

Hawks hustled him off the lot and a few day later he was admitted to the Good Samaritan Hospital. Most of his April wages were forfeited and the hospital bills were mounting. A Hollywood friend and former actress wrote Meta an embellished account: Faulkner was rushed to the hospital in an acute alcoholic state the day of Meta's wedding where he stayed six weeks. But no doubt the diminished physical state Meta's friend described when Faulkner returned to work, so thin and haggard as be almost unrecognizable, had some validity.

* * *

After their emergency exit from Germany in the fall of 1937, Meta and Rebner settled in a small Manhattan apartment at 72nd and Broadway. Since his travels basically took him to the East or West Coast, Faulkner connected with Meta much sooner than either might have imagined. They arranged a dinner date where he met Meta's husband. The two men hit it off, much to Meta's delight. When Faulkner failed to meet the couple in the Algonquin Hotel Lobby for a second dinner as planned, Meta was alarmed. She knew him as punctual. Finally gaining entrance to Faulkner's room, she found him on the bed in terrible straits. He had been drinking thinking of her belonging to someone else. He passed out and fell against the steam pipe in the bathroom causing third-degree burns on his back. Faulkner's friend, Jim Devine, a New Yorker, and Sherwood Anderson cared for him.

Anderson's involvement was a bit surprising given his admitted dislike of Faulkner. Anderson's second wife, Elizabeth Prall, had befriended Faulkner in 1921 and hired him to work—at the behest of future novelist Stark Young—in the Doubleday bookstore she managed in New York. She and Anderson married in 1924. Elizabeth believed the friendship was torpedoed because "Sherwood and Bill were too much alike."[15]

With the help of a local doctor, the two men were able to see him through the withdrawals without hospitalization. In a letter to his fourth wife, Eleanor Copenhaver, Anderson declared Faulkner an alcoholic: "Bill Faulkner has been through a big drunk, for a week. The poor chap is an alcoholic. A friend [Devine] had been sticking to him and trying to straighten him out but the friend was exhausted. Bill had been wandering—nude—about the hotel corridors."[16]

* * *

His enormous recuperative powers surged and Faulkner was determined to host the dinner he missed. When Meta and Rebner got to his Algonquin room, a room-service waiter quickly appeared with a food-laden cart. A table with flowers was set and Faulkner served the soup. Their host's attire—he was wearing only white shorts—extinguished his efforts at propriety. The agonizing burn disallowed clothes or contact of any kind. Faulkner's excruciating pain was evident and Meta couldn't imagine him suffering through an entire meal. They made their apologies and left.

Days later Meta and Faulkner strolled down Fifth Avenue and settled on a Central Park bench with a view of the waterfowl. Meta confided their financial difficulties, a subject Faulkner understood all too well. He said he was in better shape than usual and he offered assistance. Meta declined and assured him they'd make it. She also stressed that she was happy in her marriage and asked him if things were any better at home. He acknowledged Estelle's drinking was unabated but described a truce of sorts between them following the turmoil in Hollywood. Sharing intimacies stirred the romantic in Faulkner; and unable to let such an opportune moment pass, he clasped Meta's hand in his and "a bolt of his great male energy coursed through me," she recalled.[17] He quoted a character's line from his new book, *The Wild Palms*, yet another book written in the midst of heartbreak, this time the loss of Meta. "Between grief and nothing I will take grief," he told her.[18]

Six

Southern Danger: 1940–1947

Whereas 1939 had some real high-water marks with *The Wild Palms* outselling *Sanctuary*, and "Barn Burning" winning the O. Henry Memorial Award for the year's best short story, 1940 came in dark and stormy. The Faulkners were not even a full month into the year when Caroline Barr, "Mammy Callie," a beloved family fixture, suffered a paralytic stroke. Four days later she succumbed having never regained consciousness. Faulkner delivered a moving eulogy in Rowan Oak's parlor where her service was held. A choir sang "Swing Low, Sweet Chariot," as the family reflected on their deep loss. When *Go Down, Moses* was released in 1942, Faulkner's dedication to Mammy was more emotional than most: "To Mammy CAROLINE BARR Mississippi [1840–1940] Who was born in slavery and who gave to my family a fidelity without stint or calculation of recompense and to my childhood an immeasurable devotion and love." Phil Stone wrote in a 1942 letter that "the best prose in it [the book] is in the dedication to Aunt Caroline."[1] Under Faulkner's direction, her grave marker read "MAMMY Her white children bless her."[2]

* * *

Faulkner admitted to his editors it was a struggle to get back to reviewing the galleys for *The Hamlet* but he gradually returned to his desk. Three months later, April 1940, *The Hamlet*, the first of the Snopes trilogy, debuted. The Snopeses had long been a source of creativity and amusement for Faulkner and Stone who made up early stories about their shenanigans. Faulkner's ongoing fascination with the Snopes family—a clan of criminals, scalawags, merchants, and plotters—eventually yielded two additional volumes: *The Town* and *The Mansion* (all three volumes are dedicated to Stone and *The Town*'s dedication reads, "To Phil Stone He did half the laughing for thirty years.") They are also the subject of short stories, including the award-winning "Barn Burning," the searing coming of age of Colonel Sartoris "Sarty" Snopes and his vengeful father, Abner Snopes.

The Snopeses, having no regard for old South values, represented Yankee materialism. They disregarded cherished values like love of the land, politeness, honor, and family ties, and introduced moral confusion and social decay. Meanwhile, the old families floundered under a sense of dislocation and irrelevancy. Stone and Faulkner were fascinated with the rise of the lower class, as they deemed the Snopeses. Stone told Faulkner that the "real revolution in the South was not the race situation, but the rise of the redneck … to places of power and wealth. Free of 'the scruples of the old aristocracy' they were assured of victory."[3]

* * *

It seemed there was little time to savor *The Hamlet*'s accomplishment as he needed to place stories to remain solvent. He churned out five short stories in 1940 and conceived the genesis for *The Reivers*. In a May 1940 letter to Robert Haas at Random House, Faulkner broadly outlined what would be his nineteenth and last novel. *The Reivers* appeared 22 years later in June 1962. Haas had a long history with Faulkner. He and Harrison Smith founded their own publishing house in 1932 and published *Light in August* and *Pylon*, Faulkner's seventh and eighth novels. When Random House acquired Haas and Smith's publishing house, Haas became a vice president. For Harrison Smith, whose alliance with Faulkner was even longer and included publishing, along with Jonathan Cape, *The Sound and the Fury*, *As I Lay Dying* (dedicated to Hal Smith), and *Sanctuary*, the transition to Random House didn't go as smoothly. He eventually left the large publishing house for other interests but remained a close friend to Faulkner.

Financial pressures absorbed much his attention following *The Hamlet*'s release. There was great haggling over advances with Haas and he threatened to debark for Viking, only to have Viking's offer withdrawn. Bennett Cerf, a co-founder of Random House, very much wanted to retain Faulkner and was relieved to hear he was staying with them. Random house clearly was proud of having Faulkner on their author roster. *Absalom* was the first Faulkner volume they published after acquiring the Haas and Smith publishing house and great care was taken with the production. A letter from Cerf boldly assured Faulkner that *Absalom* was "the greatest thing you have ever turned out."[4] The book jacket called it Faulkner's most important and ambitious contribution to American literature. Regrettably, the auspicious event occurred during a bleak period for Faulkner. Meta's October 1936 wedding and his drinking delayed him from signing and returning sheets for a limited, 300 copy run. When weeks later Cerf

Six. Southern Danger: 1940–1947

received the requested signed pages, number one of 300 was "inscribed for Meta Carpenter, wherever she may be." She also received an inscribed set of galleys.[5]

* * *

A special honor fell November 11, 1940, when Faulkner was a godfather, along with Mississippi Congressman Wall Doxey, and two godmothers, to Emily and Phil Stone's first child, Philip Alston. Faulkner's longtime friend was a father at last! (Stone would be 55 years old when his second child, Araminta, was born.) Faulkner's relationship with his godson was not merely ceremonial. He took his role in the child's life seriously as he had with his niece, Dean, and of course his daughter, Jill. Philip was dutifully remembered on birthdays, holidays, and other special occasions. Notably, Philip received two especially generous gifts: the first carbon transcript of *The Hamlet* for Christmas 1945; and in 1948, a freshly typed and bound copy of *The Wishing-Tree*, Faulkner's rare children's book from 1927. Shaky finances eventually led the Stones to sell part of their Faulkner collection to the University of Texas. The sale did not go unnoticed by Faulkner. He wrote Ober in 1959:

> By now I should certainly have got used to the fact that most of my erstwhile friends and acquaintances here believe I am rich from sheer blind chance, and are determined to have a little of it. I learned last week (he didn't tell me himself) that another one [friend] gathered up all the odds and ends of mine he had in his possession, and sold it to a Texas University; he needed money too evidently.[6]

* * *

In his life and in his literature, Faulkner placed a great premium on tradition. The various holidays ushered in carefully cultivated celebrations. Hog-killing time—complete with its own ceremony—made use of the smokehouse on the grounds and normally fell slightly before Thanksgiving. The yearly Thanksgiving bird hunt commenced in the gallery of Rowan Oak where the men gathered before setting out. Likewise, Faulkner looked forward to hunting trips with old friends that took him deep into the woods and far away from day-to-day concerns. The November 1940 hunt was especially welcome.

The trying year was coming to a close. The clearing done by timber companies drove them farther from home, this year to the Big Sunflower River, 150 miles south of Oxford. For the 49th year, Bob Harkins led the charge, joined by three others from his generation, as well as younger participants like Faulkner and his friend, Felix Linder. The last stretch of the trip was done by motorboat. Once their camp was organized, the men looked forward to early hunting adventures—as early as four o'clock in the morning—and nights around the fire drinking whiskey, swapping stories, and playing nickel poker.

The pace of the whiskey drinking, for Faulkner at least, slipped up on him. One of the group discovered him passed out, his complexion a grayish hue. Immediately alarmed and fearing a serious health condition, maybe a kidney seizure, they began fretting over a quick exit for medical care. As if by providence, they heard a motorboat, flagged it down, loaded him aboard, and got him to the Oxford hospital. Another narrow escape for Faulkner. It may have been a perforated ulcer causing hemorrhaging. A year of angst, irritation, and too much drinking had done its work. Dr. Culley told the men that a few hours longer and their hunting companion wouldn't have survived.

* * *

Mounting financial pressure drove him back to Hollywood in July 1942. The previous year had kept him deeply involved with a book about race in Mississippi, *Go Down, Moses and Other Stories*. Despite the tagline, Faulkner considered it a novel told in seven parts, some parts divided by chapters. (When it was reissued in 1949 he had "and Other Stories" omitted.) The crowning jewel of the book was part five, "The Bear," published by the *Saturday Evening Post* just two day before the novel's release on May 11, 1942. In all, eight "chapters" from the novel's "parts" preceded the novel as magazine short stories. That year's enormous creative output resulted in a mere $300 in royalties from Random House. Notably, even after publishing 12 novels, Faulkner could not let up on magazine sales—they kept him afloat.

* * *

It would be an understatement to say Faulkner wasn't greeted with open arms for his eighth Hollywood residency in July 1942. His request for a one-year contract with Warner Brothers was countered by a seven-year contract at $300 a week—a lower salary than his first entry position—$500 a week—at MGM ten years ago. Unfortunately, he wasn't in a position to turn it down.

* * *

Glancing across the Pig-'n-Whistle, a crowded Hollywood diner, "Buzz" Bezzerides thought he saw William Faulkner, an author he greatly admired. He was familiar with everything Faulkner published, all the novels to date and the multiplying short stories. It started with *As I Lay Dying*, a birthday gift from his girlfriend while he was a student at

Berkeley. He was entranced by the characters' interior worlds, maddened by the demanding prose. He read every book with what he described as the same fury.

What luck that the Mississippian would be sitting, with Meta as he later learned, in a booth behind him. It was 1936 or 1937 when Bezzerides made his way across the diner to Faulkner's table. He told him he knew all of his work and he considered him a great writer. For once the prickly side didn't emerge at an outsider's intrusion; Faulkner stood, thanked him, and shook his hand. Years later in 1942 when the men crossed paths at Warner Brothers, Faulkner, astonishingly, remembered Buzz. The two men took a liking to each other. Buzz learned the details of Faulkner's contract, which he considered appalling, and already knew of Jack Warner's boast: he had the best writer in the country working for pennies. (Buzz's own contract at the time was $1,000 a week.) Buzz offered Faulkner a ride to the Highland Hotel where he was staying. Buzz was part of a car pool that soon included Faulkner, who had been taking a bus.

* * *

It was not just his aloofness and signature pipe that set him apart from the circle of Warner Brothers writers; Faulkner was older, and the others were a bit starstruck. They knew him as the author of 13 novels! How familiar they actually were with his work was unknown, but for Buzz, *Absalom, Absalom!* was a pure triumph. When Faulkner wrote about how much white and Black blood you can have and be forgiven, and how much Black blood it takes to be persecuted, Buzz believed he uncovered the crime that was committed against the people in the South. To understand that crime, in his opinion, all you had to do was read that book. No need to look further.

The same could be said of Faulkner's short story "Wash" and understanding caste and the Lost Cause. Both a prequel and sequel to *Absalom*, "Wash" first was published in *Harper's Magazine* in 1934, and later that same year, included in *Dr. Martino and Other Stories*. *Absalom*'s protagonist, Sutpen, a Civil War colonel, returns in 1865, his bravery recognized with a citation from General Lee. Once the largest cotton planter in Yoknapatawpha County, he has lost his land and most of his second family. What remains of the place are his daughter, Judith, and Wash Jones, a shiftless hanger-on Sutpen allows to live in an abandoned fishing cabin.

For years after Sutpen's return, Wash repeats his vainglorious refrain, "Well, Kernel, they kilt us but they ain't whupped us yit, air they?"[7] Wash's deification of Sutpen never wavered:

> A fine proud man. If God Himself was to come down and ride the natural earth, that's what He would aim to look like.... He is bigger than all them

Yankees that kilt his son and his wife and taken his niggers and ruined his land, bigger than this hyer durn country that he fit for and that has denied him into keeping a little country store....[8]

During Sutpen's absence, Wash tells anyone who will listen that he's looking after the place, a boast met with derision by the former Sutpen slaves who have long called him white trash. "Why ain't you at de war, white man?"; his shack by the river is a place the "Cunnel wouldn't *let* none of us live in"; his attempt to enter the big house stopped cold: "This time it was a house servant, one of the few Negroes who remained; this time the Negress had to retreat up the kitchen steps, where she turned. 'Stop right dar, white man. Stop right whar you is. You ain't never crossed dese steps whilst Cunnel here, and you aint' ghy' do hit now."[9]

With no real livelihood, Sutpen opens a meager general store with Wash as his help and his unlikely drinking companion. Sutpen manages to keep his stallion in decent quarters while he lives with his daughter in the dilapidated shell of their former house. At sixty years, Sutpen is still intent on recapturing a fragment of his design, a son, and he pursues Milly, Wash's 15-year-old granddaughter, giving her trinkets from his store. Two years later she gives birth to a daughter, "Well, Milly," Sutpen said, "too bad you're not a mare. Then I could give you a decent stall in the stable."[10]

The price of Wash's clarity when he finally reconciles the truth is three murders—Sutpen, Milly, her newborn daughter—and his suicide:

> It seemed to him that he now saw for the first time, after five years, how it was that Yankees or any other living armies had managed to whip them: the gallant, the proud, the brave; the acknowledged and chosen best among them all to carry courage and honor and pride. Maybe if he'd gone to the war with them he would have discovered them sooner.[11]

* * *

Buzz, 11 years Faulkner's junior, credits their evolving friendship to his understanding of Faulkner's private nature. He didn't pry and eventually the two would have dinners and drinks together. There was a certain forlornness about living in a hotel, even one just two blocks from Hollywood Boulevard, but Faulkner was very particular about whom he spent time with. He would turn down rides and take the bus if he didn't care for the driver. The Highland Hotel at 1921 Highland Avenue, now a Holiday Inn Express, cost $15 a week. Faulkner's room was on the top floor with an adjoining terrace. It had a striking view of the Hollywood Hills, probably the best that can be said of it; but the room, so close to the roof, was hot.

Wearing only white shorts, no shirt, and sometimes sunglasses, Faulkner used the terrace as his workspace with his typewriter positioned on an ottoman that matched the cane chair. Without luxury or aplomb,

Six. Southern Danger: 1940–1947

described by some as a "clean, cheap, dreary hotel," it served as home for five months until Faulkner returned to Mississippi for Christmas.

January of 1943 promised a long stretch—seven months—in Hollywood. As if Faulkner wasn't beleaguered enough, between financial straits and a job far from home, another form of torment entered his life in 1943 when he imagined what would be his 16th novel, *A Fable*. Published in 1954, the book seemed a joyless march to the finish. The thorny novel was outlined on his study's wall. It would weave its way in and out of an especially difficult decade.

* * *

Meta, now divorced, was back in his life, with a diminished hope of a real future with Faulkner. He, likewise, released her from his singular company. They seemed to have struck a comfortable bargain: she enjoyed her music and free time with friends, he accepted more invitations on his own than previously. They were not tied to an "every night" sort of arrangement. The ensuing freedom suited them both. Meta thought Faulkner seemed lighter, perhaps in part from having a guaranteed income, but if he was happier you wouldn't know it from his drinking. It was now three or four straight bourbons before they left for dinner. She noticed the bottles in his hotel room and heard he kept a flask in his office. One day Buzz found her on a set, motioned to her, and they set about rescuing Faulkner. With his arms around their shoulders and his feet skimming the floor, the two managed to get him out of the studio before news reached Jack Warner. Faulkner had been discovered head down on his desk with screenplay pages scattered around the room. This time Buzz took him to a bathhouse at Cahuenga at Yucca.

An awareness struck Meta one night after she watched him nearly drink himself into a blackout: he was at heart a family man. He loved his family, children, and southern traditions. Even adultery, as much as he enjoyed sex with Meta, was at cross-purposes with his ideas of southern respectability. Was the drinking, she wondered, a way to silence the voices telling him this was not his life? This false existence had nothing to do with William Faulkner the novelist and family man.

* * *

The more their friendship advanced, the more Buzz learned what was involved with being Faulkner's friend. A telegram reached him in February 1944. There wasn't much to it except Faulkner relating what day he would be arriving from Mississippi. When he met him at the depot and learned Faulkner hadn't arranged a place to stay, Buzz offered him an empty bedroom at their house. He sometimes heard the typewriter at three in the morning and asked what he was working on. Perhaps a little coyly, Faulkner answered it was his new fable. Buzz surely had no way of knowing when he offered the room that between 1944 and 1945 Faulkner would live with his family for ten months.

There was a comforting domestic ritual to life at the Bezzerideses'. Yvonne, Buzz's wife, liked their unobtrusive houseguest. She and Faulkner forged a friendship as well. The couple had two small children, a daughter, Zoe, and son, Peter. Faulkner, after riding home from the studio with Buzz, had dinner with them most nights. One night a bit of drama ruffled the usually serene setting. The children were seated at the table and Buzz estimated that Faulkner, who was across the room, was twenty to thirty feet away. Peter pushed back in his highchair and was careening backward. The alacrity with which Faulkner bolted across the space and caught the highchair amazed them.

They were acquainted with their visitor's more deliberate pace; Buzz felt Faulkner seemed to be moving backward when he walked. Buzz and Yvonne never forgot the "explosion of movement"[12] that averted Peter's fall. Time passed and Faulkner's presence in their home became routine. Buzz never mentioned rent and Faulkner didn't offer. Knowing the pathetic terms of his contract, Buzz understood. He'd caught a glimpse of Faulkner's small expenditure book—carefully tabulated—which always registered near zero.

That spring Faulkner was again working with Howard Hawks, this time on an adaptation of Ernest Hemingway's novel, *To Have and Have Not*. According to Meta, Faulkner literally saved the picture. Jules Furthman's adaptation of the novel raised eyebrows and objections in Washington, D.C. Furthman's script involved an amoral American smuggling rum and aiding revolutionaries between Havana and Key West. Hawks had faith Faulkner could modify the script—fix the story snag as Hawks sometimes phrased it—enough to smooth things over with the U.S. War Department (a relationship Warner Brothers needed to produce future war films).

Showing real interest and zest, Faulkner successfully reimagined the screenplay. He literally typed pages of script each morning that were read the next day by the cast, actors including Humphry Bogart, Lauren Bacall, Hoagy Carmichael, and Walter Brennan. Suddenly Faulkner was practically revered around the studio. True to his contrarian nature, the sudden change in status annoyed more than pleased him. He also seemed to understand that much was on the line with how this film came off. He developed a friendship with a male nurse, Mr. Nielsen, and when he thought his drinking might get out of hand, he would bring Nielsen along for a night out or call him as necessary. This was no time to let Hawks down and see the salary, such as it was, evaporate. (When the film premiered on January 20, 1945, Faulkner shared the film credit with Jules Furthman. It closed an eight-year gap for an onscreen credit.)

* * *

A highly anticipated summer holiday with his family in 1944 temporarily banished his homesickness. Faulkner rented an apartment in East Hollywood near Sunset Boulevard and the Cedars of Lebanon Hospital. (Foreseeing a more disciplined summer, Faulkner spent a week or so before they arrived in a hotel dispatching with a case of bourbon.) Jill was eager to experience Hollywood and her father was excited for her company. But for Faulkner, the visit came at a price. He expected Meta to understand and to keep seeing him on the side. Meta was furious at having their lives together interrupted, enough so that for the second time, she ended it with him.

* * *

The Faulkners celebrated Jill's 11th birthday in their new residence. The Faulkner and Bezzerides families spent summer afternoons together at the beach and other entertainment spots. Jill and Zoe, close in age, discovered horseback riding was a shared passion. Fortunately, there was a stable, Jack House's, near Warner Brothers. Since Yvonne also rode, sometimes she and Faulkner would accompany the girls. Estelle was comfortable enough to share confidences, and asked Buzz what Faulkner had told him about their marriage. She became emotional, cried, and told him they had loved each other but something had gone wrong. She didn't know what. Knowing all he did about Meta, Buzz must have found the conversation painful.

The summer was tarnished by a number of dreary script assignments. Even having his family with him couldn't dispel the miserable moods. And always there was the nagging pain of knowing his own work lay fallow. He had a very near brush at the studio when he almost missed a story conference. His secretary, Sylvia Rosenthal, found him in a terrible state. Buzz came by his office and witnessed, along with Sylvia, the thirty minutes Faulkner took to try and recover. When he felt stable, he asked Buzz "to take me over there and push me in." By some miracle, drunk as he was, he walked down the hall, put in a thirty-minute appearance, and carefully retraced the same straight path back to his office. It was all he had in him. The dreaded meeting and march up and down the hall finished him. Buzz whisked him away and got him back to Estelle and their apartment. Once there, sobriety and a better frame of mind couldn't arrive quickly enough. It was a trying recovery and Estelle felt the brunt of it.

As had been evident with the Hemingway novel, a decent story could brighten Faulkner's involvement. In an idle conversation with Hawks about murder mysteries, the two men discussed Raymond Chandler's *The Big Sleep*. Hawks immediately saw potential, and another opportunity to pair Bogart and Bacall. He floated the idea to Jack Warner. Soon, Faulkner was drafting a successful adaptation and would, with the movie's 1946 release, see his fifth onscreen credit.

* * *

Buzz, whom Faulkner called Bud, gradually learned more about his houseguest. Faulkner, he concluded, was sensitive to the things that mattered to him and was totally insensitive to the feelings of others. He was basically self-absorbed with a subtle knack for using people, whether it be for rides, errands, or, most evidently, by devolving into drunken states and expecting someone to pick up the pieces. He felt it was his privilege as a great writer to make demands.

A ritual developed. Faulkner would collapse, and through the kindness of others, make it to a hospital where he would be put back together again. Buzz thought the drinking bordered on suicidal. In Hollywood, Faulkner made the rounds through various hospitals and sanatoriums—a bathhouse Meta knew about, rugged places in downtown Los Angeles, a sanatorium on Van Nuys Boulevard, the Good Samaritan Hospital, Cedars of Lebanon Hospital, and others. Once that resource opened to him in 1936 there would be no turning back.

On one occasion Buzz thought he had Faulkner settled in the sanatorium on Van Nuys only to receive a call from him shortly after he left. "Bud," Faulkner said, "they stole my watch; somebody stole my watch.... You got to get me out of here." Buzz was firm about him staying, but when he came to visit later, he asked a nurse about the missing watch. No one had any knowledge of a stolen watch. Buzz discovered it in Faulkner's shoe where he'd stashed it with hopes the story would convince Buzz to spring him. A delicate transition existed between leaving the hospital and re-entering the world.

When Buzz picked Faulkner up, as he did four or five times, they might drive around Los Angeles or head out of the city. Once on Vine Street before they stopped at Sunset, two pretty girls crossed the walkway and gave them lingering looks. Almost two hours later Faulkner mumbled something inaudible. When Buzz asked him what he'd said, he repeated louder to Buzz's amusement, "I could sure do with a strange woman!"[13]

On the Ventura Highway, they took long scenic drives while the fresh air rushed in the open windows. They would stop to inhale the fragrant orange

Six. Southern Danger: 1940–1947

groves. These recovery drives were taxing for both men: Faulkner was trying to shake the hospital stay and Buzz was doing his best to help. For Buzz, like others, Faulkner's silences could be unnerving. He would find himself talking just to talk. During one such episode after Buzz's spiel, Faulkner made an odd remark, "Bud, you're an animal, but I'm just a vegetable!"[14]

* * *

With the close of the Hollywood summer vacation, Jill and her mom returned home. Jill would have colorful stories to share with her Oxford classmates. At the Hollywood stable where she took weekly riding lessons, another student was actress Elizabeth Taylor. Estelle's social life was a marvel—a dinner party at Jack Warner's with more than two hundred guests, and dinner at the home of Gary Cooper. Feeling more bereft than ever with his family's departure, Faulkner was drinking more.

Living again with the Bezzerideses, Buzz now tried to prevent disastrous scenes by limiting Faulkner's liquor supply, or when that failed, hauling him off to a hospital. Buzz was a large, burly man who carried Faulkner when necessary. During one of those episodes, with Faulkner hoisted over his shoulder, Buzz caught a glimpse of him grimacing and tugging at his own shirt collar. When Buzz asked him what he was doing, Faulkner said trying to get down. The two men erupted in laughter at the ludicrous maneuver.

* * *

In his unsteady mental state, Faulkner began to resent his friend's interventions. He lashed out at others trying to help him besides Buzz. Relief was likely shared by all when Faulkner arranged to move into a private room with its own bath and entrance at Henriette Martin's home. Henriette was a friend of Meta's and kept her informed about Faulkner, especially how much he professed to miss Meta. When Meta asked how he looked, Henriette said, "The way some boozers do. Absolutely marvelous. Your average teetotaler should look so good."[15]

That fall, after hearing Faulkner's entreaties from third parties, Meta softened toward him and they reunited for the third time. Their last year together couldn't have been easy for her as Hollywood was grating on his nerves more than ever. He was edgy, pensive, peevish. A scriptwriter, Paul Wellman, happened to run into Faulkner at a bus stop and made the mistake of asking him how he was. A tirade followed. "'I'll be glad when I get back home,' Faulkner answered. "Nobody here does anything. There's nobody here with any roots. Even the houses are built out of mud and chicken wire. Nothin' ever happens an' after a while a couple of leaves fall of a tree and then it'll be another year."[16] Likewise, Faulkner fatigue set in with film executives who saw him as "a quietly unhappy man." A supervisor noted in his early release recommendation that "he had been uncomplainingly turning out scripts which nearly any Hollywood writer could have written."[17]

Now came the time to act on the promise he'd made years ago to Meta. Jill was old enough to tell a judge which parent she preferred to live with; therefore Faulkner could hope she'd choose him should he pursue a divorce. Instead, he retreated. Meta also wouldn't put Jill through the ordeal of choosing between parents. But that fact that Faulkner made no mention of the promise when he told her, in the fall of 1945, that he was leaving Hollywood for good infuriated her. That night in her apartment she rejected him and was equally distant when she showed him out the door in the morning. Miraculously, after an apology she received in a letter at work—"Honey Love," he wrote, "If you agree that this bloke in question really means better than he does, how's for seeing your face before I leave—looking different from what it did when you brought it into the kitchen and it said, 'Good Morning, Bill'"—they managed one final, peaceful night together before he pulled out of town.

"He was forgiven," Meta recalled, "My face on our last night together was worshipful."[18]

It's hard to fathom why Jill couldn't have split her time between Faulkner and Estelle. That arrangement would have released them from their unhappy union. Whatever the reason, Faulkner wasn't bold enough to take the necessary steps. The fraught domestic scene at Rowan Oak would continue.

* * *

It would be no ordinary exit when Faulkner said his final goodbyes in September. Jill's mare, Lady Go-lightly, possibly with foal, was coming too. Faulkner was adamant he didn't want "any mare of mine to throw a foal in California."[19] Buzz, a friend to the end, drove Faulkner to the stable. The driver, Jack House's son, hitched the mare's trailer to his Cadillac and they were off. From the backseat, an unusually chatty Faulkner talked about Mississippi as if it were a mythical country. They couldn't travel fast enough to suit him. Had the Guy Clark song "L.A. Freeway" existed, Faulkner might have applauded Clark's lyrics, especially the line, "That son of a bitch has always bored me." In spite of all the dreamers, schemers, and worshipful in the famed city, for Faulkner, it equaled boredom.

* * *

He was home for his 48th birthday, swearing he would never return regardless of legal threats. Eventually, Random House helped extricate him from the seven-year contract. After 11 Hollywood stints spanning 13 years and a vast number of assignments—between 1942 and 1945 alone he worked on 17 scripts—Faulkner would accumulate six onscreen credits.

* * *

Hollywood reentered Faulkner's life in the form of a visit from the Bezzerides family. In July 1947, Buzz and his family were headed home to California after a trip to Cuba and Florida. Movie research for Paramount necessitated the trip and Buzz made a family vacation of it. It was a simple call to say hello but Faulkner seized the opportunity. They had to come to Mississippi! Faulkner, Buzz later realized, relished the idea of repaying the extraordinary hospitality they had bestowed upon him as their houseguest.

Since there was no dissuading him, Buzz and his family took the train from Florida to Memphis. They were greeted by Faulkner at the Memphis train station. Faulkner was driving a Model A Ford he bought in 1935. The driving compartment had no floorboards, and Buzz rode to Oxford with his feet on the dash. If the car was a shock, they were in for many more. The drive in the dark seemed to take hours. Finally, slightly beyond the town through the woods, they spied Rowan Oak. Estelle greeted them and they passed a pleasant evening catching up. Their daughter slept with Jill and Buzz and his wife had a room upstairs adjacent to Faulkner and Estelle's. Sliding doors separated the couples' bedrooms.

Even though he was ready to return home, Buzz felt it would be impolite to leave too soon. Buzz's perceptions while in Oxford were informed by the outsider's view and the screenwriter's eye for detail. They spent about a week with the Faulkners, who were wonderful hosts. Estelle prepared delicious meals and Faulkner would provide a ham from their personal smokehouse. Buzz perceived it was important to Faulkner that the house's image include a proper waitstaff. They had a young Black man who served the table but he was unskilled and rather inept in his approach. Faulkner was very patient and took great effort to instruct and encourage.

Estelle and Yvonne passed most of their time at Rowan Oak while Buzz made excursions with Faulkner. They made a pleasant stop at the Gathright-Reed Drug Store where Faulkner's trusted friend, William M. Reed, "Mac," was a pharmacist and part owner. Mac and Faulkner's friendship dated back to the early 1920s when Faulkner first came in the store with Phil Stone. According to Faulkner's niece Dean Faulkner Wells, by the 1930s Mac was wrapping and mailing Faulkner's manuscript submissions to New York. "After the books were published, he kept copies for sale when they were out of print, stacking them next to the cash register. There was no bookstore in Oxford. Garthright-Reed's was the only place in town to purchase Faulkner first editions."[20]

"I saw William Faulkner every day," Reed said. And he proudly displayed Faulkner's books for sale, "Goodness alive. They had the main place in the setup." Reed even passed along written questions from customers to Faulkner when they were "seeking more insight." He also said Faulkner was "always considerate" when a customer requested a signed copy. By 1955 the drugstore also doubled as a lending library and was a popular gathering spot. When Faulkner was in town he was a regular during the bustling evening hour of nine to ten o'clock.

Reed remembers Faulkner becoming so "utterly absorbed" in a book he was browsing "that he would often sink to the floor, book in hand, and people would step over him. People would come by for the chance to see him and find out just what book he had so they could read it, too." College students had more devious intentions; they stole the book check-out cards he'd signed for his signature. "I had to put a stop to that," Reed said. "I told him [Faulkner] that if he'd hold up the book he wanted to check out, one of the clerks would make a record of it."[21] If Faulkner found himself the center of unwelcome attention, he would excuse himself and walk to the post office. Buzz and Faulkner's errand that day was to refresh Faulkner's mystery book stash. Buzz asked him why he read all those "damn mysteries. 'Bud,' he said, 'No matter what you write, it's a mystery of one kind or another.'"[22]

Other stops were not so enjoyable. Buzz felt there were locals who held Faulkner in contempt; and if they recognized his celebrity, it didn't increase their fondness. An incident at an Oxford feed store heightened Buzz's perception. They had sold Faulkner corn seed infested with worms that wouldn't germinate. When he asked about it they told him to try again, almost snickering behind his back. The two men spent more than a little time on countryside drives. During one, Faulkner wanted to show Buzz a favorite fishing spot only to discover a beautiful natural stream had been dammed to stock fish. He was furious and explained all that would come of the stock dam was mud, pollution, and dead fish, "God dammit!" "God dammit! They never leave anything alone; they always destroy things, and pretty soon this country won't be anything like it was."[23] The men drove further into the woods, Faulkner was still very angry, and came to a sudden stop. An arm came through the window and handed over a bottle filled with clear liquid. The bootlegger at least was efficient. To Buzz it tasted like fire and he drank very little but Faulkner drank a lot. Buzz recalled it didn't seem to affect him. "When he didn't want to get drunk, he could drink any amount, and it didn't matter, but when he wanted to get

William M. Reed, "Mac" Reed, was part owner of an Oxford drug store and, more importantly, Faulkner's loyal friend. His drugstore doubled as a library, bookstore and informal town hangout proudly displaying Faulkner's work. Reed remembers Faulkner might become so "utterly absorbed" in a book he was browsing "that he would sink to the floor, book in hand, requiring people to step over him. People would come by for the chance to see him and find out just what book he had so they could read it, too" (Martin J. Dain Collection, Archives and Special Collections, J.D. Williams Library, the University of Mississippi).

drunk, the liquor would begin to take hold, and he couldn't stop drinking. He didn't drink just to drink; always it was to escape something."

On another afternoon, Buzz's travels with Faulkner took him to the Oxford Square, the center of which is the Lafayette County Courthouse. Like much of Oxford, the courthouse was burned to the ground by Union troops in 1864, as well as all businesses, save one, around it. It was rebuilt in 1872. The elevated statue of a Confederate soldier is prominently positioned in front of the courthouse. Quite naturally the Square is the town's social and business hub where lawyers and other professionals have office space. Residents and visitors stroll from shops, including Neilson's (1839) which boasts of being the South's oldest department store, to restaurants and pubs. Without a doubt it is the place to see and be seen.

As they drove around the Square that day, a lady in a car full of women shouted at Faulkner and asked if their California guests had arrived. After introductions, she asked "How is Estelle?" Again, to Buzz, it had the air of contempt. It meant, he realized, "Was she sober or drunk?"

Even as they handed Faulkner a bunch of gardenias for his wife, to the visitor, "there was a strange ridicule in their airs."[24]

* * *

Buzz and Yvonne were insiders to the state of the Faulkner marriage, yet even that couldn't prepare them for their final night at Rowan Oak. They all sat outside having drinks after dinner and then retired. Buzz woke to the sound of an argument next door, Estelle telling Faulkner not to touch her. The presence of their guests had necessitated them sleeping together—not the normal arrangement—and that and having a good bit to drink apparently emboldened Faulkner. He persisted, and they heard the sound of a sharp slap, followed by sexual activity. There would be no sleeping after that.

Buzz felt how deeply appalled his wife was. Estelle cheerfully served breakfast in the morning, and if she was upset, it didn't show. That was the last time Buzz ever saw Faulkner. Though Buzz was aware Faulkner came to Hollywood off and on after their 1947 visit, Faulkner never called him. Buzz, like Ben Wasson, another friend Faulkner called "Bud," was puzzled by the strange end of their friendship but reconciled to it. The need Faulkner had felt for him no longer existed.

* * *

For the Californian, the South represented imminent danger. Buzz felt it the entire time he was there—when Faulkner stopped him from nearly stepping on a poisonous snake to worry about his daughter and Jill when they were off together, that something terrible might happen to them. He sensed hazard every day, around every corner. It amazed him that the southerners didn't seem aware of it.

Seven

Enter Joan Williams: 1949

Summers in Memphis always passed slowly and Joan was restless by nature. When she was upbeat, she imagined that trait meant she was constantly seeking—more knowledge, adventure, experience—but when she was feeling critical, it seemed nothing more than an outcropping of her inherent boredom.

At least it was only a summer in Memphis. She knew it meant a lot to her parents, Maude and P.H. "Priestly" Williams, to have her home. Her mom especially was lonely. They doted on her and she appreciated it in her own understated way. Her father's success as a dynamite salesman meant a move to a distinguished home in a prosperous neighborhood when Joan was 10 years old. It felt cavernous—the three of them—in the rambling house on South Parkway, and it was quite a contrast to the cozy bungalow on Harbert with its cheerful yellow, stucco exterior. Even the neighborhood wasn't as warm and welcoming as the one she'd known. It should have helped that girls from the private school she now attended lived nearby, but somehow it didn't. By the fall, she'd be back in the Northeast and glad of it.

Finally, three colleges later, she'd found one that suited her. Southwestern at Memphis had felt limiting; she'd lived in Memphis her entire life! The transfer to Chevy Chase Junior College in Maryland as a sophomore, while promising, had been a disappointment. She wasn't interested in a "finishing school." Together with her friend, Louise Fitzhugh, who also was ready to explore beyond Memphis and Southwestern, they decided to seek the advice of Fitzhugh's uncle, novelist Peter Taylor. Taylor knew literature was a shared interest between Joan and Louise (Fitzhugh would write the children's classic *Harriet the Spy*). When the two young women approached him, Taylor was teaching English at Kenyon College in Gambier, Ohio. He felt Kenyon was the only college that would best develop their writing careers. How disappointing that in 1948 it was an all-male college! Taylor's next recommendation was Bard College in Annandale-on-Hudson, New York

Bard was a welcome change for both women. The southern strictures that had formed their lives diminished in this liberating and challenging atmosphere. Louise eventually would be able to embrace her life as an author, illustrator, and openly gay woman. Long after college she and Joan remained friends and Louise introduced Joan to a number of her romantic interests. Joan always was divided in her loyalties between southern propriety and a desire to be more bohemian. Her first noteworthy rebellion—an impulsive high school marriage—occurred when she was 17 years old.

Joan and a group of friends were celebrating high school graduation with a road trip to a small Mississippi town. Once there, they woke the town's justice of the peace so the various couples could be married. Joan had dated her boyfriend, an Irish Catholic student who attended Christian Brothers High School in Memphis, for two years. At the last moment she changed her mind, but her boyfriend drove into the ditch and said that if she did not marry him, he would simply leave her there. Upon their return to Memphis, Joan told her parents she didn't want to be married.

What was depicted as a bit of a lark lacked humor for Joan's parents, who already were aware of their only child's ability to surprise and be contrary. P.H. and Maude arranged a hasty annulment—Joan and the young man never cohabited—and the incident largely was forgotten or rarely referenced.

* * *

At her mother's urgings, summer breaks from college meant rounds of social obligations—parties, lunches, and dates with appropriate young men. Joan was a lovely young woman with delicate features and hazel eyes that Faulkner described as "violet." Maude was eager for Joan to make the perfect match and to produce grandchildren, a desire shared by her daughter. Joan wanted marriage and children. Loneliness was something she would combat her entire life, and she often felt overly focused, sometimes even desperate, to meet the right man.

Early in her childhood, Joan's parents transitioned into a comfortable material life. Her father was passionate about his work and insisted that Maude not work outside the home, which suited her as well. She passed her time playing bridge, shopping and reading. His problems with alcohol eventually crept into Maude's own drinking habits and combustible arguments might ensue. Those episodes and marital rifts occasionally disturbed the peace of the South Parkway home. At such times, Joan would dig deeper into her reading or friends might find her a quieter companion.

Seven. Enter Joan Williams: 1949

Years later she realized that for much of her childhood she'd been gripped with fear and loneliness—terrified of P.H. and Maude's fights; her father's raucous parties and his friends who would spend the night; terrified of her parents' relationship; and terrified someone would find out about her mother's drinking problem. With frequent guests coming to and from the Williamses' home, Joan continued to sleep in her parents' room until she was ten years old. Even such close proximity couldn't banish her anxiety.

Someone who didn't know Maude well might not even have noticed, but Joan could tell by dinner time her mom had been drinking off and on throughout the day. Her father was more likely to go on full-fledged binges that might require professional care. P.H.'s occupation meant he was often away and Joan's mother preoccupied. When Joan was born, September 26, 1929, P.H. was out of town on business and Maude had not been able to locate her husband. That sting seemed never to fully dissipate. Maude's anger at the time of Joan's birth took an odd form. She decided not to give her daughter what some might consider the embellishment of a middle name.

P.H. had risen above a number of obstacles—including dropping out of school at age 14 and running away from Tennessee to Colorado—to achieve success. P.H. had no fear of fighting and work. He also pledged to himself he would have financial security. At 20 years of age, he took a course in business and penmanship and was hired as a salesman for a dynamite company. P.H. believed blasting could form levees—crucial in the Delta for flood control—and it was also attractive to farmers for drainage ditches and irrigation, being faster than other means.

His territory became the levee camps that lined the Mississippi River and area farms. Should someone question the dynamite's effectiveness, P.H. didn't hesitate to shoot the dynamite himself, often using the end of his cigarette to light the fuse. His reputation soared and earned him a new nickname, Dynamite. Bigger than life in many ways, P.H. also found women were fairly easily obtained.

Still, success did not abate his worries. He pledged early on he was never going to be without money and the security it promised. Just as Joan's loneliness shadowed her, so did his nagging concerns even though his bank account spoke to the contrary. His father, Sydney Howard, had moved among various jobs, usually at the behest of his wife, Ethel, who always believed they should be doing better. Perhaps no one could have pleased her, but she seemed serially disappointed with her husband. Ethel harbored real ambitions for her family. Many years later Joan would capture her paternal family's struggles and triumphs in her second novel, *Old Powder Man* (1966).

Financial success was only one piece of the puzzle in southern society at the time the Williamses were ascending. Money didn't grant you entrée to exclusive country clubs where old family lineages were the real currency. Places like the Memphis Hunt and Polo Club and Memphis Country Club remained tantalizingly out of reach. For a man used to accomplishing his goals, Joan's father resented the rebuffs. At the Miss Hutchinson School for Girls in Memphis, Joan was surprised and unsure how to answer when a classmate asked her, "Who are your people?"[1] She understood the implications and realized she didn't have a satisfactory reply. The moment crystallized her appreciation of her parents' frustrations at the prevailing social strata. Now she knew why her father was angered by arbitrary exclusions.

Yet Joan, though shy, made friends easily and found a comfortable group. One of her friends, Kenneth W. Orgill, Jr., attended Yale and was interested in literature. He too was in Memphis the summer of 1949. At his urgings, Joan picked up a copy of Faulkner's *The Sound and the Fury*, and spent summer days absorbed in the novel on her front porch swing under a fan which succeeded at stirring the humid air. She'd never read an author who inhabited the various narrative voices with such aplomb. Faulkner realized the members of the deeply troubled Compson family with an uncanny intimacy. Joan marveled at the experimental nature of the prose. Kenneth pressed Joan to make the trip to Oxford with him. How could they not try to meet Faulkner when they were in such close proximity to sheer genius?

* * *

Years later Joan wrote about what touched her most in *The Sound and the Fury*. It wasn't the Compson saga—a doomed southern family who, according to Faulkner, "refused to accept now and tomorrow. And there is no place for them in now."[2] Nor was it Faulkner's narrative magic—which she readily admits she didn't understand at 20—but how the story made her feel. Benjy, the delayed Compson son, narrates what was for Joan the most astonishing section of the novel. "I didn't understand it… I felt it, and only Benjy's section. I knew what had moved me was his inarticulateness because I felt it to be my own."

Kenneth, more versed in Faulkner's literature than Joan when they made the drive to Oxford, was likewise deeply affected by the author's novels and stories. He came from a prosperous family who in 1847 founded Orgill Bros. & Co., a hardware distribution company and Memphis's oldest operating business. The prominent family even had an eponymous avenue in midtown Memphis. Perhaps to Maude Williams' disappointment, Kenneth and Joan shared a friendship rather than a romance. Joan intuited the pressure Kenneth felt to excel and move into the family business after college even though his interests veered more toward the humanities. Nothing, though, might have prepared her for his death a decade after their visit to Rowan Oak.

On January 31, 1960, at about 2:20 p.m. witnesses saw Orgill run from his 1955 Ford and vault the railing of the Memphis-Arkansas Bridge. In interviews with Memphis newspapers, Mr. W.L. Wadsworth of West Memphis [Arkansas] recounted how Orgill "slammed on his brakes and stopped all at once. Then he jerked open the door and never stopped running until he went over the rail."[3] Mrs. Wadsworth said the young man slammed the front door of his car as he ran. "He placed one hand on the rail and leaped over feet first."[4] The drop from the bridge to the Mississippi River is about nine stories. Mr. Wadworth said it happened "so quick I couldn't tell what he was wearing, except that he had on a suit. There wasn't anything anybody could have done."[5]

Kenneth had been to Sunday service at Calvary Episcopal Church, hence the suit, and had lunch with his parents. He told them he was going for "a little drive."[6] Nothing alerted them to his intentions though his mother said he "had been despondent the past week. He seemed worried ... depressed."[7] Kenneth was 33 years old and working as a toy buyer for the family business. Police found an "assortment of toys such as a cooking set, dart board, and Western-style pistol and holster set" in the trunk of Orgill's car. During a New York buying trip the previous year, he had suffered a nervous breakdown and spent the next three months in Baptist Hospital's psychiatric ward followed by continued psychiatric care.

The timing of his "suicide leap" was sadly ironic. At that very moment, the Civil Defense River Rescue Squad was practicing body recoveries nearby. One of the squad members, Roy Malone, said "I walked out to the front of the boat and heard screams from the bridge." Mr. Malone said the victim "looked like he was trying to swim."[8] Within two minutes of witnessing the jump, 11 men on three boats attempted a rescue. The high river yielded only a dark beaver hat with the initials "KWO" on the inner band about five miles south of the bridge.[9] Despite efforts by the CD squad and Marine Rescue Squadron, who searched a thirty-five-square mile area, a body was not recovered.

Outside eyes would see a picture-perfect family. Before his undergraduate years at Yale, Kenneth attended Salesbury Preparatory School in Connecticut. The rector of Calvary Episcopal Church, Dr. Donald G. Henning, described Kenneth as "a very likeable extrovert and a good businessman."[10] He was a member of the Yale Club and a second cousin to Edmund Orgill, a Memphis mayor. Kenneth was married to Nancy Wilson, a lovely young woman, and father to Kenneth W. Orgill III, five years old, and Elizabeth Orgill, three. The family's comfortable life belied tragedy. As shocking and sad as his suicide was, a second and unfathomable death followed. Twelve days later, his 31-year-old wife jumped from the same bridge. Nancy, educated at Miss Hutchison's School, was a Phi Beta Kappa scholar at Southwestern at Memphis and also attended Randolph-Macon College. She was socially adept as well. She belonged to the Chi Omega Sorority and was a newly named member of the Junior League. In fact, her selection appeared in the Memphis newspaper the day before her suicide.

A Jonesboro, Arkansas, couple were eyewitnesses to Nancy's desperate plunge into the Mississippi river. Mr. and Mrs. Rex Cavenor saw the car stop at 9:45 p.m. Thursday evening. Mrs. Cavenor said,

> It all happened so quickly, that even if we had known a suicide was under way, we could have done nothing to prevent it. We were in the left lane 200 or 300 yards behind the Orgill car, which was in the lane next to the rail. We saw the car stop ahead of us. By the time we were even with it, we saw a figure in a full-length blue or black coat jump over the rail.

When Mr. Cavenor stopped at the Arkansas Highway Patrol weigh station he was told to contact the Tennessee police "since the leap was from the Tennessee side."[11]

Nancy's wallet was on the front seat of the 1955 Oldsmobile that had been abandoned—still running—with the front passenger door facing the rail open. The west-facing vehicle was discovered about halfway across the bridge. A Yellow Cab driver with a fare to West Memphis, Arkansas, was stopped by five or six people gathered around the car. Police theorized Nancy's grief-stricken state and unrest that her husband's body hadn't been recovered led to her fatal jump. Mere speculation seemed as close as anyone would come.

Her father, Gilbert Wilson, was a retired executive of the American Snuff Company and past president of the Tennessee Conservation League and the West Tennessee Sportsman's Association. Wilson had had lunch with his daughter the day of her death and said she was in excellent spirits. "While she has undergone terrific grief and strain she seemed to be holding up well," Wilson said. "However, she was under strain for a long time while her husband was undergoing treatment."[12] Nancy's close friends were in disbelief and echoed her father's assessment, "She seemed a very stable woman. She seemed to bear up well after her husband's tragedy. But she wasn't one to unload her troubles on others."[13]

"Unlike her husband," Wilson said, "she had never undergone any psychiatric treatment. There was nothing wrong with her, nothing." Nancy had called her sister-in-law, Dorothy Orgill White, Kenneth's only sibling, and Dorothy's husband, Thomas White, about 8 p.m. that evening to see if they would look after the children. She told them she wanted to visit relatives but didn't mention any names. Several boats from the Red Cross Marine Rescue Squadron as well as a Civil Defense rescue and body recovery unit were on the water within thirty minutes. It was two months later in the Mississippi River near Scott, Mississippi, that Nancy's body was discovered; Kenneth's body was never recovered.

* * *

The manner of Kenneth's death is hauntingly reminiscent of Faulkner's character Quentin Compson, who serves as one of the narrators in *The Sound and the Fury*. Quentin, the intelligent, sensitive, but tormented Compson son, attends Harvard for one year before he throws himself off a bridge over the Charles River in Cambridge, Massachusetts. Faulkner described Quentin as "existing half way between madness and sanity," as an "educated half-madman."[14] When Quentin accepts that he can't escape the present—"the now"—and return to the past, his only recourse, according to Faulkner, is suicide.[15] The Compson family is doomed. A plaque on the bridge wall in Cambridge memorializes the fictional character's demise:

> Quentin Compson
> Drowned in the odour of honeysuckle
> 1891–1910

Faulkner's depiction of Quentin's state of mind as he contemplates and eventually commits suicide veers from evocative to practical. Over and over the forces driving Quentin to despair are revisited—the state of his dysfunctional family, his incestuous but unacted upon urges toward his sister, Candace, "Caddy," his conflicting feelings about the South; and especially, the tragic fate of his brother, Benjy. Though christened Maury at birth after his maternal uncle, his name is changed to Benjy five years later when his parents recognize his mental impairment. Quentin's Harvard tuition is covered by the sale of Benjy's pasture; a parcel of land known to soothe and comfort his brother. Quentin is haunted by the transaction— Benjy's once idyllic escape commercialized as a golf course. "Let us sell Benjy's pasture so that Quentin may go to Harvard.... Harvard is such a fine sound forty acres is no high price for a fine sound. A fine dead sound we will swap Benjy's pasture for a fine dead sound."[16]

Benjy, who also narrates a chapter of the novel, conveys his loss and grief in shattering fragments moving back and forth in time. He is preternaturally perceptive and operates on a sensory and emotional level. Dilsey (the Caroline Barr "Mammy Callie" character) is a primary caretaker as is his sister. "You a big boy," Dilsey said. "Caddy tired of sleeping with you.

Hush now, so you can go to sleep." The room went away, but I didn't hush, and the room came back and Dilsey came and sat on the bed, looking at me. "Hush," Caddy said. "I'm coming.... She snuggled her head beside mine on the pillow.... The room went black. Caddy smelled like trees."[17]

Quentin's chapter, "June Second, 1910," denotes the date of his suicide. The trail of his waning mental acuity is interspersed with dominant Faulkner themes of southern honor, womanhood, and virginity, personified by Caddy, and Quentin's vainglorious attempt to believe in the Old South. The random events in the chapter are fairly insignificant since what is germane is Quentin's stream of consciousness. He dresses carefully that day, so carefully that his roommate, Shreve, remarks on his attire, "Say, what're you doing today, anyhow? All dressed up and mooning around like the prologue to a suttee."[18]

At one point he is transported by the University bells, "The chimes began again, the half hour, I stood in the belly of my shadow and listened to the strokes spaced and tranquil along the sunlight, among the thin, still little leaves. Spaced and peaceful and serene, with that quality of autumn always in bells even in the month of brides."[19] And as the chapter nears conclusion, Quentin appears to lose narrative control: "A quarter hour yet. And then I'll not be. The peacefullest words. Peacefullest words. Non fui. Sum. Fui. Non sum. Somewhere I heard bells once. Mississippi or Massachusetts. I was. I am not. Massachusetts or Mississippi."[20]

Final preparations in his dorm room include brushing his teeth and securing the hat that designates his year of study.

> Then I remembered I hadn't brushed my teeth, so I had to open the bag again. I found my toothbrush and got some of Shreve's paste and went out and brushed my teeth. I squeezed the brush as dry as I could and put it back in the bag and shut it, and went to the door again. Before I snapped the light out I looked around to see if there was anything else, then I saw that I had forgotten my hat. I'd have to go by the postoffice and I'd be sure to meet some of them, and they'd think I was a Harvard Square student making like he was a senior. I had forgotten to brush it too, but Shreve had a brush, so I didn't have to open the bag any more.[21]

* * *

The influence of *The Sound and the Fury* on Joan's literary path was profound (and a few years after they met Faulkner gave her the handwritten manuscript of the novel). Faulkner's ability to create characters who illuminated human nature in all forms—a narcissistic mother who feigns martyrdom, a psychopathic son, a rebellious daughter, a mentally delayed son, a suicidal son, and a saintly caregiver in *The Sound and the Fury* alone—was a skill she honed in her own fiction. And while her background may have seemed ill-suited to a famously liberal college in the East, it is to her parents' credit that they encouraged and supported her aspirations.

When her Bard College graduation rolled around, Joan remembered her father's discomfiture at the prospect of attending. P.H. finally agreed to go but only if he didn't have to talk with her professors. He told Joan he didn't know how to "talk with people like that." In 1948, even against the backdrop of many other excellent liberal arts colleges in the area, Bard stood out. Students essentially were free of residential rules. What a pleasant contrast for Joan from the old-fashioned regulations of Chevy Chase! Students were free to come and go at will. The college had no grades and analytical papers by and large replaced exams. Tutorials were as significant as traditional classes and seminars eclipsed any sort of lecture platform.

Besides attracting like-minded students from Manhattan and the area, Bard likewise attracted a creative and liberal faculty. Joan's world was blown open by meeting such different and intellectual people (a theme she would return to in *The Wintering*, her 1971 novel about her relationship with Faulkner [Jeffrey Almoner] as well as her friendship with Kenneth Orgill [Quill]). Bard had a six-week field period in January during which students sought a vocational experience. She spent her field period in New York City working at a progressive elementary school and as a receptionist in a law firm. She savored the opportunity to explore the city. Even as she took great pleasure in the way her world was expanding, Joan was dogged by the prospect of returning to Memphis for the summer. There she felt neither fish nor fowl.

Bard allowed her to dig deeper into literature and she was rewarded when her innate talent as a writer flourished. Joan's professor and advisor at Bard, Joseph Summers (later she would study under novelist William Humphrey), encouraged her to enter the *Mademoiselle* college fiction contest. For that, she simply sat down and wrote a short story, "Rain Later," about the uneasy relationship between her mother and her maternal grandmother, Arvenia Moore. Arvenia spent her life in the small Mississippi town of Arkabutla, thirty miles south of Memphis, where she was born in 1873. She was a vigorous woman who reared four sons and two daughters. When her husband died at 59 years, she continued on with the home place, raising chickens, livestock, gardening, canning, and helping out at her church. For her daughter, Maude, born in 1903, she envisioned a different life. Maude spent four years in boarding school, followed by two years of college, not de rigueur for women at that time.

Whether it was the mother and daughter's disparate lifestyles—once married Maude spent most of her time playing bridge as the Williamses had full-time domestic help—or more fundamental personality gaps, the tension between the women as well as all the lost opportunities reverberates throughout "Rain Later." Faulkner summarized it best when he wrote Joan that it was "...moving and true, made me want to cry a little for all the sad frustration of solitude, isolation, aloneness in which every human being lives, who for all the blood kinship and everything else, cant really communicate, touch."[22] For her part, Joan remembered the story "just came out right," and was a spontaneous success. Indeed, "Rain Later" captured the *Mademoiselle* prize and was published in the August 1949 magazine, and many years later, holding its integrity, or, as Joan said, "standing up on its hind legs," it would be included in *Pariah and Other Stories* (1983).

Joan's success with *Mademoiselle* in the spring of 1949 accelerated her appetite and ambition to become an author. That, along with Bard's nurturing environment, allowed her to see the world less as a coed and more as a writer. Thus, her friend's suggestion that they try to meet Faulkner in Oxford seemed to make sense. Joan agreed it would be foolish to miss such an opportunity. The summer was dragging on and she had a connection, her cousin Regina Moore Holley, who could facilitate an introduction. Regina recently had married John Reed Holley. Holley had grown up next door to Faulkner's in-laws, the Oldhams, and knew the family well. He was willing to call Mr. Bill and see if they might be welcome.

Faulkner apparently was not in the mood for company. He told Holley he was going to Sardis, a nearby reservoir. The weather hadn't cooperated that day and there was a fine drizzle. A boat outing at Sardis seemed unlikely. The Holleys exchanged a look—by then Joan and Orgill had been at their Oxford house a while and everyone was restless—which acknowledged they didn't believe Faulkner's excuse but they also understood his motive. Holley told the disappointed visitors that they might as well drive by Rowan Oak and see the house. As the afternoon diminished, Holley drove the carload (Regina and John Reed's toddler was also in tow), past the "no trespassing sign" into the Faulkners' turn-around drive.

While the Holleys certainly weren't surprised to see Faulkner in the yard, it led to an awkward exchange. John Reed got out of the car and walked over to greet Faulkner. He repeated his favor, that Faulkner speak to Regina's cousin. "What does she want to meet me for?" Faulkner asked Holley. "To see if I have two heads?" Things didn't improve much when Faulkner made his way to the car and spoke briefly to Regina, Orgill and Joan. (Faulkner explained his behavior when he answered Joan's letter the end of August. What he expected from Holley's request was meeting "a grim beldame of 40 or 50 summers, president of some limited literary circle, come out of curiosity."[23])

Joan was far from the dreary introduction Faulkner anticipated. If he had conjured a new love interest someone very much like Joan might have materialized. Her auburn hair was set against a creamy rather than pale complexion. Fine boned, with the elegant, polished countenance of a model or actress—indeed Joan dreamed of being an actress and wrote fan letters to many—she epitomized the beauty standards of the time. None of this was lost on Faulkner. More significant than Joan's age and appearance was how much she and Faulkner—though thirty years apart in age—had in common. Joan knew the South—would always be deeply a southerner at heart regardless of domicile—and she knew Manhattan and the Northeast, just like Faulkner. She had a writer's temperament and sensitivity. They shared a number of traits—though highly talented, both could be shy and insecure—and both expressed feelings of inadequacy, sadness, and a desire to escape when pressures mounted.

Hindsight might declare Faulkner and Joan's meeting the perfect storm. Faulkner at midlife was restless and often unhappy in his life with Estelle. Suddenly, there was a 20-year-old aspiring writer—who happened to be female—gazing up at him with wonderment and embarrassment. What Joan saw was a handsome, older man in khakis and a tee shirt who was somewhat annoyed by the uninvited company. He didn't appear to be the person her aunt Ethel Moore had warned her about—an irresponsible drinker and someone to avoid. The moment might have passed had not Joan written Faulkner a letter of apology. The letter set a five-year romance in motion, one that would rock the Faulkners' marriage and test Joan's ability to balance Faulkner's demands and her own aspirations. "You take too much, and are willing to give too little," Faulkner wrote Joan near the end of their affair. "People have attributes like animals; you are a mixture of cat and mule and possum—the cat's secretiveness and self-centeredness, the mule's stubbornness to get what it wants no matter who or what suffers, the possum's nature of playing dead—running into sleep or its pretense—whenever it is faced with a situation which it thinks it is not going to like."[24]

That afternoon in Oxford resurrected more than a few of Joan's childhood anxieties—she would find herself unsettled by Faulkner's difficult moods and desires that often didn't match her own. For Estelle, the unstable and often volcanic domestic situation at Rowan Oak would be tested as never before.

Eight

New York and Trouble Follows: 1948–1949

In the years since he said his Hollywood goodbyes, Bill and Estelle's life together had gone on much as usual, with the tone and pace determined by Faulkner's moods. There might be long draughts of silence or he might take a genuine interest in a domestic matter. Generally, without arguments over Meta, the waters were calmer. It was his new book—his opus as he sometimes called it—causing stress now. *A Fable* certainly was extracting its pound of flesh.

When he took a break to write his detective story *Intruder in the Dust*, what a contrast that was. He wrote it in three months! That satisfying experience was followed by a financial windfall. In the summer of 1948, MGM bought the movie rights for $50,000 before the book was even published in the fall. Estelle and Bill enjoyed quite a celebration with that happy news. They were ecstatic. Bill kicked off his shoes, and when Sallie Murry Williams dropped by, he told her anyone who could sell a book to the movies for $50,000 had a right to drink and dance barefoot. The money gave Bill the courage to admit his old Ford was well past any kind of repairs, and he bought an almost new Ford station wagon.

* * *

Another source of frivolity entered their lives as well. Three of Bill's friends, Hugh Evans, Ross Brown, and Dr. Ashford Little, along with Bill's off-and-on assistance, built a three-ton houseboat with a lugger engine. (A truck capable of hauling the boat eleven miles to water had to be ordered from Memphis.) The finished craft had six bunks in a bedroom below, lighting, heating, and a water system. Bill's role was usually ceremonial and he donated an inscription for the boat:

> Out of Confusion by Boundless Hope: conceived in a Canadian Club bottle
> She was born A.D. 15th August 1947 by uproarious Caesarian Section in prone
> position with her bottom upward in Evan's back yard eleven miles from the

Eight. New York and Trouble Follows: 1948-1949

nearest water deeper than a half-inch kitchen tap & waxed & grew daily there beneath the whole town's enrapt cynosure.[1]

Working with the wives' first names—Minnie Ruth Little, Maggie Brown, and Mary Evans—Faulkner named the vessel the M/S *Minmagary*. The *Minmagary* eventually would launch at Sardis Lake, a flood control reservoir on the Little Tallahatchie River that covers almost twelve miles. An early spring scouting trip for the summer launch ended with Evans' truck submerged under the swollen spring waters. He failed to notice the road was under water. If Faulkner, who was in the truck's cab beside Evans, noticed the water in time, he didn't alert the driver. Evans later asked Faulkner what he was saying before the plunge, "I said, 'God Damn, he ain't gonna stop!'"[2]

The vessel's actual christening in July 1948 went much more smoothly. Faulkner, again in costume, this time a Navy cap and jacket with a blacked mustache, composed the commissioning papers—"appoint her to be a Ship of the Line in the Provisional Navy of the Confederate States of America"[3]—while Mary Evans smashed a champagne bottle across the bow. The lively party stretched into weeks as they all enjoyed and possibly overcelebrated the houseboat. Faulkner wrote Robert Haas that he'd been more or less out of circulation for the last two weeks.

Faulkner's enthusiasm for news of a Faulkner course at Harvard University, the first in the country, paled in comparison to the *Minmagary*'s inauguration. Faulkner and Professor Carvel Collins met at Rowan Oak and passed a pleasant afternoon together talking horses rather than literature. When pressed for his thoughts on an entire course dedicated to his work, Faulkner said, "I don't know anything about universities. I ain't surprised at anything they do."[4]

* * *

During some of the darker days in Hollywood when Bill fretted about neglecting his real work, a new friend and advocate came into his life. Malcolm Cowley, *The New Republic* editor and critic, admired and believed in Bill's talent, offering him assurances when he was most in need. Bill still hadn't met Cowley in person—that would be rectified in the fall when he was in New York—and Estelle also hoped to one day meet him and thank him for being a source of optimism. His interest had been a godsend and stayed some of Bill's restless energy. (Indeed, unbeknownst to Estelle, he wrote Cowley that life at Rowan Oak was dull and that he needed a new young woman.) Bill's lack of progress with his cantankerous book made for trying days.

For four years the two men, who were contemporaries in age, wrote back and forth. Cowley proposed a long essay on Bill which the *Atlantic* turned down, believing it wouldn't sell. He wrote it regardless and eventually part of the article appeared in *The New York Times Book Review*, titled "William Faulkner's Human Comedy." Undaunted, Cowley queried Viking Press about their interest in *The Portable Faulkner*. (Cowley edited *The Portable Hemingway* in 1944.)

For the Faulkner volume, Cowley needed Bill's help. Bill drew a map of his "little postage stamp of native soil," the fictional kingdom of Yoknapatawpha County, for the book; but when it came to answering personal questions, he resisted. To Estelle's surprise, he did insist Cowley remove a passage about his plane crash and combat injury during World War I. When Cowley resisted he admonished him in a letter, "You're going to bugger up a fine dignified distinguished book with that war business."[5] He was discovering the fabrication he started in 1918 was hard to dispel.

Even though all 17 of Faulkner's books except *Sanctuary* were out of print, Viking Press agreed. For the first time, a publication would exist that illustrated his sweeping vision of the American South. Cowley harbored lofty goals for the book and his bold introduction ignited interest, "There in Oxford, Faulkner performed a labor of imagination that has not been equaled in our time."[6] The Yoknapatawpha saga was arranged in chronological order. That structure yielded an entirely new and more accessible way of reading Faulkner. Cowley believed the volume, at seven hundred–plus pages, would incite a reevaluation of Faulkner's entire oeuvre to date and rekindle dormant interest. Some would say it resuscitated Faulkner's career.

When the advance copy arrived at Rowan Oak April 23, 1946, proselytizing was neither here nor there in the Faulkner home. Faulkner was immensely pleased with the book and expressed his gratitude in a letter to Cowley: "The job is splendid. Damn you to hell anyway. But even if I had beat you to the idea, mine wouldn't have been this good. By God, I didn't know myself what I had tried to do, and how much I had succeeded."[7] Novelist Caroline Gordon's review made the cover of *The New York Times Book Review* (May 5, 1946). While there was no immediate bump, over time *The Portable Faulkner*'s influence was indisputable.

* * *

The October 1948 trip to New York was planned to coincide with the publication of *Intruder in the Dust*. Ever since Estelle made the exhausting trip to New York in 1931 to bring him home, and after the third-degree burn he suffered at the Algonquin in 1937, her anxiety soared when she thought of him there. She could tell he was excited about seeing friends and colleagues. That would mean trouble if he wasn't careful.

But Faulkner wasn't in the mood to be careful. He looked forward to the amenities and freedom the city afforded and he clearly planned to enjoy himself. For some time he'd remarked in various letters that he hadn't had anyone to talk to in years. He made sure to connect with Jim Devine, a reliably lighthearted companion, and his rescuer from the Algonquin burn incident. He turned down Bennett Cerf's offer to stay with him and his wife and booked a room at the Algonquin. He thanked Cerf but told him he'd had enough of the nest-and-hearth.

When he arrived at the hotel, Faulkner called Cerf as promised. Cerf and his wife, Phyllis, had another houseguest that night, Sinclair Lewis. Lewis was the 1930 Nobel laureate for literature and the first American author to receive the award. Cerf asked Lewis, whom he called Red, if it would be all right to have Faulkner over for a drink. Lewis was not about to accommodate, telling Cerf that it was "his night," and that "Bennett, don't you know you should have only one author at a time?" The couple naturally acquiesced to his wishes. Still Lewis was uneasy that his time with them might be compromised. He went to the guest bedroom and then got back up in his pajamas. He told Cerf, "I just wanted to make sure you didn't duck out to see Faulkner after I went to bed."[8]

Lewis need not have worried. Faulkner had plans with actress Ruth Ford. Ruth's contract at Warner Brothers had overlapped on occasion with Faulkner's but she already was known to him. She'd dated his brother, Dean, and attended Ole Miss. Now, living in New York, Ruth's talents were expanding. During the fall of 1947 she'd appeared in Sartre's *No Exit* on Broadway. Faulkner and Ruth had dinner together his first night in town where he commented on their long friendship. "Ruth," he said. "I've been your gentleman friend for quite a while now. Ain't it time I was promoted?"[9] The young actress charmingly demurred.

Random House too was keeping him busy with meetings and social events. A dinner party his second night in town united many key players. At the Haases' Fifth Avenue apartment, Faulkner met Malcolm Cowley and his wife, Muriel, for the first time. Dinner drifted into after-dinner drinks, and when the Cowleys left at two a.m., Faulkner, Devine, and Hal Smith, a former Random House partner, moved the party to Smith's apartment. The next day meant lunch at 21 Club, the storied restaurant on West 52nd Street, where, since its 1929 inception, every United States president, save one, has dined, as well as a host of other celebrities, dignitaries, actors, and artists. (Sadly, after ninety years, the restaurant permanently closed in 2021.)

On one visit not many years after 21 opened, Hemingway made quite a night of it. He set the tone by declaring, "Since I'm not drinking, I'll just have a tequila."[10] He became enamored of an alluring woman dining and struck up a conversation. One thing led to another, and he asked co-owner Jack Kriendler if they could linger after closing time. Kriendler agreed they could stay and it is said they had sex on the restaurant's "very steep" kitchen steps. When Hemingway returned the next day to find out her name, Kriendler told him she was the girlfriend of notorious mob boss Legs Diamond. Diamond put a hit out on Kriendler and the club's other owner, Charlie Berns, for getting their prohibition liquor through a police department arrangement rather than the mob, and a hit on Hemingway for the 21 Club tryst with his girlfriend. Fortunately for the men, Diamond was killed first in Albany, New York, in late 1931.

* * *

After lunch with Don Klopfer, co-founder of Random House along with Cerf, Faulkner grudgingly granted an interview to *The New York Times*. His unwillingness to do interviews—or much of anything—to promote his books was vexing at Random House. While on some level he enjoyed veneration, and understood the need for increased book sales, Faulkner disliked the required social interaction. Interviews could be especially troublesome since he couldn't control the outcome. To Ralph Thompson, the *Times* reporter, he said, "Look, I'm just a writer. Not a literary man. I write about the people around Oxford. I know them, and they know me. They don't much care what I write."[11]

He bemoaned the loss of his earlier days when he was a "free man" with only one pair of pants, shoes, and an old trench coat with a pocket large enough to accommodate a whiskey bottle. It was hard to tell if his comments merely captured his mood at the moment or reflected a sincere sentiment. Regardless, that sort of discomfort started him drinking. Even when he was among people he genuinely liked, the social pressure he felt or perhaps imagined could prove his undoing. Cowley's scheduled lunch date with Faulkner two days later was one of the many meetings—including a number with Random House—he missed.

For the next three days, friends couldn't rouse him at the Algonquin. He had been drinking and not eating. Finally, a hotel manager let them into his room and arrangements were made for the Fieldstone Sanitarium. The attending doctor assured them he understood such cases. He had cared for Thomas Wolfe. When Faulkner pleaded for an early release the next morning—he spent only one night in the facility—Ruth called Cowley to see if he could recover at their Sherman, Connecticut, home. Faulkner seemed unhinged and desperate to leave the sanitarium. It was painful for his friends to witness Faulkner pacing around the room.

Amazingly, the Cowleys, having only had the one dinner with him, agreed. They had friends go through similar episodes and understood the artistic temperament. Cowley remarked that artists and writers as a tribal

Eight. New York and Trouble Follows: 1948–1949

group have certain defects of character, most notably they drink too much. Faulkner suggested a drink at every tavern they passed en route from Manhattan to Connecticut. The Cowleys knew to space his drinks and provide nourishing food. As he started to come around, Faulkner talked a good deal about his work and home, smoking cigarettes rather than his pipe as was his custom when recovering. He was back in Oxford for his deer camp and the holidays.

* * *

Faulkner's trips to New York were almost always high-wire acts. The transition from his quiet Oxford existence, where he was at the very least misunderstood, if not shunned, by townspeople, to New York, where important and influential people sought his company, often unnerved him. Soon the city would become even more perilous. New York, as it turned out, provided the most accessible backdrop for his pursuit of Joan Williams.

* * *

A great deal of hullabaloo occurred during the spring of 1949 when MGM came to Oxford for seven weeks to film *Intruder in the Dust*. Juano Hernández, an Afro–Puerto Rican actor, portrayed Lucas Beauchamp, a self-sustaining farmer who is zealously charged and jailed for the death of a local white man. Race relations were such in 1949 that Hernández was lodged with a Black undertaker's family in Oxford and socialized little off the set. (Hernández didn't return for the movie's Oxford premiere.)

Faulkner took a real liking to Hernández, even helping him cultivate a Mississippi Black's accent (Faulkner thought his portrayal of Beauchamp sounded Shakespearean). He admired movie director Clarence Brown and assisted with casting, scouting local locations, and reading the film's script. Faulkner wrote Cerf that "Brown is one of the best to work with I ever knew. Right off he asked me to read the script and tell him what I wanted changed; I think he meant it. There was nothing to change.... I myself am so pleased with the job that I would like all the credit to stay where it is: with Brown and the cast."[12]

He and Estelle entertained the entire cast and crew on the *Minmagary* and planned for a second social event at Rowan Oak. That idea was highly discouraged by civic leaders, including Sallie Murry Williams' husband Bob Williams, the Oxford mayor. Their objection was over Hernández socializing at Rowan Oak, which would mean including his Black Oxford host family. Eventually the party occurred with the exception of Hernández. The Faulkners also hosted a small party for Claude Jarman, Jr. Jarman played a white teenager intent on proving Beauchamp's innocence. Other partygoers included Jill and a group of her high school friends. (Normally entertaining friends could be precarious for Jill; she never knew what her parents' condition might be, a source of anxiety and sometimes embarrassment.) Jarman recalled that Faulkner was around a lot during the film's shooting and that Faulkner and Clarence Brown "kind of bonded." Meanwhile, "Jill was my age and she used to have parties at the house [Rowan Oak] on weekends so we used to go to those. Dancing, that sort of thing."[13]

* * *

Finding himself directly in the public spotlight provoked Faulkner's discomfort. The more attention and excitement the movie generated, the more withdrawn he became. All told over five hundred local individuals appeared in the film. The Memphis newspaper described the amateur actors as often looking as "self-conscious as a bunch of high school girls walking past a fraternity house."[14] The high-pitched frenzy failed to excite Faulkner. He also harbored ill-feelings for the way Hernández was treated during the filming. "He was very upset and disappointed about the Hernández incident, how it reflected badly on his hometown and on his state,"[15] Vicki recalled.

Thus, his cooperation was lackluster at best. He finally agreed to pose for a publicity photograph and attend a news conference scheduled for the visiting newspapers. MGM hoped for an author photograph suitable for an eighteen-inch blowup on the Lyric marquee. Faulkner countered that they should use an image of the book. That tug of war ended when Oxford photographer J.R. Cofield snapped an unshaven Faulkner wearing a t-shirt and tweed coat while holding his book's dust jacket.

The interview at the Mansion restaurant held the afternoon of the premiere didn't go much better. Long periods of silence followed Faulkner's responses to questions. Rather than engaging with the press, he swirled ice in his drink and looked like he'd rather be a million other places. When asked why he was drinking club soda rather than his trademark bourbon, he said he was temporarily on the wagon—not drinking or smoking. November meant deer camp where he would make up for lost time.

Sallie Murry and Bob Williams owned the Lyric and had worked tirelessly to prepare the theater, even having it painted. When Sallie overheard Faulkner say he'd given away his tickets for the premiere she was alarmed and quickly called Estelle and told her she'd have to get Aunt Bama to intervene. Sallie reminded Faulkner of her family's investment in the event—"William," she said, "you've gotten your money out of this and it doesn't mean anything to you, but it means a whole hell of a lot to us"[16]—to which he made no reply. He merely ambled out of the restaurant toward the Square. It was classic contrarian behavior.

* * *

The rest of Oxford, however, celebrated the occasion with great enthusiasm. Schools were dismissed Monday afternoon for a mile-long parade with three marching bands and three floats. A first for the small town. Monday evening included speeches on the Square followed by a block dance. All in prelude to a formal ball at the University complete with a grand march led by the Mississippi lieutenant governor. Twenty-five newspapers covered the movie's world premiere, and some reporters asserted that not since the Yankees burned Oxford had there been such excitement.

On the evening of October 11, 1949, searchlight beams and floodlights illuminated the Lyric. All 800 seats were occupied, and close to 8,000 Oxford moviegoers saw the film its first week, eclipsing even *Gone with the Wind*. The movie was nominated for ten awards, including two Golden Globes, with two wins. Finally, a well-groomed Faulkner wearing a white shirt, tie, and jacket made his appearance. He was accompanied by six Faulkner women—Estelle, Jill, Dean, Aunt Bama, Maud, and Vicki—in dresses of taffeta and silk. "I mean everyone really put on the dog!" Vicki said. "Grandmama made a dress for me with taffeta I'd brought back from Hong Kong."[17]

Earlier in the evening he had hunkered down in his bedroom, refusing to go. None of their entries stirred him. It was his great-aunt Alabama, in town from Memphis, who moved the mountain. A legendary and formidable woman, Faulkner once said not entirely in jest, "When she dies, either she or God has got to leave Heaven, because both of 'em can't be boss."[18] Aunt Bama arrived at Rowan Oak insisting they all go to the theater together, and that since she was wearing one of her best dresses, her nephew and escort should dress accordingly. In her finely beaded dress and large hat, Aunt Bama led the charge to the Lyric where the program promised a speech from the author. Vicki remembered that her grandfather "made a very insignificant speech. In fact, his remarks were more just an inaudible mumbling of words, very quick and short."[19] The film went off without a hitch, Faulkner took a bow to thunderous applause, and the family filed quietly out when it was over.

* * *

Before the film's premiere, Faulkner's granddaughter, Vicki, said Faulkner was regarded by many in Oxford "as an eccentric failure."[20] He was considered a loser, a drunk, someone who walked about immersed in thought and who ignored such basic courtesies as even a nod of greeting or hint of recognition. That same cold shoulder could be turned on his own daughter. One day Jill, wearing shorts rather than a customary skirt for a trip downtown, passed her father. He seemed to not know her. When a few weeks later she ran into him again, this time dressed in a skirt as was deemed appropriate, he was wearing a pith helmet, threadbare shirt, and cropped khaki pants held up by a stretch of rope. When Jill pointed out the incongruity of her clean, presentable shorts, and his beggarly attire, her father took the high road. "Missy," he said, "you've got a point."[21]

Now, having brought such fame and attention to Oxford, Faulkner was celebrated by some but vilified by other who didn't care for the film's message. *Intruder in the Dust* is as much a racial awakening as a whodunit. Chick Mallison, played by Jarman, initially operates as an entitled white teenager entrenched in the social milieu of the day. Change occurs when Chick becomes an advocate for Beauchamp. He and a few like-minded souls race to prove he is an innocent man before there is a mob lynching. The movie evoked widespread distrust over Faulkner's liberal leanings—though he cast himself as a centrist—and his stand on civil rights issues.

If he was already considered rude and standoffish by some, Faulkner's indignation at racial prejudices made him all the more suspect. The very tenor of his work drew him into the racial maelstrom. Vicki said her grandfather was actually a moderate, though, "Being a moderate in Mississippi in those days meant being considered a flaming liberal."[22] Members of his own family, like his brother, John, and his wife, Lucille, were segregationists. That introduced tension within and beyond the family. Some of Faulkner's former friends turned against him. "There's no doubt," Vicki said, "that almost all of Pappy's associates, friends, and many who didn't know him at all found him traitorous and his public sentiments reprehensible."[23]

In the coming years, he would feel more and more distressed by racism and would write letters of protest to newspapers. The murky ambiguity that enhanced his fiction was out of place in the world of politics. He was so misunderstood that segregationists and desegregationists alike claimed him. An inebriated interview in 1956 probably hastened the end of his outspokenness. Racial tensions in Alabama were at peak with the admittance of Autherine Lucy to the University of Alabama. He wrote an article, "A Letter to the North," which Ober sold to *Life* magazine. The article addressed the Civil Rights activists and advocated caution and a slow approach. Something akin to, let the southerners come to this position on their own, in their own time. It wasn't hard to imagine how the "go slow" message was received. The region's history of violence against Blacks—victims of lynchings, murders, rapes, and assaults—and their ongoing frustration at being targeted, persecuted, denied, poorly compensated, and unfairly imprisoned—demanded immediate and forceful change.

Likewise, Faulkner attempted to explain the traditional southerners' likely response should the federal government intervene. It would stir latent feelings of being underdogs and under siege with possibly tragic results. Indeed, rioting ensued when the federal court ordered Autherine Lucy's admission. Faulkner was convinced that the young student might be killed. He also started drinking. Talking with Russell W. Howe of the *London Sunday Times* in Saxe Commins' New York office at Random House, Faulkner said, "The government will send its troops and we'll be back at 1860… As long as there's a middle road, all right, I'll be on it. But if it came to fighting I'd fight for Mississippi against the United States, even if it meant going out into the street and shooting Negroes." Unfortunately, he continued in that vein, "I will go on saying that the Southerners are wrong and that their position is untenable, but if I have to make the same choice Robert E. Lee made then I'll make it."[24]

Could he possibly have imagined the clamor those words would provoke? He wrote three letters to national magazines trying to explain his disastrous statement. His comment about shooting Negroes was more "a misconstruction than a misquotation"; a "foolish and dangerous" statement. In an effort to further calm the waters, Faulkner wrote a letter to *The Reporter*, "They are statements which no sober man would make, nor, it seems to me, any sane man believe."[25] Vicki understood Faulkner's passion for his native land and heritage, "He never wanted to be thought of as a traitor. He felt a deep love for Mississippi, but he also knew that the route Mississippi had taken was wrong, basically, humanly wrong, and could not help speaking out."[26]

In his review of *Intruder in the Dust* for *The New Republic*, Cowley captured the duality of Faulkner's position: "The tragedy of intelligent Southerners like Faulkner is that their two fundamental beliefs, in human equality and in Southern independence, are now in violent conflict."[27] Nothing captures the torment of Faulkner's feelings about the South better than an exchange in *Absalom* between Quentin Compson, a Harvard college student from a prominent and highly dysfunctional southern family, and his Canadian roommate, Shreve McCannon. Shreve, fascinated by the South, probes Quentin:

> "Tell about the South. What's it like there? What do they do there? … Jesus, the South is fine, isn't it? It's better than theater, isn't it? … Now I want you to tell me just one thing more. Why do you hate the South?"
>
> "I dont hate it," Quentin said, quickly, at once, immediately; "I dont hate it," he said. *I dont hate it* he thought, panting in the cold air, the iron New England dark: *I dont. I dont! I dont hate it! I dont hate it!*[28]

* * *

November 1949 brought more than the annual deer camp. *Knight's Gambit*, a collection of five detective stories and a novella by the same title, was released. Faulkner clearly wasn't in a mood to leave the mystery genre behind. It was evident too that the rapid-fire writing techniques he'd honed in Hollywood were still at his command. Only eleven months separated the publication of *Intruder in the Dust* and *Knight's Gambit*. The *Knight's Gambit* stories are bound by Gavin Stevens, a small-town southern attorney, who provides drama and moral instruction. Stevens was also a prominent character in *Intruder in the Dust*.

Reviews ranged from exuberant "Six masterly whodunits hot from the master's hand" (*New York Times*), to disparaging "very inferior Faulkner" (*The New Yorker*).[29] Regardless of critical reception, both books kept Faulkner from *A Fable* and provided necessary diversions. He would soon find another in *Requiem for a Nun*, a play that served as a means of courting Joan and also providing material for—and possibly receiving favors from—Ruth Ford.

More notoriety came Faulkner's way as rumors swirled about the 1949 Nobel Prize for Literature. The initial pool of impressive candidates included, among others, Hemingway, John Steinbeck, Boris Pasternak and Albert Camus. Cowley predicted Faulkner would be the recipient; but the award required a unanimous vote, and three members held out. In the end, there would be no award for 1949. That would be rectified in 1950 when the academy selected co-recipients Faulkner (1949) and Bertrand Russell (1950).

* * *

In between those events, Faulkner and Joan's relationship inched along, primarily through letters and a couple of awkward meetings in Memphis where they drove about aimlessly in Joan's mother's car. Faulkner apparently was quite serious when he wrote Cowley about the need for a young woman in his life. At 51 years, he was bent on romancing the 21-year-old college student. Was it an extreme midlife crisis? Was he truly locked in a sexless marriage? Or did he want all the comforts of home while maintaining the intrigue and fantasy of an affair?

Nine

Per Aspera ad Astra: 1950

Miraculously, the new, young woman Faulkner sought materialized in the drive at Rowan Oak. He quickly determined Joan's appearance and personality matched his desires. It didn't matter he knew little about her or had little chance to know her. She might well have been part of his phantasmagorical world. But the magic ended there. The relationship hardly advanced as he imagined. It made slow, agonizing progress, with Joan saying no more than yes. It was difficult for them to see each other, and when they did, seldom satisfactory. Memphis turned out to be the least attractive option. Later they would meet halfway between Memphis and Oxford, in the woods near the small Mississippi town of Holly Springs. New York would offer the most freedom.

Nothing was simple about it, yet they reached an uneasy truce. She knew Faulkner opened many doors: he could help her learn the craft of writing, help her gain access to agents and publishers. In return, she needed to keep the promise of sex alive. Those expectations ushered in pitches of euphoria and despair. The twin demons of his fifties, conquering Joan and *A Fable*, set in motion a draining five-year stretch.

Painful or not, his infatuation increased. It was her face, he told her. After he saw it five or six times he realized it was pretty. And then beautiful. And then he wished he'd never seen it. "Every letter from you is a violet and everytime I think of you is one, the color of your eyes, your hair, the shape of your mouth, the shape (imagined) or your body under your clothes, girl woman of course but not screaming at you as most are." When silences occurred between them, he'd refresh memories, here of a visit to see her in New York and at Bard: "We need 2nd Ave., a Berkshire hill, something like that—snow, a little boot of a bug trying to go somewhere in the snow, God knows where or why, snow in your hair and not making any noise at all like your face, lips, so that even the snow smells like a young girl, woman.... Hello, Joan, Miss Williams, sweet love."

If she felt his attention flagging, Joan's letters sounded a new note of affection:

> Bill—you are practically all that's left in this ridiculous process of living.... We're wasting time—this is life to grab while it is here—and I don't want to look back ten years from now and wonder why we didn't see each other when we are so close—.... These days are so beautiful! I keep thinking of the Oct. after that first Aug. [1949] that you said you stood up in the woods one day and started to come to N.Y. to see me. I want us to walk through the leaves some afternoon—always with love—joan.

Three years elapsed before he could claim Joan "half-conquered." "If we could meet whenever we like, it might be different with me," he wrote her, "though probably not. But as it is, I wont get any peace until we have finished the beginning of it. Maybe I can do more for you then, after there is no more barrier, no more mystery, nothing to remain between." For him, the relationship yielded heartache from deferred hope. "I have puzzled and anguished a good deal in trying to understand our relationship, understand you and what must have been your reasons ... for your actions."[1] Only when Joan's desire, spontaneity, and fervor matched his own would he consider her conquered.

Life seemed to offer less to savor and more to endure. His drinking was on the uptick—and frequently blamed on Joan's refusals of him—and often ended with a last resort professional stay. Life with Estelle went from bad to worse, only to find a decent plateau toward the end of his life. In countless letters to Joan, he used the words unhappiness, loneliness, and grief.

* * *

There had been a rapid exchange of letters between Faulkner and Joan after her impromptu 1949 visit. When he answered Joan's first letter, a note of apology for intruding on his privacy at Rowan Oak, he offered to answer her questions as they occurred to her. Something "charming" came out of her letter, "like something remembered out of youth: a smell, scent, a flower, not in the garden but in the woods maybe, stumbled on by chance, with no past and no particular odor."

Later he would write that from her very first letter he knew he was going to fall in love with her. Faulkner's reply to her second letter startled her. It surprised and scared her, and it came too early. He clearly envisioned a love affair. "These are the wrong questions," he wrote. "A woman must ask them of a man while they are lying in bed together. Not the first time but after several, and when they are lying at peace or at least are quiet or maybe on the edge of sleep so you'll have to wait, even to ask them."

Letters were their lifeline and Faulkner wrote that "as soon as I look at the blank sheet of paper, I want to write you a love letter on it." What he needed was three days alone with Joan, "by the ocean all bleak and winter and cold."[2] That plan didn't develop any better than the one he outlined in his fourth letter to her on New Year's Eve 1949; that she come to Sardis Lake and they'd spend the holiday on the *Minmagary*. He didn't anticipate anyone else wanting it in the winter. His note included a detailed bus schedule and he even suggested an appropriate wardrobe for her.

Though forewarned and troubled, Joan still hoped to know Faulkner better. Another opportunity soon presented itself. At the outset of February, he met with Saxe Commins and Donald Klopfer about releasing a collection of 42 short stories previously published in magazines (*Collected Stories of William Faulkner*, 1950). The stories dated back to 1930 and Faulkner told his editors he'd enjoyed staying up reading them again and laughing about the mules, much of the material forgotten. "It's all right. The stuff stands up amazingly well after a few years, 10 and 20."[3]

Faulkner lodged at the Algonquin for almost two weeks and Joan made a visit from Bard along with three friends. At one point they had drinks at the Biltmore Hotel and Faulkner said they talked of a story line for a play. Hoping to see more of her, he took the train to Bard, explaining it as an opportunity to explore the college for Jill. Their third meeting that February was a dinner party in Faulkner's honor hosted by Bob and Merle Haas. Faulkner was enchanted with Joan's demeanor—"an extremely well-bred, well-behaved child"—and appearance—"I didn't even have a chance to tell you what a pretty girl-white white—slip, isn't that it?—you had on that day."[4]

A united front of friends and business associates made sure Faulkner enjoyed the city. He went to several parties, often with Ruth Ford. Leaving one, they headed for drinks at her apartment along with Harvey Breit, *New York Times* assistant book review editor, and Truman Capote, 25 years old, whose best-selling novel *Other Voices, Other Rooms* was published by Random House in 1948. When the conversation in the taxi turned to Hemingway's recently serialized novel, *Across the River and into the Trees*, Capote spoke disparagingly of what he'd read thus far. Eventually Faulkner felt compelled to speak up for his contemporary and sometimes rival: "Young man," he said, "I haven't read this new one. And though it may not be the best thing Hemingway ever wrote, I know it will be carefully done, and it will have quality."[5] A hush followed.

* * *

If anything, Faulkner and Joan's time together in early February introduced greater confusion which now required sorting out in letters.

He was more smitten; she was more intent on distance. His increased talk of a love affair rather than friendship agitated her. In an effort to calm her fears, Faulkner wrote that he would be "whatever you want me to be to you," but that he was "capable not only of imagining anything and everything, but even of hoping and believing it." She also questioned his motives. Was it simply her looks and age that drew him to her?

In a mid–February 1950 letter, after congratulating him on the Nobel nomination, she ended her letter with a surprisingly emphatic declaration: "Bill, I do love you." It became a predictable pattern. She would encourage only to later retreat. He replied:

> I dont know anything about the Nobel matter. Been hearing rumors for about three years, have been a little fearful. It's not the sort of thing to decline; a gratuitous insult to do so but I dont want it. I had rather be in the same pigeon hole with Dreiser and Sherwood Anderson, than with Sinclair Lewis and Mrs. Chinahand [Pearl S.] Buck.[6]

The spring and summer of 1950 brought more recognition and success. In late April, he learned he would receive the William Dean Howells Medal from the American Academy of Arts and Letters. The prestigious award for the most distinguished works of American fiction was only awarded every five years. He chose not to attend the ceremony in New York most likely because Joan didn't encourage the visit. He tentatively asked if she would meet him should he attend? That was one of the many times Joan failed to directly answer such questions.

The issue was resolved when he wrote Joan that he wouldn't be coming up for the medal thing. He sent his regrets to the academy: "I am a farmer this time of year; up until he sells his crops, no Mississippi farmer has the time or money either to travel anywhere on. Also, I doubt if I know anything worth talking two minutes about."[7]

The farmer identity was one he assumed off and on as needed. In early 1938, Faulkner purchased a 320-acre farm 17 miles from Oxford that his brother, Johncy, managed. The property, named Greenfield Farm by its proprietor, was part bottom land, part hills, with a running creek located in what was considered the toughest part of Lafayette County. Stranger yet, Faulkner insisted on raising mules and producing their feed. Johncy and Uncle John told Faulkner that the Mississippi soil lacked lime, and therefore the mules' bone structure would be small and inadequate. Plus, tractors were becoming the preferred method of working crops.

They recommended cattle but Faulkner said he had no feeling for cows. Instead, he purchased twelve brood mares and a large Spanish jack the help nicknamed Big Shot. Despite his size, 14 hands tall, Big Shot was gentle but his living quarters were abysmal. Faulkner told Johncy the pen he built should be eight-foot-high solid walls so Big Shot wouldn't get excited by the mares.

Before long Faulkner relented and also began running cattle though with diminished enthusiasm. It was clear he mythicized the idea of mule farming. He once sent Joan a letter with a sketch at the bottom. It's Faulkner walking behind a plow pulled by a mule. He's wearing a straw hat, smoking a pipe, and atop the plow sits a jug of moonshine. A bonus to the Greenfield Farm was the surrounding hill people. They were often the subject of his fiction and he admired their independent nature. "They made whiskey from their own corn and didn't see why that could be anybody else's business," Johncy said. "They fought over elections and settled their own disputes. We had a killing just across the creek from us, over redistricting a school zone."[8]

The farm and its neighbors added a distinct dimension to Faulkner's life, but about two years into farm ownership, his money played out and his brother moved to Oxford to find work with the WPA (Works Progress Administration). Going forward the farm became more of an idle hobby. The Black families who lived on it managed it as they saw fit. As property caretakers, they would receive off and on infusions of cash depending on Faulkner's circumstances. What Estelle thought of his costly side ventures—an airplane and a mule farm—is anyone's guess. The apparent patriarchy allowed for his eruption over a new sofa and radio, but little known reaction from her over such sizable expenditures.

* * *

The *Collected Stories of William Faulkner* appeared in August 1950 complete with a ready audience. The Book-of-the-Month Club adopted the collection as an alternate fiction selection. By and large the book was greeted with enthusiasm and favorable reviews. Less successful were Faulkner and Joan's sputtering attempts to form a bond. Faulkner continued to plot and fantasize about meetings that rarely occurred. That the relationship was more imagined than real made little difference to Estelle. She was convinced he was in an intrigue. Her drinking escalated as well as feelings of helplessness. Hoping to diffuse what had become an intolerable existence, Faulkner attempted to assuage Estelle's suspicions. That he believed was best accomplished by Joan visiting their home.

* * *

It raised Estelle's hackles when Bill approached her with the idea of inviting Joan Williams to their home the summer of 1950 for an outing on the *Minmagary*. When she suggested last month a visit from Joan to put an end to the Oxford gossip, he'd rejected that idea. He refused to believe there was Oxford talk but she knew better. Now, Miss Williams, as he ridiculously called her, would not only be coming but also bringing her college boyfriend, Brandon Grove. Estelle knew of Joan's literary aspirations but she never believed Bill's interest in the young woman was innocent. Bill claimed to be working with her on his play, *Requiem*, which Estelle found an outlandish assertion. Estelle wrote Saxe about the situation—about her husband's "absorbing interest in Joan"—hoping Saxe might shed some light. She related to Saxe that when Bill told her and Jill that Joan was his collaborator "we both were a little amazed—as Pappy heretofore, brooked no interference."[9] And he had never, to her knowledge, been interested in helping an aspiring writer. If anything, he avoided literary conversations and events.

Now when she thought the roughest waters were behind them—his affair in Hollywood and the pain it provoked—a new source of conflict appeared at her very house! In the turnaround driveway last summer, a young girl who was kin to some Oxford folks showed up, uninvited, dreaming about meeting a great author. Good God, at 53 years she now had to contend with a college student. Her mental resources had been sorely tasked by the Meta affair and she saw this one as even more hazardous. The girl, Joan, was no doubt pampered and unrealistic. She had no idea what Estelle had been through with Bill and she apparently had no respect for marriage. Something was off about the invitation and it reminded her of the dreadful dinner party at their Palisades rental. It still outraged her to think of Bill, Meta, and Ben Wasson plotting behind her back while she prepared dinner and offered genuine hospitality.

* * *

Estelle had grounds for her concerns. She knew Faulkner and Joan maintained a steady correspondence despite Faulkner telling Joan not to use Bard College letterhead or a return address. (For a while her letters to Oxford arrived general delivery on Wednesdays. He first suggested addressing them to Quentin Compson, realized that such a famous Faulkner character might be recognized, and switched to A.E. Holston, a play on poet A.E. Housman. Eventually he secured a private P.O. box.)

Estelle's instincts rarely let her down and she couldn't shake her disquietude. When an Oxford neighbor alerted her that Faulkner was seen with a young woman in Memphis, the revelation proved explosive on the home front. A simple trip to the beauty parlor in June turned treacherous when Mrs. Smallwood told her someone saw the couple in a Memphis juke joint. The Cotton Bowl was actually more a lunch place and college favorite for the nearby Southwestern students. Indeed, Joan had taken Faulkner there over her Easter break.

When confronted by Estelle, Faulkner dismissed the account by reminding her that she'd failed to call on Mrs. Smallwood when she moved near them. This was her retribution, he told his wife. That explanation hardly appeased her. Estelle accused Faulkner of having an affair that she would put a stop to by phoning Joan's mother or father and "telling them what kind of (her words) old goat I am." As he related this to Joan, he shifted the blame to Estelle's drinking, "She will of course get drunk again, it seems to follow her old menstrual periods, every month. She seems quite crazy except for an inability to do anything successfully—co-ordinate, rationalize—is really capable of anything that will make enough people unhappy."[10]

Faulkner was indeed being disingenuous. By placing a snapshot of Joan near the only telephone in the house, Faulkner was flaunting his love interest in the domestic sphere, and deliberately antagonizing his wife. Their granddaughter, Vicki, and niece, Dean, were disturbed he would hurt Estelle and show her such little respect. Despite his declarations of his wife's inadequacies, Estelle's resiliency had not gone unnoticed by Faulkner. "Your mother," he acknowledged to Jill, "is like a piano wire."[11]

Estelle made good on her promise and talked with Joan's mother, Maude. The conversation was pleasant enough but Maude was alarmed that her daughter might be mentioned in a divorce suit. It was much the same threat Faulkner had repeated to Meta. He also harkened back to another familiar line from his affair with Meta. His hands were tied when it came to dealing with his wife because of his child who still needed him. (Jill at this time was 17 years old.) If not for Jill, he asserted, he would have been out of the marriage fifteen years ago. Maude advised Joan to quit writing or seeing Faulkner. That was unlikely to happen. At the Cotton Bowl with Joan, Faulkner commented on the Mills Brother song that was playing, "You Always Hurt the One You Love." He told her that song could be for her because he was going to fall in love with her, or possibly already had. Joan likewise seemed reluctant to end things as her mother requested.

One day Joan received a call from Estelle, who asked her to meet for lunch. That first lunch date abruptly was cancelled by Estelle, but in due time, the two women met at the Peabody's Black Cat restaurant. Estelle took Joan's arm for support as they made their way to the table. Dignified and direct, she asked Joan if she wanted to marry her husband. Joan assured her that was not her intention. It was simple, she wanted to be a writer and felt fortunate to know a famous writer. Then it was Joan's turn to ask a question: If Mrs. Faulkner wanted to be a painter, wouldn't she want to know Picasso? No, she answered, and she wasn't the least bit swayed by the writer-student ruse. She told Joan her husband was going through male menopause.

On the drive back to Oxford, Estelle's friend, Kate Baker, asked her how the lunch had gone. "She will not destroy my marriage," Estelle asserted and left it at that.[12] For Joan, if nothing else, the meeting must have made her reconsider the way Faulkner described his wife. The decorous woman she met at the Peabody was far from the raving madwoman he depicted.

* * *

Reality and fantasy did collide the August 1950 afternoon when Faulkner, Estelle, Joan, and Grove took a skiff out to board the *Minmagary*. Grove arrived in Memphis by train after classes dismissed at Bard. He already had met Faulkner during one of his visits to New York and looked forward to seeing him again despite the complications of both men pursuing the same woman, "I was in love with Joan, he was in love with Joan, so it was a bit of a triangle." Yet, Grove never sensed jealousy, "I did not feel threatened and whether he did toward me I have no reason to think that." He surmised that Joan was "conflicted but also flattered."

During the drive from Memphis to Oxford, Grove noticed she was nervous:

> I mean there was tension all over the place. I knew what was going on. It was pure theatre. We went first to his house, Rowan Oak, and I was so impressed by it, a long, straight driveway and big trees. I thought it was a southern mansion. It was sparsely furnished. And inside I saw his typewriter which was old. In his own surroundings he seemed weighed down, restrained, tense. He was a quiet, gracious host.

Estelle also went out of her way to ensure a nice outing. She prepared a picnic lunch with "a huge basket of sandwiches."[13] She was quiet but very friendly to Joan and Grove.

While by all appearances the day was a success, Joan continued to be a source of conflict between the Faulkners, especially when they were both drinking. The Wright's Sanatorium notebook used to record distributed drugs and the dosage amount, labeled the Drug Book, reflects a long stay for Faulkner beginning August 23. He primarily received morphine shots, as well as Dolophine (an opioid analgesic used to treat severe pain and opioid use disorder), and codeine.[14] During this same time period there was a lull in the letters exchanged between Faulkner and Joan, quite a dearth, especially on his part. In September, their letter stream picks back up with Faulkner acknowledging that they had suffered a temporary hibernation.

Though only 75 miles apart, they were unable to celebrate their September birthdays together. Faulkner, who turned 53 on September 25, especially was frustrated by the long separations. In Memphis, a telegram arrived wishing Joan, who was 22 on September 26, a happy birthday (she would receive one every year until the end of his life). By October, restless and bored with her job at a Memphis insurance company, Joan planned a visit to Bard. Faulkner responded angrily to her plans; he didn't want her fifteen hundred miles away! Retrospectively, Joan realized the most important and direct writing guidance Faulkner ever gave her was at this juncture when he said, "Don't leave your own people." It took her years to appreciate his meaning. In an effort to placate, she sent him an emotional letter dated November 1:

> I hope that last letter was not really one of anger, but just an outburst of the same hopeless frustration that I feel. The same frustration at not being able to make my mother stop drinking, of not being able to talk to my father.... I want to see you too. I want to somehow reach you, lose my restraint, timidity—all the things that keep us from being close. I would give anything to be somewhere alone, to do, think as we pleased.[15]

* * *

Life would change dramatically in November. As it turned out with the Nobel Prize, there really was enough smoke to be fire. He took the early morning November 10 call from Sweden in the pantry off the kitchen. He was receiving the award "for his powerful and artistically independent contribution to the new American novel."[16] The monetary award was $30,171. When asked how he felt about the trip to Stockholm for the ceremony, he resorted to the same excuse he'd used for the Howell's medal, the Mississippi farmer business. Without saying a word to anyone, he and Estelle drove Jill and Vickie to school and ran some errands afterward. Jill went about her day until the school principal summoned her to the office to tell her.

Faulkner's selection meant he was only the fourth American author to receive the award. To Estelle, he acted like he'd received a life sentence! Instead of graciously accepting the honor and appreciating the financial reward that accompanied it, he mulishly refused to go to Stockholm. He disparaged two of the three previous American authors awarded, Sinclair Lewis and Pearl Buck. Only Eugene O'Neill escaped censorship.

It seemed everyone was jubilant except the recipient. On their return to Rowan Oak, the phone didn't stop ringing. Reporters, family, friends, and acquaintances. Bill took the call from Phillip "Moon" Mullen, editor of *The Oxford Eagle*. Phil had followed Faulkner's career since his father, Curtis Mullen, purchased the *Eagle* in 1933. Since he couldn't shake his nickname—the source of which was his plump, round face, and glasses— Phil embraced it, even calling his *Eagle* column "Moonbeams." For close to thirty years, Phil would write off and on about Faulkner's stories and novels. He, along with Phil Stone, was among the first in Oxford to recognize Faulkner's potential. He and his wife, Faye, were Faulkner family friends.

Pylon's March 1935 publication, Faulkner's eighth novel, was duly noted in "Moonbeams": "His descriptive passages are as long and as unintelligible as ever to me ... yet as paragraph after paragraph is read, the reader begins to fall in step with the characters and rushes on to some illogical and inconceivable climax."[17] And three years later, Phil's column carried this startling declaration, "Today William Faulkner is doubtlessly Oxford's most widely known citizen. It is entirely possible that in the far future, when you and I are dead and gone, that William Faulkner will still be the most famous of Oxonians."[18]

Phil was therefore probably less surprised than many when he received a call from the Associated Press in Jackson, Mississippi, asking for a story on the Nobel laureate. His call to Faulkner was unequivocal; he told Faulkner there was one damn newspaper man he was talking with. Faulkner relented and told him to come on out to Rowan Oak. The two men sat in the library by the fireplace. A painful hour passed as Phil tried to gather material from his reluctant subject. As friends would have it, Phil agreed to let Faulkner see his piece before sending it to Jackson that afternoon. Only a few hours elapsed before Faulkner was in Phil's office reading what would be one of many Nobel articles. He objected to one line about the RAF, "Change that to I was a member of the RAF. I did not see any service." After a pause he added, "The story is all right,"[19] before exiting the newspaper and making his way around the Square to the post office, never mentioning a word of the news to anyone.

* * *

Back home, Faulkner insisted he was going fishing. Estelle managed to talk him out of that and he went outside and started chopping wood. Before long a group of Memphis reporters showed up at the house. They talked with Estelle who affirmed her unwavering faith in her husband's talent and gratefulness that it was being recognized. She also acknowledged her gratitude for the accompanying money. "Anybody who comes down here can see we're not rich," she told them. Faulkner told the reporters he didn't think he would make the trip to Stockholm. When his brother, Johncy, dropped by the next morning, Faulkner's misgivings were evident, "There just isn't enough gas left in the tank to go all that distance,"[20] he told him.

Estelle knew it was more than the distance, it was the intense spotlight and attention he dreaded. Despite the November 16 letter he sent Stockholm regretting the ceremony appearance, Estelle and the rest of the family kept up their lobbying efforts. The Faulkner family doubled down on measures to ensure his participation in Stockholm. Phone calls were exchanged with the American embassy, and a number of prominent people, including Secretary of State John Foster Dulles, entered the fray. In the meantime, Faulkner had the cherished distraction of his November sojourn.

* * *

The deer camp, an excursion braced by masculinity and freedom, held many charms for Faulkner. Tradition, hierarchy, and an escape from the nest-and-hearth were all a part of the experience. With his old friends, Faulkner received no favors or special treatment. It was a grueling trip November 17 to the Sunflower River. The group traveled partially by boat and later with a team of mules pulling the supply-laden wagon. Once at Cypress Lake, there was camp to assemble, daily chores, and meals to prepare and clean up. All of which he apparently savored.

His fellow hunters wouldn't have had a chance to toast the Nobel winner if someone hadn't brought a newspaper along. Faulkner hadn't mentioned it. Congratulations ensued and Bill gave one friend a key to his whiskey box. The toasts and nightcaps went on until three in the morning. When at last they retired, Faulkner chose to sleep outside rather than in a tent. They woke to sleet and snow. Nine days after the hunters had departed on November 17, when Faulkner was expected to return, there was no sign of him. At the Cypress Lake camp, his whiskey box hadn't closed again since the night of their arrival. It was evident he wasn't up to the arduous trip home. His drinking was out of control and he'd developed a worsening cold. His friends nursed him as best they could.

By Monday morning, November 27, he was in bed at Rowan Oak with possible pneumonia. Despite his poor condition, Estelle and family members pressed their case. Surprisingly, he capitulated. It might have been the miserable cold and the drinking, though more surely it was the way Estelle framed the trip. She told him she personally didn't care to go but Jill very much did. She argued that there would never be another opportunity like it. The Swedish ambassador to the United States, Walton Butterworth, a New Orleans native, offered to personally handle all of Faulkner's travel arrangements. Faulkner sent a telegram off that very day with his acceptance.

Yet victory wasn't claimed. He was deep into his cycle and without a hint of stopping. In nine days, on December 6, he needed to be on the plane from Memphis to New York. Estelle called Phil Stone to intervene, "Won't you please try to help us with Billy? He's drinking and swears he's not going to Sweden." Phil initially refused, saying, "Stelle, I'm sorry, but, no, I won't. Bill doesn't want to quit or he would. There's nothing to do until he decides himself to stop." But Faulkner's old friend softened when Estelle told him Jill had her heart set on the trip. "Well," he said, "that puts a different face on it. I'll come over and talk to him."

His visit no doubt helped turn the tide. Faulkner promised he'd take his last drink Monday night, December 4. It was a reckless plan—by then he would have been drinking for eighteen days—and no one could predict how difficult his withdrawal might be. (Curiously, Wright's medication dispensary records show a Faulkner in residence December 4–December 10. However, on December 10, Faulkner was delivering his Nobel speech in Stockholm.)

Fearing the worst, the family devised a scheme to move the calendar forward. They told him it was Monday and he needed to start getting sober. Faulkner started tapering off a bit, but he happened to ask where his stepson Malcolm was. When someone said the high school football game, he reared in indignation. Knowing they didn't play football on Monday, he announced he had another three days to drink.

Meanwhile, the details were crowding in on them. Off and on during the intervening days he'd worked fitfully on his acceptance speech. The Stockholm ceremony fell on an anniversary and would include invitations to all living laureates including the 12 past recipients for literature. Faulkner needed a tuxedo and refused to buy one. Once again Saxe came through, getting Faulkner's measurements from Estelle and renting him one in New York. Likewise, Faulkner and Jill's social calendar was filling. The Haases planned a dinner party for Wednesday and the Cerfs arranged a predeparture dinner for Thursday.

His disinclination to focused attention and social interactions made it easy to imagine his mental and emotional state. Heightened anxiety, nervousness, and ill-temperedness were part and parcel of sobering up. "My soul is not my own until the whole mess is over," he'd say to no one in particular.[21] To Joan he described all the preparations as "hurrah and uproar"; and in interviews before his Oxford departure, Faulkner reiterated his sentiment regarding the prize: "It doesn't matter so much who does it, what his name is, what sort of bloke he is in private life—so long as the work uplifted, strengthened or did something to other hearts."[22] Joan said,

> When I first met Faulkner, he was still this town oddity. To me it was not the Nobel Prize that changed things. It was when *Intruder in the Dust* was made into a movie. Then people could really understand. And I remember after he won the prize he and I were in Memphis at Sears-Roebuck and when he got the clerk to send the things to his house, he said, "Oh, aren't you the man that they made a movie out of his book?" The Nobel Prize was entirely over his [the clerk's] head.[23]

The letter she received December 5 was nearly illegible which she attributed to his drinking, "Have wanted to call you, see you, but your name came up once and all the old stink started again. I dont know when I will see you, but you are the one I never stop thinking about. You are the girl's body I lie in bed beside before I go to sleep. I know every sweet red hair and sweet curve on it. Dont forget me. I love you."[24] A letter from London after the hurrah of the ceremony was over reiterated his love but also introduced a rival. He had discovered in Stockholm, he wrote Joan, that he wasn't as old as he thought he was.

* * *

The night before the flight to New York, according to Blotner, Faulkner and Estelle played pool and partied at a friend's home until three a.m. No doubt that would help with pretrip jitters, but it couldn't have made the early morning takeoff easy. By 8:30 a.m., having navigated icy roads, they were at the Memphis airport. Reporters gathered with questions. Faulkner said he didn't understand why he needed to be in Stockholm since the award recognized his work not his person, the "husk" as he came to characterize his physical presence at the award ceremony. And he reiterated that he was donating the prize money. (As promised, Faulkner found worthy uses for a good deal of the money. Some was distributed among the poor in Lafayette County. A young, African American principal, whom Faulkner had once asked to teach Mammy Callie to read, received college funding for Hampton College and the University of Michigan. The Faulkners also established a music scholarship in Dorothy Commins' name at the University of Mississippi.)

* * *

His cantankerous mood continued. Bob and Merle Haas greeted them at LaGuardia Airport in New York. Soon there were reporters as well and he was no more inclined to conversation than he had been in Oxford or Memphis. Merle accompanied Faulkner and Jill to the Algonquin. She quite frankly told Faulkner he looked ill and he didn't disagree. She kept an eye on him at their dinner party that night and noticed he was drinking Jack Daniel's and water. Things were worse in the morning. His fever was 102. Merle managed to get him in to her doctor, who prescribed penicillin and bed rest. From the doctor's office, they went to the Algonquin, where Merle believed Faulkner went straight to bed as advised.

Imagine her surprise, then, when only a short time later, she and Jill returned to the suite from a shopping trip and found him dressed and talking with seven reporters in the smoke-filled room. Was it being in his own room at a favorite hotel? Or finally resigning himself to the Nobel ordeal? Merle and Jill couldn't say for sure. It was a welcome if worrisome sight. He wasn't getting the prescribed bed rest but was actually enjoying himself as he entertained the press. Telling jokes and repeating a now familiar message: it was the work that was being honored not him.

The rest he needed proved ever elusive. Having accepted the Cerfs' dinner party invitation before he left Oxford he felt obliged to attend. As the honoree, he had to do more mixing than he would have preferred. Author John O'Hara made a long-winded speech and insisted on giving Faulkner his father's cigarette lighter. Faulkner didn't want the lighter but said he was "cooked either way. If I took it, he [O'Hara] could say, 'The son of a bitch took my father's lighter.' If I didn't, he could say, 'The son of a bitch wouldn't take my father's lighter.'"[25] To others at the dinner Faulkner seemed numb, no doubt exhausted from the travel, socializing and ill health.

The Haases, Cerfs, and Harold Ober, his New York entourage, accompanied father and daughter to the airport Friday morning. With good wishes, they saw them set out at 11:30 a.m. on the Harald Viking SAS DC-6 for the taxing journey. Faulkner would take comfort in working on his acceptance speech during their flights to Stockholm while Jill slept. In that draft he wrote, "A few years ago, I was taken on as a script writer at a Hollywood studio. At once I began to hear the man in charge talking of 'angles,' story 'angles,' and then I realized that they were not even interested in truth, the old universal truths of the human heart without which any story is ephemeral—the universal truths of love and honor and pride and pity and compassion and sacrifice." The mistake for young writers, he continued, was that they wrote "not of the heart but of the glands; they write as though they stood among and watched the end of man."[26]

In its final form, the speech seemed at odds with the man who drafted it: "I believe that man will not merely endure: he will prevail. He is immortal, not because he alone among creatures has an inexhaustible voice, but because he has a soul, a spirit capable of compassion and sacrifice and endurance."[27] Faulkner's novels and stories never shied from revealing dark and difficult truths: cruelty, injustice, sorrow, and depravement. Here was a speech about mankind triumphing over odds, restoring compassion, and being immortal. It left some puzzled. "This optimist rhetoric from an author who had described life as 'the same frantic steeplechase toward nothing everywhere' surprised many of his readers even as it won wide favor,"[28] wrote Paul Gray, who was a student in Faulkner's teaching sessions at the University of Virginia. In time, Gray became *Time* magazine's book critic and was a former Princeton University English faculty member.

* * *

The Nobel schedule was daunting for even the most robust and loquacious laureate. Faulkner was neither. He had yet to fully recover from the cold and extended drinking episode, and even excellent health couldn't alter his social aversion. "He was a very shy man and unaggressive in his daily life," Joan recalled. "If he went to a party and there were a lot of people he really was so nervous by just having all these people around, he would really perspire and his hands would shake. He just didn't like to be around a lot of people." The coming days, with seemingly endless eyes upon him, would be full of some of his least favorite activities: talking with strangers, formal social events, no fewer than five official and a number of unofficial press events, delivering his first speech (which he frankly said scared him), and keeping his behavior above reproach. There would be few if any periods of solitude to dot the marathon ahead.

Friday's rigorous travel schedule involved flights from New York to Newfoundland; Newfoundland (the thirty-minute layover included a radio interview) to Glasgow; Glasgow (where reporters and photographers joined them on the plane) to Oslo; Oslo to Stockholm. Touching down in Stockholm might have elicited an emphatic sigh of relief if it hadn't meant facing a welcome reception with dignitaries and press.

Ambassador Butterworth was instrumental in getting Faulkner to Stockholm and he was determined to see Faulkner through the coming days. (Faulkner and Jill would stay at the ambassador's residence while the three other American laureates for 1950 lodged in hotels.) Butterworth, his wife, and a representative of the Swedish Foreign Office were among the many to greet the travelers. The Swedish Academy sent President Gustaf Hellström and Dr. Anders Österling, the academy secretary and president of the committee for literature.

A stiff and tense Faulkner endured the many introductions and the throng of press, his mind no doubt already drifting to a quiet stroll around Rowan Oak. Without Butterworth's dedication, the next few days might have proved disastrous. To him, Faulkner, unshaven, appeared nervous and tired. He assigned his butler, Geoffrey Button, an Englishman in his forties, the role of Faulkner's valet. Fortunately, the two men liked each other, and Button did his best to keep Faulkner on schedule and presentable.

Back at the ambassador's residence, there was little time to rest before the afternoon press conference. Faulkner met Embassy Press Secretary Wilfrid Fleisher who attended the conference along with Butterworth. The questions mirrored the ones Faulkner had been answering since the announcement. One reporter queried Jill about her familiarity with her father's book; whether or not she was allowed to read them. With aplomb, she answered that he would neither discourage nor encourage her. "It's not an author-reader relationship," she said. "Sometimes I read the books, sometimes I don't."[29]

Darkness fell early and might, along with the cold, have signaled an end to the long day. But it was not to be. Faulkner's Swedish publisher, Kaj Bonnier, had planned a dinner party. Before the taxi came for Faulkner and Jill, Butterworth gave a lesson in Swedish etiquette, stressing the formal social usage. Rather than nodding and hoisting a glass, possibly saying "cheers," the Swedes looked a member of the party in the eye, said, Skål, then drank, returned the eye contact again, and put the glass down. Special rules were observed for the hostess so that the necessary reciprocating wouldn't leave her inebriated. In a taxi to the Bonniers, Faulkner told the Bonnier publishing director accompanying them that he never listened to the radio. The quiet ride signaled a pricklish mood for the guest of honor.

Once in the residence, a lovely house that afforded views of the sea and Stockholm harbor, Faulkner hit the wall. Rather than mingling, he wandered around looking at the family's art collection. With the host in bed with the flu, entertaining fell to his wife, Ulla, who took Jill under her care, and Kaj's elder brother, Tor. Other guests included Bonnier authors and conversations flowed primarily in English. Little could be done to save Faulkner's evening, until a charming widow, Else Jonsson, appeared. She was a captivating presence, a tall, striking beauty in her mid-thirties with a vivacious personality. Though it took time for him to put the two together, Faulkner realized he had met Else's late husband in Oxford four years earlier. Thorsten Jonsson was a correspondent of Stockholm's *Dagens Nyheter* in New York for a time. He also was an early translator of Faulkner's work.

In 1946 Jonsson was traveling with a group of Swedish journalists. He stopped by Mullen's office to inquire about Faulkner, stating, "I have come 7,000 miles, all the way from Sweden, to see your William Faulkner."[30] When the two men met, Jonsson told Faulkner he would one day receive the Nobel. That evening Faulkner learned the couple had a four-year-old daughter. He sensed Else was struggling. They spent the evening in conversation. Her red hair and violet, blue-gray eyes surely made him think of Joan.

* * *

The next day meant the Nobel ceremony and a final go at the Nobel speech. A Sunday morning photo session caught a sweet image of Jill on a sled with Faulkner behind her, arms around her shoulders and pipe in his mouth. His trademark trench coat, torn and oil-stained to Butterworth's dismay, was unbuttoned and didn't seem warm enough for the snowy scene. In the afternoon, the speech finally came to the fore. Butterworth enlisted the help of his press secretary Wilfred Fleisher. Fleisher quickly deemed the pencil-covered sheets of Algonquin Hotel stationery impossible. He then asked Faulkner to read aloud as his secretary typed. Butterworth suggested shortening the draft; Fleisher, more punctuation. He pointed out there was no place for Faulkner to take a breath. With what time remained, Faulkner worked on his delivery with Fleisher.

* * *

Button's services were now of the utmost importance. The ceremony started at 4 p.m. and Faulkner was due there an hour in advance. It seemed he suffered a real fit of nerves and Button found him in the library. "What is this all about, Button?" he asked. "I can't stand this."[31] The valet offered him a drink. Unable to convince Faulkner to shave, he did his best otherwise. He helped him with his formal wear and white bow tie. When departing couldn't be delayed any longer, Faulkner put on the opera hat he'd purchased and the well-worn trench coat. The latter drew a moan from Butterworth.

First stop, the four-hour award ceremony at the Concert House. Faulkner sat next to the 1950 laureate for literature, Bertrand Russell. Russell, born in Wales, came from a wealthy and influential family. Russell sensed Faulkner was intimidated by the grandiosity and made efforts to befriend him. Faulkner maintained his remoteness. What Russell took for intimidation may well have been Faulkner's impatience with the excessive pomposity. Naval trumpeters sounded when the king and queen entered—the nine laureates were already seated—and the Royal Swedish Symphony Orchestra played enthusiastically after Hellström introduced Faulkner, "the unrivaled master of all living British and American novelists as a deep psychologist" and "greatest experimentalist among twentieth-century novelists."[32] The audience rose as Faulkner made his way toward King Gustav Adolf.

It was a short ride from Hötorget square to the Town Hall in Stadshuset for the banquet and the laureates' speeches. An enchanting scene, especially for Jill, awaited. Silver candelabras on flower-strewn tables were the only source of light for the elaborate meal served with stately fanfare and dinner music ending with toasts. In due course, Faulkner made his way to the microphone but stopped a little too soon. Without amplification, the 550-word speech was virtually inaudible. That handicap, coupled with a speedy four-and-a-half-minute delivery, southern accent, and a voice growing even fainter toward the end, sealed its fate. It would be the next morning before anyone knew what he said. All was forgiven, however, when the text was available. And it garnered more esteem over the years, many calling it the best Nobel speech ever. Faulkner may have heeded Stone's advice: "For God's sake, make it short. I never heard a bad short speech in my life."

After the speech appeared, Stone concurred with others, saying it was "The best damn thing Bill ever wrote."[33] (Later, Stone accused Faulkner of "Nobelitis in the Head."[34]) After another burst of song, this time a choir of students from universities near Stockholm, the dinner concluded. The students, Jill wrote for *The Oxford Eagle*, "marched down the stairs, through the hall, and out of sight under the arches until their voices could be heard only faintly echoing along the long corridors."[35] The assembled gathering adjourned to the gallery for coffee, Faulkner spent his time talking with Else.

* * *

Monday's itinerary was abundant but not as unnerving. In a morning session, Faulkner talked about the Sardis Reservoir to an impressive group of mariners who sailed in the Swedish archipelago. He surprisingly told them he wanted to come back to Sweden to sail. His day got even better when he took Else to lunch and experienced the country's customary Christmas food. Even though Tuesday was a day of travel, the Swedes weren't finished with Faulkner yet. Monday night was the Nobel family dinner held in Stockholm's Grand Hotel. After dinner, there was an audience with the king and queen in the Palace Throne Room. Jill didn't remember a lot of her conversation after being presented to the royalty but she recalled the king talked a long time with her father about farming, sailing, Mississippi, and Sweden. From there it was on to the National Museum for a 10:30 p.m. concert where they made a brief appearance before returning to the embassy. Button's prepared grog tray greeted Faulkner in the drawing room. Butterworth told Faulkner to tell him "when" as he filled his glass with bourbon. To what seemed the equivalent of four drinks, Faulkner added a splash of water. He enjoyed another before they retired around 2 a.m. Faulkner and Jill's route home included stays in Paris and London.

Tuesday was a scattered, hectic day. Faulkner had to return to the Nobel House to gather his check. Though some packing was complete, he couldn't find his Nobel medal (later discovered by Button in a potted palm), and there was still the matter of returning signed books to some students. Another search was underway only to have the books turn up in Faulkner's suitcase. At last, fond farewells were extended to Button and the Butterworths. Faulkner once again promised to return to go sailing. In Paris, a decidedly more light-hearted Faulkner talked with reporters. His description of the Nobel festival drew chuckles, especially in Sweden. "It was as long as a Mississippi funeral."[36]

TEN

Spooked: 1951

Though Faulkner possessed an uncanny ability to compartmentalize his life, the fissure cracks intensified with passing years and wreaked havoc on his mental and physical health There was Meta in Hollywood; Joan in New York and Memphis; Else in Sweden; and Ruth in New York or wherever her acting career took her. Above all, there was Estelle. United, the couple represented tradition and continuity, an established family with Oxford lineage. Their marriage and Rowan Oak were part and parcel of Faulkner's southern identity: landowner, farmer, citizen. Estelle once wrote Saxe that without Bill and Jill she was a total nonentity. Despite his accolades, Faulkner may have felt likewise, and it explained why he clung to a marriage he openly disparaged.

* * *

Fallout from the Nobel meant increased opportunities and recognition. In 1951, the French bestowed the Legion of Honor, and the National Book Award went to *Collected Stories*. The year also yielded a more active private and professional life. Despite having sworn off Hollywood, when Hawks called about a lucrative offer with Twentieth Century-Fox, Faulkner didn't pass. Hawks believed Faulkner could doctor the script for *The Left Hand of God* (the 1955 movie starred Humphrey Bogart with the screenplay credit attributed to Alfred Hayes), and offered him a two-month assignment at $2,000 a week. The contract was to start February 1. There was also a potential bonus if the work was finished earlier. Even Faulkner seemed surprised when he completed the work in a month and met the bonus deadline. As usual, he cared little about the contrived plot and less about Hollywood. He was focused on the generous remuneration and possibly seeing Meta again.

To hedge his bet on Meta, he suggested a California rendezvous to Joan. He sent a flurry of letters to Joan at her parents' South Parkway home in Memphis. They would have to be discreet in Hollywood as he was not yet able to burn bridges; he still had paternal obligations. (In a letter she received a few days in advance of the Hollywood invitation, Faulkner told Joan he'd dismantled the telephone at Rowan Oak. Estelle said she was calling the Williamses' home and he wasn't sure if she was serious or not.)

Should Joan join him, it could be their chance to melt her emotional block. For her part, Joan couldn't imagine arranging a trip to Hollywood. She didn't have the resources—Faulkner didn't volunteer any assistance—and couldn't ask her parents. "I don't know what I would have said to my parents. 'Guess where I am, I'm in Hollywood with William Faulkner.'" When she declined the invitation, he wrote sorrowfully about his inability to help her. It is a little sad, he wrote, a fading scent and a little grief, even a little death. He expressed hope that she would meet someone soon to remove the block.

His sole copy of Act III of *Requiem for a Nun* was in Joan's possession and he asked her to mail it to California. "Here I am until March 1st," he wrote on Beverley-Carlton stationery. "Fantastic place, fantastic work, almost worth the 2000 a week they pay me. Send the 3rd act to me here." A few weeks later, he strikes a tone more typical of letters from Hollywood: "This is a nice town full of very rich middle class people who have not yet discovered the cerebrum, or at best the soul. Beautiful damned monotonous weather, and I am getting quite tired of it, will be glad to farm again."[1]

* * *

Meta and Wolfgang's second marriage in 1945 was no more successful than the first. She and Wolfgang were living in the same house but estranged when Faulkner called from the airport. She didn't hesitate to meet him at his hotel. They picked up where they had left off five years ago. Faulkner had no real explanation for the long, agonizing time apart. Meta thought he looked like the Nobel photographs she'd seen, more mature and distinguished. Likewise, their romance held autumnal overtones. It lacked the fervor they'd previously known but was now a comfortable and affectionate union. Once again, Meta let herself imagine a future with Faulkner. They spent the evenings and weekends together.

One surprise of his visit was a conversation about Estelle. In the past, he talked animatedly about Jill; and, if about Estelle, usually to insult or lodge a complaint. Meta was surprised that there was little talk of Jill, who now seemed closer to her mother than father. Instead, he talked of an injustice to his wife. He'd criticized Estelle for lack of attention to her appearance and a dusty, untidy home. When they discovered cataracts that kept her from seeing clearly, Faulkner genuinely rebuked himself for his criticism. Somehow Meta seemed an unlikely audience for his admission. When he left Hollywood, they agreed there would be no more long separations.

* * *

After strenuously objecting to the Nobel travel, Faulkner did an about-face, traveling a good deal, domestically and abroad, over the coming years. An April 1951 trip to Europe was in part research based. He wanted to see Verdun, a goal he shared with Else before the trip: "I still have one more to do, the big one (Verdun) and then I have a feeling I shall be through, can break the pencil and cast it all away, that I have spent 30 years anguishing and sweating over, never to trouble me again."[2] But the two-week trip was not all work. In Paris, he enjoyed time with his host family, made a new friend, a young novelist-editor, Monique Salomon; and, perhaps most to his liking, Else was able to join them from Sweden. She and Faulkner were corresponding since meeting in Stockholm and Else was a friend of Monique's. The beautiful spring weather lightened everyone's spirits. Monique recalled Faulkner's fondness for martinis, coq au vin, and visiting Chartres. Faulkner absorbed the past displayed before him at Verdun; the site of multitudinous death and suffering. It was a powerful and emotional visit to Douaumont Cemetery with identifying crosses for 100,000 men, and Douaumont Ossuary, a resting place for 400,000 unidentified soldiers. The haunting visit would prove fruitful for *A Fable*.

* * *

It may have been the splintered state of Faulkner's personal life that led to *Requiem for a Nun*, a novel-essay-play that defies classification. He conjured the title in 1933, and imagined the book would be "on the esoteric side, like *As I Lay Dying*,"[3] but other projects intervened. Upon publication 18 years later, *The Kirkus Reviews* described *Requiem* as "A strange book even to come from the pen of the unpredictable Nobel prize winner" (September 1, 1951).[4] Though four central characters harkened back to earlier publications, those connections lacked the cohesive relationship of "Wash" and *Absalom*.

In the end, *Requiem* is most commonly evoked for the lines delivered by Gavin Stevens, an overtalker from a number of Faulkner's later novels and stories, "The past is never dead. It's not even past"; and, incongruously, for the prose sections tucked in the pages of the "play." These passages include the most comprehensive history of Yoknapatawpha County Faulkner ever provided. Faulkner's intentions to write a play for Ruth Ford were genuine. It would be her dearest wish realized, she told him. She would be cast as a latter-day Temple Drake from *Sanctuary* (1931).

In *Requiem*, Temple is now married to Gowan Stevens, the nephew of lawyer Gavin Stevens, and faces a tragic situation. Her infant has been murdered by the child's nurse, Nancy Mannigoe, an African American character from a 1931 short story "That Evening Sun." That there is no motivation for the infanticide is just one of its many problems. Faulkner was acutely aware of the play's weaknesses. Despite his screenwriting work in Hollywood which naturally involved dialogue, he began admitting "I realise more than ever that I cant write a play … it may be a novel as it is."[5]

Vicki didn't believe her grandfather was finding writing as rewarding as he once had, and that the various women he pursued were "poor substitutes for the more substantial rewards he was searching so hard for to fulfill his life.… I don't think he cared as much about *Requiem*. I really don't! Frankly, Ruth Ford had bothered him for years to do that one because she wanted to be a star, and she thought it was a good story. Sure, Pappy had it as a story before he actually started a play, dialogue, and Ruth pushed and pushed him. It was not one of the things he really wanted to do, because he knew that his forte was not straight dialogue."[6]

As for her role as collaborator on the troublesome creation, Joan was reluctant at best. Faulkner stood by his assertion that the play's idea originated with something Joan said over drinks at the Biltmore, though she could never recall what it might have been. She did however remember exchanging her first kiss with Faulkner in his Biltmore Hotel room that night, a light brush of their lips. In many ways she was frustrated with the play he foisted upon her. She would have rather had him reading her original work. When the play drafts arrived, she didn't make any real attempts to change them. "It was already his idea, his everything. His characters." She didn't think anyone would believe Nancy, the "nun" of the title, murdered the child, as it made no sense to her. And when she contributed a two-page critique, she focused on ways to expand and develop Nancy's character, to give her a voice in the play. However, there is nothing to suggest Faulkner paid the least attention to it.

When Ruth shared *Requiem's* manuscript with Broadway producer Lemuel Ayers during the summer of 1951 he was interested. (This was the beginning of a prolonged and rocky road that would span eight years before its New York premier.) Faulkner appeared ebullient with the news. "It will be pretty fine," he wrote Ruth, "if we can make a good vehicle for you. I would like to see that title in lights, myself. It's one of my best, I think: *Requiem for a Nun*."[7] Ayers interest in the play presented a bonus for Faulkner; a trip to New York to see Ruth Ford. Even in his excitement to share the good news with Joan in a letter, there are barbed comments. "I have a bona fide offer from the man who produced Kiss Me Kate, to produce what I still think of as our play, even though you have repudiated it."

Why, he asks in closing, didn't she stick with him and the play? Before he and Estelle left with Jill for her first year at Pine Manor Junior College, he said his goodbyes to Joan, who was only slightly older than his daughter, "I am too old to have to miss a girl twenty-three years old. By now, I should have earned the right to be free of that."[8]

* * *

The Faulkner family made their way north to Wellesley, Massachusetts, at a leisurely pace. In South Sudbury, Massachusetts, Robert Linscott, a Random House editor, joined them and suggested they spend the night at the Wayside Inn. Linscott personally helped arrange a room that he thought would be a special treat for Faulkner. The inn now was primarily a Henry Wadsworth Longfellow museum, and when the manager showed the Faulkners their accommodations—Longfellow's own bedchamber preserved exactly as it had been when he wrote *Tales of a Wayside Inn*—Faulkner said it would make him uncomfortable to sleep in Longfellow's bed.

After traveling farther down the road, it became apparent they wouldn't find another hotel or inn. When they returned, the Faulkners were given a room adjoining Longfellow's. It seemed everything about the inn set Faulkner's teeth on edge. Linscott perhaps overthought the ambiance when he suggested they sit by the fire in the old barroom and enjoy a drink. Since *Tales of a Wayside Inn* is a collection of poems told by patrons of the inn tavern, that would seem a fitting end to the day. But Faulkner wanted no part of it and instead walked the unfamiliar roads in the darkness. When he returned, hoping for sleep that didn't come, he spent the night reading mysteries. He admitted to Linscott that Longfellow's ghost had him thoroughly unnerved. Faulkner relished telling ghost stories at Rowan Oak and effortlessly channeled long-departed characters for his novels and stories. Whatever spooked him at the Wayside Inn made for a harrowing, sleepless night. Was walking the backroads a sign of a mental breakdown?

Parting with their daughter exacerbated the canyon between Faulkner and Estelle. Over the next four years Faulkner was gone more than he was home. Vicki felt he was spiritually and geographically adrift.

> He was a pitiful man at that point. He was lost. He didn't seem to know where to go. And he was traveling. He was a celebrity, meeting people, influential people, and he was also meeting women. And most of all, Pappy was away from his family. His country had turned against him. I mean his country in terms of Mississippi and Oxford. I think he sank into a despair and that was the cause of his excessive drinking. His health was just going to pot because of it.[9]

***

Faulkner's respite from *A Fable*, the big book that eventually would be outlined on the walls of his office, might have come to an end with *Requiem's* publication (September 27, 1951), had the play not asserted itself again. With her energy and connections, Ruth was lobbying for a production at the Brattle Theatre in Cambridge, Massachusetts. She'd previously worked with Albert Marre there in his production of *Macbeth*, with Ruth as Lady Macbeth. Marre was willing to direct *Requiem* but knew it needed a substantial overhaul. Faulkner must have realized how daunting it would be to bring the play to stage. He took a suite in early October at the Hotel Continental, close to Harvard Square and the theater. Marre came to feel Faulkner primarily was appeasing Ruth and that he didn't believe in the play. He and Marre worked on it for a few weeks until Faulkner's frustration with it led to exponential drinking.

An evening with Thornton Wilder, a prominent playwright and novelist, proved painful and embarrassing for Marre, who set up the introduction. Wilder, who was born the same year as Faulkner, wanted very much to meet him and was a great admirer. In return, Faulkner remained virtually silent the entire evening until the discomfort was such Wilder ended the evening. When Marre questioned his behavior—"Bill," he asked, "why do you have to be such a bastard?"—Faulkner gave Marre a nonanswer accompanied by a malevolent smile. "He's a nice man," Faulkner said, "He's a gentle man, isn't he?"[10] Before leaving for Oxford, Faulkner promised to return after his visit to New Orleans for the Legion of Honor ceremony. The play wasn't much improved from where they started.

***

The Wayside Inn seemed a harbinger of more odd behavior. Shortly after leaving Cambridge but prior to the Legion ceremony, Faulkner made a puzzling side trip, also to New Orleans. He stopped over in Oxford to touch base and then drove toward to the Crescent City alone. He left his car outside of New Orleans and boarded a train into the city. There appears to have been no particular reason for the visit. Once there, he connected with friends Helen and Guy Lyman, owners of the hunting cabin in Picayune, Mississippi, where he'd left the sole manuscript of *Absalom* in 1936. It didn't take long for the Lymans to surrender; they couldn't or chose not to keep up with his revelry.

Faulkner's penchant for costumes returned during his stay in the French Quarter at the historic Monteleone. Situated on the corner of Royal and Iberville, the hotel dates back to 1886. It was a favorite for literary luminaries like Tennessee Williams and Hemingway. Truman Capote's mother was a long-term resident there during her pregnancy with him.

Ten. Spooked: 1951

The Monteleone's lively atmosphere includes the Carousel Bar with a rotating merry-go-round for seating. Given the environment, it's easy to imagine Faulkner's enthusiasm.

He was spotted leaving the hotel by another guest—weaving here and there—in a white-linen planter's suit and came close to a tragic accident with one of the city's famed streetcars. The macabre near-miss evidently was embellished by the witness who said the oncoming streetcar line was Desire (the Desire Streetcar line ended in 1948). Still, it made for a great story. Guy Lyman, now very concerned, contacted another friend in New Orleans, George Healy, telling him "Your friend's here and he's getting so I can't handle him." Healy reached out to another friend who contacted a sympathetic doctor. Faulkner resisted as usual but the doctor was able to get him admitted to the Southern Baptist Hospital. The rest and care he received there allowed him to return home with a second trip to New Orleans close on his heels.

At the French consulate days later, Faulkner delivered his short acceptance speech in French. Family members, including his mother who had traveled to Memphis for a new dress and shoes, Estelle, his brother, Jack, and his wife, Suzanne, all attended appropriately attired. By contrast, the honoree wore rumpled slacks, scuffed shoes, and a well-worn hunting jacket. Even his sister-in-law, Suzanne Faulkner, who knew his eccentricities, was astonished by his outfit. After the ceremony, they were treated to dinner at Antoine's, one of the city's oldest (1840) and finest restaurants. The weekend ended in a surprising manner. Faulkner and Estelle harmoniously drove back to Oxford with a loaded station wagon. Estelle's shopping spree in the various French Quarter shops for chairs and love seats for once didn't incite her husband's ire.

* * *

November and December were quiet as if aware of the careening year ahead. There was another trip to Cambridge for work on *Requiem*, "that damn play ... of which I am quite sick now,"[11] he wrote Else; his annual deer camp where the hunters failed to spot a single deer; and a smattering of letters to Joan. Stymied at having failed to advance the romance, either because he feared the domestic eruptions, or "mess" as he phrased it, that seeing her would provoke, or due to Joan's resistance, it no doubt crossed his mind that she was slipping away.

Eleven

Superlative: 1952

How many lives can one man maintain? And at what price? The complexity of Faulkner's mind craved endless intrigue, while his soul sought solitude, quiet rambles around Rowan Oak, and domestic comforts. As his relationship with Meta cooled, and the vast distance from Else proved challenging, he captured the romance he coveted with Joan. Their primary involvement in 1952–1953 fulfilled his prophesy of grief over nothing. The push and pull of their time together left him depressed and fragmented. These tumultuous years involved nine recorded hospital and sanatorium stays, two in-residence recoveries, and reported electroshock therapy. Episodes of blackouts followed by retrograde amnesia were occurring. Faulkner learned from a prominent psychiatrist that his brain was hypersensitive to intoxication and near the borderline of abnormality. What's more, "worry, unhappiness, any form of mental unease produces less resistance to the alcohol."[1] He was advised to stop drinking for three or four months and repeat the test. Such a measured response was never his way and his self-destructive course was not to be altered.

* * *

In May 1952, Faulkner passed on an opportunity to meet Meta in New Orleans where she was working on the film *The Steel Trap* with Joseph Cotten and Teresa Wright. When she related the lucky opportunity in a letter, he told her he couldn't make it work. He already had committed to addressing the Delta Council in Cleveland, Mississippi. It was hardly the answer she expected after his letters full of yearning since they parted over a year ago. Upon *Requiem's* publication, he wrote, "You are beautiful. I want to sleep with you. I didn't sign your book. I was waiting to be with you to sign it." When he was troubled by nerves and depression, she was the balm he imagined: "I wish I could spend about two weeks with you, lying on my face with the sun on my back. That would do more good than anything." And, "I want to see you. I have not forgotten any of it, never will, never."[2]

Meta was accustomed to Faulkner's passionate letters—"Dear Meta: As soon as I touched that envelope, I knew who it was from. I dreamed about you last night and had to get up and change pajamas"[3]—but alarmed when he repeated the same stories. That was something previously unimaginable. To her, his sharp mind registered every line he wrote and thought he had. In time he acknowledged telling the same stories. He believed the spells of forgetfulness were due to a fall from a horse only to learn from specialists that there was no skull injury.

The speaking engagement at Delta State University wasn't something he embraced; in fact, when he was first asked he declined, and the compensation, $400 plus expenses, was hardly a windfall. It seemed odd he would choose the Delta Council over a rare opportunity to see Meta. Yet he did.

* * *

Faulkner's back-and-forth with Bob Farley, who extended the council's speaking invitation, exasperated Farley. And it was not the first time. Farley, law school dean at the University of Mississippi, was also a riding companion. The two men often took morning rides along Old Taylor Road. Almost inevitably Faulkner's outburst, "Let's let 'em go, Bob,"[4] would break the spell of a pleasant ride. Farley looked on as Faulkner raced past him at a mad gallop on the uneven gravel road. Farley recognized the danger; and if Faulkner did, he still felt compelled to act on his impulse. It was much the same bravado that would accompany his drinking episodes. "When I have one martini," he once said, "I feel bigger, wiser, taller. When I have a second, I feel superlative. When I have more, there's no holding me."[5]

* * *

Roughly six weeks out from the event Faulkner expressed reservations about the speech and asked for another week to consider. Time passed. Since Farley never received a definitive "no," he showed up at Rowan Oak the morning of May 15. Faulkner was in a mischievous mood, asking if this was the day of the event. Another interesting outfit marked the occasion: a badly frayed shirt made from parachute silk, seersucker slacks, and a belted jacket, now too small, he'd purchased in New Orleans. The outfit was crowned with a felt hat Farley believed dated to 1915.

There was no doubt Faulkner took some pleasure in being the outlier. He after all identified with the hardscrabble north Mississippi farmers rather than the wealthy Delta planters. Delta Council Day brought those cotton planters together along with a host of prominent merchants, bankers, and professionals. Dating back to 1935, it is a virtual who's-who of Delta citizenry marked by food, festivities, and even an award for the best-dressed man and woman wearing cotton clothing. None of this went unnoticed on Faulkner's part. He kept close company with his old friend, Ben Wasson, that day. As he surveyed the crowd, he told Wasson,

> They're not a bit like the farmers in my part of Mississippi. These Delta folks all *look* rich. There's something about them suggesting Midas must have touched them. Rich like the Delta soil. Rich. Productive. And maybe self-satisfied. The hill folks think all you people are godless and headed for fire and brimstone. I expect most Deltans are touched with hubris.[6]

On the stage, Faulkner stood between Governor Hugh White of Mississippi and Governor James F. Byrnes of South Carolina to address the five thousand people in attendance. Faulkner's speech, "Man's Responsibility to Fellow Man: Freedom Is Each Citizen's Charge," lambasted federal welfare programs and the Truman administration. He spoke of independence, the intentions of the founding fathers, and the hard work of early pioneers. He asserted that the forefathers expected each individual "to be responsible for the consequences of his own acts, to pay his own score, owing nothing to any man" and that "I believe that the true heirs of the old tough durable fathers are still capable of responsibility and self-respect, if only they can remember them again."[7]

Like the Nobel address, due to technical issues with the sound system, Faulkner's remarks were heard only by those within close earshot. Not to be outdone, Byrnes echoed Faulkner's sentiment and even spoke of forming a new party to represent the people of the South. Something about Byrnes rubbed Faulkner the wrong way, and when Wasson labeled Byrnes a Snopes, Faulkner concurred, "He sho' is."[8] Enthusiastic receptions greeted both speeches on the beautiful spring day. (Delta Council Day expects nothing less.) Wasson noticed Faulkner's enjoyment in the afternoon and his friendly interactions with those who approached him.

Many attendees complimented his speech. He apparently was so caught up in the moment he told the council president not to worry about his fee, that a few bottles of whiskey would suffice. That was news to Farley, who already was put out with Faulkner after all of his negotiations. A case of bourbon was loaded in Farley's car—guarded until they departed for Oxford—and the council president, confused about how to handle the check, gave it Farley. Farley told Faulkner, handing him the check, that for all the trouble he was keeping half the case of bourbon. Faulkner told him to keep it all, ending the day on a magnanimous note.

* * *

Faulkner may have parted with the case of bourbon easily because four days after the council event, May 19, 1952, he was in Paris for the *Oeuvres du XXe Siècle* festival. As a guest of the French government and speaker at the Writers' Congress, his expenses were paid. The original hope was that *Requiem* would be performed at the Théâtre des Champs-Elysées along with the festival's other offerings. When funding for the play failed to come through, Faulkner didn't alter his course. He seemed very much taken with the idea of a month in France and Else's company.

Joan, who was living for a few months in New Orleans, must have sensed his drifting attention. Her impassioned letter reached him in early May: "And is the violet finally wilted—is there no need in you any more? Tell me—for we have agreed on the honesty, too, great man whom I do still love, in the depths that no one else has touched." Not wilted, he assured her, though if he wanted peace, he would wish it faded and gone. Probably hoping to arouse jealousy, he wrote Joan that he would be seeing another pretty woman in Paris who also had red hair and beautiful violet blue gray eyes. The woman had everything except she was not Joan. He even proffered a negligible apology; he admitted it was shabby and dishonorable to carry the image of one woman to another.

At this juncture, both Joan and Faulkner were at a lull with their writing. She was looking for inspiration in New Orleans; he was farming and tending to his horses. Faulkner recognized these activities belied the work to come. He hadn't "anguished" over putting words together for a long time,

> Which probably means that I am getting ready, storing up energy or whatever you want to call it, to start again. Which, I believe, is what is happening to you [Joan]. To have written something once which you dont need to hate afterward is like having cancer; you dont really ever get over it.[9]

* * *

Albert Marre likewise was in Paris on the earlier assumption that he would be directing *Requiem* there. Faulkner confided that he was "relieved we don't have to do the play. I don't think it's any good." Marre insisted that Ruth felt otherwise. "I don't think this play is going to do Ruth any good," Faulkner said, "but she can go ahead with it if she wants to."[10] Meta remembered how absorbed he was with *Requiem*, "more than any novel-in-progress that I had known about…. For all his struggles to write a well-made play with theatrical thrust and power, it was one of his failures, and the final setbacks to production depressed him."[11] Having dispatched with *Requiem* for the time, he was savoring this holiday. It was light on official duties, an address to the writers' conference, and little more. Yet even that didn't go without a hitch. When the Writers' Congress secretary tried to rouse him for his appearance, he threw a bottle at her. He probably wouldn't have made the conference at all if he hadn't been scheduled to follow French novelist André Malraux, whom he admired.

It was classic behavior, drinking in advance of an obligation he disliked, and also because his nagging back pain was accelerating. Whether the cause was a fall from a horse or down the stairs at Rowan Oak, he was in agony. At the Clinique Remy de Gourmont on May 31, doctors took multiple x-rays and discovered he had a broken back. The professional advice was surgical fusion. Faulkner was hardly receptive to that idea. He agreed to a period of bed rest and the usual course for coming off a bender.

Nothing would interfere with his planned four-day trip to Biddenden in Kent and from there to Oslo for ten days. He continued to tempt fate with all the travel and soon the back pain erupted. He called Else from his London hotel room in excruciating pain after almost drowning in the bathtub. In Oslo, Else and Faulkner stayed in a hotel where she arranged a week of daily visits with a masseur. His relief was palpable and he would sing the praises of the Swedish masseur for years to come. He had promised a return to Norway at the end of the Nobel affair. Now, without responsibilities or pressure, it was the return he imagined.

With his back pain eased for the first time in years, he could appreciate the striking country as a relaxed visitor. And it didn't hurt to have Else by his side. Of the various women in Faulkner's orbit, Else kept their friendship the most private, but her remarks to Blotner after Faulkner's death made it clear how close they were. Without promise of a future, she chose to embrace the affair, "It was my own decision," she said, "to take this unhappy genius, this former household god, as a lover."[12] Not one to miss an opportunity when it came to women, Faulkner used Else to fuel a rivalry with Joan.

* * *

As was customary on his return to Mississippi, Faulkner spent a night in New York, this time at the New Weston Hotel, before flying to Memphis. The hotel was a favorite of Faulkner's where on occasion he could be found having a solitary dinner at the bar. Tonight was a more social event. His dinner companions included Robert Penn Warren and top Random House editor Albert Erskine. Erskine, a Memphis native, along with Warren and others, founded *The Southern Review* (1935) while teaching at Louisiana State University. Besides Faulkner, Erskine edited top-tier authors like Warren, Eudora Welty, Ralph Ellison, Malcolm Lowry, Cormac McCarthy, James A. Michener, and John O'Hara. His authors were fiercely loyal to him.

Upon meeting Erskine in New York at a dinner party in 1950, Joan recalled being awestruck by his former marriage to Katherine Anne Porter (a four-year union that was said to end when he discovered Porter was at least 20 years older than him), and also because he was "very handsome."

The night of pleasant literary conversation ended with a ferry ride—Faulkner's suggestion—to Weehawken and two bottles of champagne in the hotel bar. He apparently was feeling celebratory, perhaps because when he wired Joan to meet him at the Memphis airport the next evening, she agreed. They would have the uncommon treat of private time together without the usual espionage.

* * *

A familiar blast of heat and humidity greeted Faulkner when his plane arrived the evening of June 17. Even for Memphis it was on the warm side, with a high of 96 degrees. As promised, Joan was there to meet him. A blush of summer of sun brightened her fair skin and the stylish summer outfit suited her uncharacteristically ebullient mood. It had been three months since they last saw each other and Joan was happy to see him. For once she didn't shy away from his embrace. It all boded well for their evening. Almost three years had passed since they met. Since the relationship hadn't advanced in any real way this might have been the time to end things. The two had dinner; and later, in her car, after all her reluctance and avoidance, Joan spontaneously turned to Faulkner without reserve.

It was, he wrote, incredibly beautiful to find each other at last; she kissed him and he touched her and she accepted. What's more, he asserted that his entire body of work—all the years of creating—was in anticipation of that night in Memphis. Had Faulkner's time in Oslo with Else convinced Joan to initiate intimacy? That perhaps she'd made Faulkner wait too long? What wish fulfillment to have carried one woman's image to the next and boast of two successful liaisons. Else and Joan were redheads with violet gray eye color but quite different physiques. Else was tall and curvaceous. Joan was slight and small boned with lovely legs. Both had their charms.

* * *

Faulkner and Joan's had been a strange courtship. Dates were random drives on small country roads outside of Holly Springs. The area was heavily wooded without signs posting ownership. "And it was hot then," Joan remembered. "It was before the days of air conditioning and it'd be just miserable driving along and you know dying of the heat." The small roads yielded discoveries like abandoned houses and structures they liked to stop and explore. "We liked doing that," Joan said, "not many people would." Faulkner would bring a picnic lunch and some beer. And they would spend the afternoon talking though he would prefer to take things in a different direction. It was during one of those drives that Faulkner reached over the seat and retrieved *The Sound and the Fury*'s handwritten manuscript, saying "I've brought you something. I have something I want to give you."[13] The sentimental gift was even more so because he called the novel his heart's darling.

The Mississippi day trips are frankly depicted in Joan's novel *The Wintering*. She often said she and Faulkner romanticized the woods more than any other place, even New York and the freedom it afforded. While these rendezvous were sometimes pleasant, they could also incite a truculent Faulkner. One such meeting recounted in the novel takes place in November. Jeff Almoner, Faulkner's stand-in, tells his wife he is scouting out roads to a deer camp. When he meets Amy Howard, Joan's character, at the bus stop he is wearing outdoor gear. As usual he has a lunch packed for two, but for the chilly weather he also brought a bottle of whiskey and a blanket. The sight of an abandoned schoolhouse, a welcome shield against the cold, drives them inside where they manage a small fire in the pot-bellied stove. The bottle is passed between them and they stretch out on the floor in their winter coats using the blanket for cover.

> Against the stove's warm sides, the soles of her feet had begun to burn uncomfortably, though the floor beneath her was hard and cold. The two inconveniences loomed large in her mind, and Jeff's hand touching her was bothersome. He seemed trembly and shaky, like an old man. This time: she repeated that to herself over and over. Must she blame herself that when she tried to return his kiss, she felt nothing at all? Coldly, she removed his hand from her leg. She said all the things she always said: she was sorry but she couldn't and she just didn't feel that way. Her longing, however, was for abandonment.... Old shame filled her as she stood and drew up her pants, uncomfortable that he did not look away. Not speaking, she gathered things to take to the car.[14]

The drive to the bus stop that would return her to Delton [Memphis] was nearly silent. And he left her there before the bus arrived without a recognizable goodbye.

The male character's thinly disguised anger is verbatim dialogue from Faulkner's letters to Joan. Jeff describes her as a "poor baby who can't melt." He tells her she thinks too highly of her body—"It's after all, flesh and blood"[15]—worries she'll never love anyone—and, while he doesn't believe she's frigid, he sadly realizes he isn't the one to help her. He imagines something from her childhood has done this to her, and it is also the source of her writing block. These are themes Faulkner returned to over and over. He assured her that if she ever released her sexuality, her writing would flourish.

* * *

The tenor of their relationship changed after the night in Memphis but there was little time to savor the nascent closeness. Whatever her motivation—to appease him or to satisfy her curiosity—sex with Faulkner was not something Joan frequently sought. She felt their age difference was too great and his marital state disturbed her. What she found more awkward to tell him was that she simply wasn't attracted to him. They were again at cross-purposes. Whereas he thought her acquiescence signaled a promising new beginning, he soon acknowledged his mistake. The affair left him baffled, puzzled, unhappy, heartsick, and frustrated.

Faulkner's letters chronicle the aftermath of their next three disappointing meetings in the woods. She once again had reverted to rejecting him. His inability to conquer—his word—Joan was a nagging failure. She epitomized the qualities he sought: youth, beauty, a writer's sensibility, and an inherent loneliness like his own. Why couldn't she love him? Faulkner accused her of giving him crumbs and using subterfuge. On one of his drives home he had a flat tire and changing it ignited his back pain. But the real pain, he wrote, was the unhappiness of her refusal: "very unhappy, but after all they are your mouth and your bottom and yours the right to say no about them and anyone that dont like it should better go back where he came from and maybe stay there, hadn't he?"[16] Her rebuffs stirred his oft-used refrain, "Haven't I been telling you something too: that between grief and nothing, I will take grief?"[17]

Soon enough Joan was characterizing his letters and their meetings as burdensome "pressure," a description Faulkner did not dispute. Twice he admitted to forcing her compliance. The first time he deliberately set out to break down her mind, the rational, moral forces that he believed obscured her desire. His determination made her cry and she consented. The next time he succeeded not by physical force, but by relentless insistence. He realized later he'd crossed a line. They would only be together again, he promised, if she turned to him as she did the first time. The emotional seesaw was hard for Joan; but for Faulkner, it was devastating. His drinking increased along with tensions at home. Indeed, a clean break with Joan that summer might have been a better outcome than the "terrible amount of no-peace"[18] he felt.

* * *

If he thought this intense three-month pursuit of Joan was lost on Estelle, Faulkner was wrong. Her suspicions and his dodgy behavior kept her off balance. While the misery he felt was dutifully recorded in one letter after another to various recipients, she no doubt felt the same or worse. Given the turmoil at home, and her vulnerability with alcohol, by early August she needed professional help. Wright's Sanatorium opened in Byhalia in 1948 and was about half the distance of the drive to Memphis. Whether it was Estelle herself (unlikely given her condition), her son Malcolm, or Faulkner, someone in the household determined Wright's offered the care she needed and was more convenient.

Whereas most patients spend a week or more, Estelle was admitted to Wright's August 3, 1952, and spent only one night there. When she woke up sober the next morning, she vehemently insisted on returning home (Faulkner phrased it as screaming in a letter to Joan). Dr. Wright apparently accommodated. Her diagnosis was alcoholic avitaminosis (vitamin deficiency) and her condition upon discharge was noted as "poor." On August 5, Faulkner made an account deposit to Wright's for $135, and ten days later received a $65.90 refund.[19]

* * *

The vexing relationship with Joan and the fits and starts of *A Fable* were intricately bound. "I still felt so rotten yesterday morning that I had to do something," he wrote, "so suddenly I dug out the mss. of the big book and went to work at it; suddenly I remembered how I wrote THE WILD PALMS in order to try and stave off what I thought was heart-break too."[20] (A reference to his first separation from Meta.) Encouraged with the book's progress, he reminded Joan that he needs someone to write not *to* but *for*. And she is that someone. Vicki and other family members knew of his involvement with Joan. "I think even Pappy realized the hopelessness of that," Vicki said. "Joan was saying no."[21]

Whatever role he assigned her, Joan struggled for release. She was seeking a change and by early September was living in New York in a small apartment. The move turned out to be good for her. She had a job at *Look* magazine in the reader's mail department personally answering subscribers' letters; and, with the help of Faulkner's agent, Harold Ober, placed her short story, "The Morning and the Evening," with *The Atlantic Monthly*.

The first letter she received in New York from Faulkner, composed on Gartly-Ramsay letterhead stationery and dated September 25, 1952 (his 55th birthday), related dire news. On September 18, he arrived at the hospital by ambulance. He told Joan his back had collapsed but actually he had suffered a convulsive seizure. His home remedy of alcohol and Seconal, meant to assuage the back pain, ended as it often did.

The next day, September 26, Joan received his customary telegram wishing her a happy birthday and sending love. He told her he was home from nine days in the hospital. They were indeed living in parallel universes. He imagined that if she still lived in Memphis they could have been together every day of his hospital stay. Maybe such thoughts were a way for him to deny his deteriorated health. While in the hospital, he had suffered another seizure, and decided against the recommended diagnostic spinal tap. He wanted to go home, and though the doctors advised differently, he was steadfast.

The massages and heat compresses he'd received offered temporary relief but within days the back pain surged. Jimmy Faulkner saw him sitting in front of the hearth warming his bare back and Joan remembered his frequent complaints about the pain and taking Seconal for relief. The physical pain clearly was compounded by Joan's move to New York just two months after they were finally intimate. He tries in a letter to reconcile having had her for a moment and then losing her. What's to blame, he asserts, is her frozen heart. Sometimes his letters read like sermons. He admonished her for running from herself; from fact, reality, truth, ecstasy and godhead. But mostly for running from him. The artist must embrace the experience of the soul and spirit to be brave, truthful, and generous. His letters brimmed with grief and loss, "I still feel rotten, and will until I see you again. I dont think it is my back really, I think my heart broke a little."²²

* * *

This time, not even two weeks later, his reckless combination of pills and alcohol led to a fall down the full flight of stairs at Rowan Oak. Coming on the heels of his self-discharge from the hospital, it left Estelle overwhelmed. She wrote Saxe Commins for help and on October 7 he made the trip from New York to Mississippi. From Rowan Oak, Commins wrote detailed letters evocative of southern Gothicism. To his wife, Dorothy, he related a "ghastly" tale of a "harrowing" night full of "strange and pathetic happenings":

> [Bill] pleads piteously for beer all the time and mumbles deliriously.... His body is bloated and bruised from his many falls and bears even worse marks.... The disintegration of a man is tragic to witness. It was pitch dark when I arrived in Memphis and now I am getting my first glimpse of Southern daylight. So I have no impression whatever of the country. The house, however, has left a strong and rather distasteful impression on me. It is a rambling Southern mansion, deteriorated like its owner, built in 1838 and not much improved since. Ours is a heavenly mansion in comparison, if very much smaller. The rooms are bare and what they do contain is rickety, tasteless, ordinary.²³

Likewise in his letter to Robert Haas and Bennett Cerf, Commins spared no details. He intuited the tragic severity of Faulkner's condition:

> The fact is that Bill has deteriorated shockingly both in body and mind. He can neither take care of himself in the most elementary way or think with any coherence at all. This may be only evidence of his condition in a state of acute alcoholism. But I believe it goes much deeper and is real disintegration.... To move him even as far as Memphis is unthinkable. New York or Princeton is totally out of the question. So this morning I'm going into town to talk to his local doctor and try to find out what can be done medically. I'll know better what to do after I get his advice. Estelle is really desperate and doesn't know where to turn. Malcolm, her son, and a very fine fellow, is doing all he can but he too is helpless.... Under the circumstances, particularly the one that would make me terribly sorry if anything happened and I did not make the trip, I am glad I came down here. It's the least one does for a friend.²⁴

Commins assumed responsibility but was at a loss for viable options. He originally thought Faulkner might fly to New York with him for care—that he determined impossible once he saw him—and the seventy-five-mile drive to Memphis seemed almost as daunting. Likewise, he knew the Oxford hospital couldn't handle the patient. If there was any discussion about taking Faulkner to Wright's, it is unknown. Somehow, Commins got him back to Gartly-Ramsay where he stayed almost two weeks. Besides managing his withdrawal, doctors addressed the recurrent back problem. They were in agreement with the Paris physicians that surgery was his best option.

He was no more agreeable now than he was then. That failing, orthopedic specialists at the Campbell Clinic in Memphis resorted to fitting him for a back brace. Faulkner referred to it as a corset. The back pain, he was told, was something he would have to learn to live with. In a raw letter to Joan during this stay, he left little doubt about the depth of his feelings for her: "I love you. Sometimes I think I have never loved anyone before. Maybe I never have. In a way I made you, as you have made me, over."[25]

* * *

The trouble visiting the Faulkners lingered like a bad house guest. Faulkner's second hospital stay gave Estelle plenty of time to think. And plenty of time to read Joan's letters to her husband. Two arrived postmarked from New York while he was in the hospital. Naturally she wanted to know what this young girl felt for Bill and believed it was in her best interest to find out. She was confident he was filled with romantic notions about Joan. But was it reciprocated? Should Bill ask for a divorce, what would she have? It terrified her to imagine navigating life alone, financially and emotionally.

Her insecurity accelerated at an alarming rate when she read Joan's letter, "About your coming, I want to see you and anytime; I only don't like the fortnight idea. Can't you get another medal or something and stay here to work for a long time. Whatever you decide about and when coming, I'll be here."[26] The hurt and betrayal she'd felt with Meta resurfaced. He always had a reason for a trip to New York, and now more so with Joan waiting for him there. She would confront him and he would deny everything. The girl's letter—that's what she was to Estelle, a girl—showed she knew only Bill's better side, "So, silver-head, I saw you standing in a dark hall with the phone," Joan's letter continued, "with a hurt back, aching heart, sad voice, and kind—kind all over, inside and out."[27]

* * *

Her discovery of Joan's letters—proof positive—left Estelle feeling defenseless. She already had panicked earlier in the month when she received a letter from Saxe Commins addressed to Mrs. Estelle Faulkner. "I was a little startled when I saw your letter addressed to Mrs. *Estelle* Faulkner—Aren't you being a bit premature," she wrote, "or has something happened that I'm in the dark about? Right now, though, I know I'm super-sensitive—Excuse me, if that unusual (to me) form of address worried me without cause—."[28] Estelle's niece, Dean, summarized her aunt's precarious situation, "Being *Mrs. William Faulkner* seemed to be all that mattered to her. As long as she held the title to the throne, though her position might be challenged, no one could take her place."[29] Wells believed of all the women in Faulkner's life Joan posed the greatest threat to the already "troubled" marriage. "As his literary 'protégé,' Joan held a unique position in his life, and her proximity to Oxford was a double threat ... with Aunt Estelle's awareness of what was going on under her nose, Rowan Oak turned into a war zone."[30]

Predictably, Estelle's drinking rocketed. What a pair they were! Faulkner returned home from Gartly-Ramsay to find his wife teetering on the edge. His attempts to get her sober were mixed. His medication hangover clouded his thinking and Estelle took some pleasure in taunting him; not only about having read Joan's letters, but also about possessing them. He managed to retrieve them by blackmail and admitted to Joan he was a bit ashamed of his tactics. He withheld Estelle's drink for seven hours until she relented. Of course, that small victory didn't stop the battle from raging. "This is a terrible situation," Faulkner wrote Commins, "never can I remember being so unhappy and downhearted and despaired. I have done no work in a year, am living on my fat, will begin soon to worry about money, and I do not believe I can work here. I must get away...."[31]

The whipsaw of his back and drink, whether he was in Oxford or elsewhere, was thematic for 1952 and the years to come. Whatever improvements he'd achieved at the hospital couldn't withstand the firestorm at home. His November 14 letter to Joan from the Gartly-Ramsay marked three months of consecutive stays at the Memphis hospital. No doubt the latest fracas over Joan's letters contributed. He writes that he can barely manage to hold a pen and admits he never imagined his life could feel this empty. Regardless, he thinks of her always, loves and misses her. He hopes to be out of the hospital over the weekend and make a break for New York. Ostensibly, it was to work on *A Fable,* but Faulkner was desperate to see Joan and escape the tensions at home.

* * *

Once again Saxe and Dorothy Commins came to his rescue. Saxe suggested he stay with them in Princeton while he worked on *A Fable*. Vicki credited the couple with "literally" saving her pappy's life in the fifties, and Faulkner told family members Dorothy was one of the kindest women he'd ever known. His lodging assured, he arrived in November, writing Joan that Princeton was a good location with the close proximity to New York. He suggested they spend weekends together when possible. Later, he moved from the Comminses' home to the Princeton Inn.

Knowing Faulkner was sentimental about holidays and would be missing Rowan Oak, the Comminses invited Faulkner and Joan for Thanksgiving. Over the leisurely holiday, Joan didn't remember Faulkner doing any actual writing but he did reconnect with the manuscript. "He dug it up and he suddenly said out of anguish 'I've started working on the big book again.'" The first order of business was getting it in some sort of order.

> He arrived with it either in a suitcase or a box. [It] was just an enormous jumble of manuscript which we spent a whole day trying to put together because some of the pages weren't numbered. We fit them together by one page after another. That was when he started back on that [*A Fable*.] It seemed to please him so much that I had helped him. Who wouldn't help Faulkner straighten out his manuscript? He had come to a point where he hadn't written anything in a long time. He knew he couldn't write with the same fire and passion that he'd written with when he was young.[32]

Joan felt in a way he was fooling himself about the book. "He thought *A Fable* was going to be the greatest thing he'd ever written.... He had worked on it so long; he didn't want to ever give up." Many agreed with Joan's assessment of the novel: "*A Fable* had not come out as he had wanted," Vicki concurred. "He had had such high hopes that *A Fable* would be his greatest novel. He dedicated it to Jill because he thought it was going to be his *chef d'oeuvr*, but he was not satisfied when it went to print—it wasn't good. That was another source of depression. Things really hit an all-time low, I think, in [19]54."[33]

Over drinks with Stone while Wasson was visiting Oxford, Stone offered his opinion of *A Fable*:

> I'm afraid it's a lot of gibberish, from what I know about it. Bill must have slipped a mental groove to be writing such stuff. He won't listen to me when I try to tell him he's gotten way off the track.... It's about Jesus appearing during a battle in World War II and about how the soldiers lay down their arms, and a lot of other puzzling events.[34]

His two weeks near Joan offered hope for the fragile relationship. More and more Faulkner worried she would marry. Worse, that she would marry a "champion of the middle class" who would stifle her ambitions as a writer. For Joan, who was just getting established in the city, finding free time for Faulkner wasn't easy. Tensions arose over Joan's accessibility. Soon Faulkner's predictable drinking had Saxe and Joan scrambling for appropriate care. Though there was an unfortunate familiarity to the process, his stay at the Westhill Sanitarium would be one of the most controversial.

* * *

Located in Riverdale, a residential neighborhood in the Bronx, Westhill was a private facility. Faulkner's admittance there was arranged by Dr. Eric P. Mosse, a Manhattan psychoanalyst Joan was seeing at the time for her own issues with depression. Dr. Mosse wrote novels and plays and liked treating artists. Joan said,

> This man [Dr. Mosse] was like a vulture. He couldn't wait to get his hands on Faulkner. I mean I don't know what he thought he was going to find, like he was going to open his brains and see something fantastic. And he kept insisting to me that Faulkner couldn't have any children and I kept insisting well he does have a child. He just had all these preconceived ideas about the man.

Regardless of her reservations, she called Dr. Mosse when Faulkner's binge escalated. She told him that Faulkner "was on this thing" and she didn't know what to do. This was in stark contrast to the many times she said Faulkner "could drink socially perfectly well. He could decide that he wasn't going to drink at all and go for long periods when he didn't drink. He just went on binges." She attributed many these spells to his back pain.

> And otherwise I don't know why he went on them. There was never any warning. Just suddenly I might phone where he was staying and if the phone didn't answer for a day and a night or something like that I knew he wasn't away, I knew this is what had happened. Sometimes he just drank beer. Now what I always was aware of, he took Seconal when he went on these binges, so it's even questionable how much he actually drank and how much was the combination of the two.
> And he would often say "I don't know why I did it and I don't know how dangerous it might have been to combine the two." But we always had to get him to a hospital. He never raved, he never ranted. I don't know what torment it was that might have made him do this.... I asked him once if he had a happy childhood and he said yes, that he had a very happy childhood and he never had any of the cobwebs and things to work through that I had before he could get to his writing.[35]

In his effort to help Faulkner with his drinking and depression, Mosse said he administered probably six sessions of electroshock therapy. Dr. Mosse told his wife that after the sessions Faulkner was gentle and affectionate. Some still question whether or not this therapy occurred. Dr. Mosse's enthusiasm for it argues one way, but it would seem counterintuitive to Faulkner's nature. In general he distrusted psychiatrists. He thought their fees were exorbitant and he told Joan it was destructive for writers to see them and "give away" the pain and emotions they needed for their work.

Whether he would have been in any condition to consent or refuse electroshock at Westhill is unknown. Joan, who visited Faulkner there, felt she would have noticed if such radical treatment occurred. Years later Jill discounted the idea because of what she considered her father's faultless memory (that stands in stark contrast to Meta's depiction and Faulkner's own admission of forgetfulness to others). Faulkner was aware of his lapses, writing Else that "Something is wrong with me; as you saw last spring, my nature has changed. I think now that when I fell off the horse last March [1952], I may have struck my head too."[36] Buzz Bezzerides felt the electroshock treatments contributed to Faulkner's mental decline:

> Oh, the drinking for years had certainly dulled off his sharpness. When I read that he had had shock therapy applied to him by a psychologist who hadn't even asked for permission to do it, had done it without getting permission from the family, I asked a lot of questions about what shock therapy does to a person. One of several very bright doctors put it this way: "It deletes memory, the memory of the past, pain."

He believed Faulkner's great literature came out of the memory of pain, and once deleted, the sweet memories Faulkner now harbored were at odds with future narratives. For Buzz, it explained Flem Snopes' transformation from "monster" in *The Hamlet* to a loveable character in *The Town*. "Certainly Bill must have realized in some strange, profound way that he had lost something terribly important," he said, "and this loss drove him to his special kind of suicide."[37]

Given the frequency of electroshock therapy at the time for clinical depression—Ernest Hemingway is said to have endured twenty sessions—it is as likely as not that Faulkner did indeed receive such treatments. What was indisputable was Dr. Mosse's enormous bill. Faulkner and Commins were aghast. Dr. Mosse responded that it was a two-hour trip each way to see Faulkner at the sanitarium. In the end he relented, agreeing to whatever fee the two men found reasonable.

* * *

Released from Westhill with two more scheduled weeks in the New York area, Faulkner writes Joan from Princeton that he would like to book a hotel near her Greenwich Village apartment so they could be together every evening though he knows that's impossible; she has a life outside of him. Instead, he booked a room at the New Weston on Madison between 49th and 50th street. That gave him easy access to Commins' office at Random House where he worked on his novel. The elegiac letter borrows the phrase "to part is to die a little." That is what happened to him when she left Memphis and will happen to him again when he returns home.

He writes about knocking on her door at 4 a.m. on a Sunday if for no other reason than to touch and lie beside her, another tactic used often with Meta. (Since Joan shared a tiny one-bedroom apartment, it's doubtful she welcomed his advances.) A long, sexualized description of her body follows—her breasts, her girl hair, and the intimacy they had resumed. A postscript noted as 7 a.m. acknowledges what a dreary letter he's written; it's worse even than her phone call to him at that jail place [Westhill] when she cried so terribly. For Joan, seeing him admitted to such places was deeply disturbing because he often blamed his lapses on her rejections.

In many regards, Joan left Memphis that September to free herself of the entanglement with Faulkner. Yet, just a month and a half after she moved, Faulkner was at her doorstep. His agent had helped her place her story. There was gratitude but also a sense of obligation. Extricating herself, especially now that New York offered them freedom as a couple, would be difficult.

* * *

Christmas at Rowan Oak did little to lift his spirits. He thoughts were erotically centered on their time together in New York; the New Weston bar, sleeping together in beds not meant for two up and down the city. Instead of the beleaguered suitor, he vividly relived satisfying encounters in Princeton—the taste of her navel and her nipples growing hard between his fingers and tongue—and in Bob Linscott's New York apartment, a generously offered accommodation, a chance to admire her in a transparent shift. French painter [William Adolphe] Bouguereau would have appreciated her legs and thighs, he writes. One can tire of short-brained, long-legged girls. It's too much thinking of her 1,500 miles away. He hopes they never spend another Christmas apart.

* * *

His New Year's Eve resolution seemingly was to break from Rowan Oak and the ceaseless arguing with Estelle. Both were drinking. His December 31 letter to Joan describes fights that left him huddled in an overcoat walking the outside gallery until Estelle went to bed. Likewise, his work suffered, "What I expected seems to have happened. I have run dry I mean about the writing. What I put on paper now is not right. And I cant get down what I know is right. I cant work here.... I will be able to do nothing until I get away."[38] The letter's most shocking news appeared in parentheses—Estelle's son, Malcolm, according to Faulkner, said his mother should be sent to Whitfield, Mississippi's state asylum, a notoriously dire and frightful institution.

Faulkner rejected the drastic measure. He intuited that Malcolm didn't want to take responsibility for his mother upon Faulkner's return to

New York. And another familiar frustration surfaced. His work is impossible because all anyone there wants is money. There is no warmth, affection or sympathy. He needs someone to give to; someone who will return his refrain of yes, yes, yes. Will being needed send her into flight as being wanted does?[39]

Twelve

I Wont Stop In: 1953

It was evident by Faulkner's restlessness and inattentiveness to Christmas—a holiday he usually savored—that he sought escape. Not for the first time he imagined a new location would solve old ills. He planned a six-month sojourn in New York, the kind he professed to dislike in Hollywood. The life he envisioned there with Joan usurped his dedication to Rowan Oak and the solidity he garnered from his domestic sphere. He was willing to embrace uncertainty and dislocation in hopes of securing her affections. Where some people heed warning signs, Faulkner crashed head-on into heartbreak. The year would bring bittersweet endings.

A number of family issues, not the least of which being Estelle's worsening eyesight, delayed the hasty departure he imagined. For some time she kept her trouble to herself. She'd been diagnosed with cataracts but surgery was delayed until it would be most effective. Faulkner, however, speculates in a letter to Joan that Estelle decided on the mid–January date to keep him from leaving. The separate surgeries occurred within a two-week period. Estelle would need his help during recovery. He also was attending to his farm and completing taxes. Not too long after Estelle's recovery, Faulkner's brother Johncy paid a visit. Johncy found Faulkner in his office, staring out the window. "I've done Estelle an injustice over the last few years," he told his brother. "See how clean this place is? Estelle cleaned it. It's the cleanest it's been in I don't know when. Here I had thought she'd got to be a bad housekeeper. Now I find out she's been about half blind."[1]

Faulkner too dealt with age-related conditions. His teeth eventually necessitated a partial plate he called his "eating teeth," or his "Sears-Roebuckers." For the new teeth, Faulkner insisted on the whitest shade available, "Doctor, I want real white teeth. Every time I lose a tooth I want the whitest I can get, and finally I'll have a set of white teeth."[2] Given that his pipe smoking caused heavy discoloration, the bright shade he selected made the color variations quite pronounced. It was a curious dilemma for his Oxford dentist, Dr. Wilbur Abernethy, who settled on subduing the shiny new teeth just enough to escape Faulkner's notice.

* * *

From Rowan Oak, Faulkner wrote Joan a string of lovesick letters detailing his unhappiness at their separation. There will be an explosion, he predicts, when he tells Estelle he's leaving for New York. He is back at work on *A Fable*, and while his talent can be summoned, the fun has retreated.

> The work, the mss. [sic] is going again. Not as it should, in a fine ecstatic rush like the orgasm we spoke of at Hal's [Harrison Smith] that night. This is done by simple will power; I doubt if I can keep it up too long. But it's nice to know that I still can do that; can write anything I want to, whenever I want to, by simple will, concentration, that I can still do that. But goddamn it, I want to do it for fun again like I used to: not just to prove to bill f. that I still can.[3]

When his letters start associating his ability to work on the unwieldy novel—the big book—with having her nearby, it was another form of the pressure Joan dreaded. He began to link her body and sex with his writing success: "I still have the power and fire when I need it, thank God, who is good to me, lets me be able to write still and to be in love."[4] Once after a brief meeting in Holly Springs, he returned home and wrote the three temptations scene from *A Fable* with the old urgency he used to know. This he credits to merely touching Joan intimately (her girl-hair) for a second. Does she realize what she does to him?

If Faulkner was truly in the midst of a midlife crisis as Estelle believed, it may have centered more on the personal than professional. He acknowledged his gift in letters to both Joan and Saxe: "Damn it, I did have genius.... It just took me 55 years to find it out. I suppose I was too busy working to notice it before."[5] One day in Saxe's Random House office, he looked up, pointed to a shelf filled with his books, and said "That's quite a legacy for a man to leave the world."[6] That shelf would further expand with *A Fable* (1954), *The Town* (1957), *The Mansion* (1959), and *The Reivers* (1962) for which he would receive a posthumous Pulitzer Prize. While the later novels weren't the exhilarating epics of his earlier years, Faulkner was still writing during the last year of his life.

* * *

January brought Joan her own acclaim. Her *Atlantic Monthly* short story "The Morning and the Evening" appeared and Faulkner promised a worthy celebration on his return: a bed of a thousand violets and a bottle of champagne. While no doubt speaking in metaphor, Faulkner, who was normally quite frugal, especially about possessions, would splurge on people he cared about and his cherished horses and hunting dogs. As he told his nephew Jimmy, "Whenever you can swap money for pleasure, do it."[7]

He is now referring to New York as "home" and anticipating their reunion. Her soft body and his hungry hands. He wonders if his absence has made her eager for him? Faulkner's outpouring of letters was overwhelming and Joan made a sparse contribution in return. When she apologized for not writing often, there was a hint of coercion in his reply. Her letters should be spontaneous and written out of the ache and need to tell him something, talk with him. "Of course you like mine. Who wouldn't like to read the letters Faulkner wrote to the woman he loves and desires? I think some of them are pretty good literature, myself; I know what I would do if I were a woman and someone wrote them to me."[8]

Pressure mounts when he suggests they spend five straight days in Hal Smith's apartment. As it happened, Smith, Faulkner's friend and former editor, planned a vacation in Bermuda and offered the free lodging. Faulkner would make 9 East 63rd Street his first stop when he arrived in New York the end of January.

It was during this time that they came as close to being a "couple" as they ever would. Familiar problems still haunted them—her middle-class repressions and his Mississippi ghosts as he described it—but there was a real opportunity to build something. If she could shake the old values that disavowed an unconventional union, and he could truly break from Estelle, Rowan Oak, and his Mississippi ties, the future held promise.

* * *

Rather ironically, Faulkner and Joan found themselves working side by side in New York. Random House was located across the street from the Look Building on Madison Avenue and 51st Street. If they had plans— often they walked to the nearby New Weston bar—Joan would see Faulkner waiting for her.

> He would wait outside of Random House on the corner for me sometimes and I came out once and there was this huge, imposing old building ... and there was Faulkner. He was so small, standing against that blank wall. And I thought it just seems so odd that here is the most important person they have and he's just standing there like this little sort of forlorn figure.[9]

Their shared background made for comfortable times together; he called her his soulmate and countryman. They both understood the north Mississippi hill country and the allure of the Delta. Growing up Joan spent summers at her maternal grandmother's in Arkabutla, a town smaller than Oxford. A certain easiness accompanied their similar upbringings. Facing strangers made him nervous, and if she was by his side, Faulkner was much more at ease. She accompanied him to parties and they enjoyed other aspects of New York. It was this extended period—without the complications that plagued them in the South—that allowed her to truly know Faulkner. She found him not to be the unhappy soul his letters to her suggested. Rather, she noted his wry sense of humor and amusement at life.

> When I think of him it's always as laughing. Never laughing out loud I mean never could you imagine him laughing real hard real loud. It was sort of like when he laughed it was a little chuckle. Almost to himself. And it was as if he were internalizing the thing and saw far beyond what you saw. Humor. Beyond the immediate situation. And his eyes always would light up. If you turned and looked at him there was just this glow in them. He was amused by a great deal. I never think of his face as being tragic or unhappy or of him being an unhappy person. He enjoyed small things.

Their close proximity gave her a clear glimpse of his surprising work habits. He was not only able to deal with disruptions but also instigated them. "He would talk, get up, walk around, do anything. Go uptown, come downtown, sit down, write a few words. This was *A Fable* and that's the way he wrote it all the time that I saw him. He was never bothered by interruptions and things like that."[10] There was loneliness about him too. Nights when they weren't together, or he wasn't with a friend from Random House, he would choose a solitary dinner. Or as he phrased it when asked about his evening, "I dined alone." Joan imagined a number of people would have been delighted to have dinner with him.

She also took note of his humbleness. Even in a stylish city like Manhattan he went about in shirts with frayed collars. One night they were at Sardi's, a famous New York restaurant in the theatre district. Joan recalled the host was preparing to seat them upstairs: "They have a place upstairs if you're sort of nobody and Mr. Sardi came rushing forward and ushered us downstairs. But he [Faulkner] was not going to say a word. He never would have pulled weight or asked to be seated downstairs."

* * *

The honeymoon period in Smith's apartment was short-lived. A scene from *The Wintering* depicts it in unsparing detail, "She lay there wishful for love and staring into the darkness. Jeff's hand moved cautiously. Her brain became alert. If only she could stop thinking.... She cried silently, Don't! with her teeth gritted. Her soul and her spirit were unmanageable and ungiving."[11] Faulkner and Joan's conflict over intimacy and her accessibility had the usual outcome. Soon he was talking about his aching back and heart.

In the scramble for his care this time, Joan and Bob Linscott arranged for Dr. Benjamin Gilbert to visit the apartment. Dr. Gilbert, known as Dr. Broadway, was a physician to celebrities and the house physician at the Algonquin as well as other hotels. He had met and cared for Faulkner

Twelve. I Wont Stop In: 1953

on Faulkner's return from Norway in the summer of 1952. Dr. Gilbert arranged for a nurse to stay with him and oversee the usual attempt at sobriety. He would be only one of many physicians attending to Faulkner's care as the year progressed. The dreaded cycle was more entrenched than ever. The year was a revolving door of doctors, in-home care, hospitals, and sanitoria. Was Faulkner's reckless emotional abandon with Joan the primary trigger? He would tell her again, as he had four years ago, that for him he feared this love affair was for keeps.

* * *

Dr. Gilbert's approach with comfortable accommodations offered a temporary reprieve. Friends dropped by, including Albert Erskine, who was amused that Faulkner wasn't too sick to appreciate how striking his nurse was. That same nurse contacted Joan and asked if she'd join Faulkner for dinner in the apartment. The nurse arranged the delivered meal and Faulkner ordered Lindy's famous cheesecake for dessert. Those sorts of amenities are few and far between in hospitals or sanitariums—jail places—as Faulkner called them. It's questionable whether or not he was ever sober at the end of the hiatus. The National Book Award ceremony arrived February 7 which he attended with Saxe. At a cocktail party following the event with five hundred or so attendees, Faulkner was the literary star. *The New Yorker* characterized him as the "lion of the afternoon," and another wrote, "it was hard to get a word with him, so closely packed around him were his admirers. His famed reticence and dislike of publicity were much in evidence, as were his dignity, poise and shy friendliness."[12] The patched-together façade soon devolved and he experienced another blackout. Dr. Gilbert realized the situation called for more aggressive care and had him admitted to a private hospital, Charles P. Townes, on Central Park West.

Saxe's baptism at Rowan Oak when he saw Faulkner through the October 1952 ordeal failed to inure him to future episodes. Joan said:

> We took him to this hospital on the Upper West Side, and when we left, Saxe said to the woman at the desk, "Now I don't want you telling or talking to any newspaper people who come here" ... and the woman drew herself up and said, "I certainly won't because I've never heard of William Faulkner. I don't know who that is."
>
> Saxe said to me later, "I'm glad this didn't happen in Princeton, my wife has never seen anything like that." And I [Joan] thought, God, what a privileged lady. You know. I was upset when he did that, but it was not like something I couldn't face or hadn't seen before or didn't think I understood. I had grown up with my father and mother going on binges.

As was his custom, Faulkner insisted on leaving the hospital too early. He tried his luck back at Hal Smith's apartment but Smith slipped a note under the bedroom door—he had behaved so badly he would have to go somewhere else. Bob and Merle Haas took him in but realized his condition, slurred speech, and persistent issues with forgetfulness were abnormal. At the Doctors Hospital on the Upper East Side, Faulkner underwent a series of physical tests that proved unremarkable. Doctors and friends in New York recognized the focus must shift to his mental health if he were ever to confront his demons.

This might have represented a turning point. In Manhattan, Faulkner had access to some of the finest care. Dr. S. Bernard Wortis, a psychiatrist and neurologist at New York University Medical School, oversaw his evaluation. Dr. Wortis gathered that life was very painful for Faulkner and alcohol was a narcotizing device. He labeled Faulkner's brain near borderline abnormality and suggested he abstain from alcohol for several months before repeating tests. Together they needed to uncover root causes for the blackout drinking and confused thinking. Dr. Wortis wanted to talk about Faulkner's mother! Possibly nothing could shut things down faster.

Bezzerides held strong opinions about Faulkner's obstinacy. "I do feel that Bill couldn't benefit from therapy of any kind. He simply couldn't examine why things happened. He couldn't face the realities of his life: it was too painful." Probing into his past was pure terror.

> Pure terror at knowing the reality that you come from. Pure terror! Can you imagine how it must have been to be a child, an infant, to be in the presence of a dominating, angry mother and an incompetent, drunken father who failed at everything he did. Faulkner heard this even before he was born, when he was rocked in the amniotic stage. Can you imagine how terrifying it must have been to explore into that—terrifying! No wonder he didn't do it.[13]

* * *

Faulkner's piecemeal approach to his chronic condition continued without respite. His response to Dr. Wortis' treatment was to complain about the bill. He again cautioned Joan against psychiatrists and advised her in a letter to stick with Dr. Melchionna who first admitted him to Doctors Hospital: "Stay with Melchionna, who is a simple doctor. He gave me a complete physical overhaul, charged $85 against Wortis's $450, out of which I got one bottle of Seconal capsules."[14]

* * *

After staying with the Haases and at the Algonquin, Faulkner sublet a Greenwich Village apartment from writer Waldo Frank. Joan was by then settled in her own Village apartment. Ironically, Faulkner had consistently discouraged her from living there. He thought it was passé and that the artists there talked more about creating art than really accomplishing it.

Still, if he walked around and came across a place he recognized (he lived there briefly in 1921 with a job at a book store), he enjoyed stumbling across it like a lost treasure.

And when Faulkner met Else Jonsson in 1950 in Stockholm they discussed Greenwich Village. Else and her husband had lived in a famous Village landmark, the home of poet Edna St. Vincent Millay, who was highly revered in the Jonsson household. Beyond the impressive provenance, the residence at 75.5 Bedford Street was a mere 9½ feet wide, making it the narrowest townhouse in New York City. Faulkner also was a Millay enthusiast from way back. In 1921 he published a paper in *The Mississippian*, the Ole Miss student newspaper, praising her inventive play, *Aria da Capo*.

Joan's small apartment at 55 Horatio Street, painted by Faulkner one day on a whim, became a social hub of sorts. Joan's Memphis friend and fellow Bard graduate, Louise Fitzhugh, would stop by with friends of her own. Fitzhugh was an author and illustrator with a fascinating personal narrative. Louise's life of privilege—she was reared in her paternal grandparents' Memphis home with a coterie of domestic help—was not without caveat. Louise was deprived of an opportunity to know her mother. Her father, Millsaps, a successful Memphis attorney, was heir, along with Louise, to the Fitzhugh millions. Louise was a baby when her parents' contentious divorce was final. Her father gained custody and denied her mother, Mary Louise, visitation. For years Louise believed what her father told her, that her mother was dead. With maturity she realized the unknown woman she saw at the front door—rebuffed by the household staff—was Mary Louise hoping to see her daughter.

The southern social scene Joan found stifling affected Louise in a similar manner. While exhibiting the expected behavior—dating appropriate young men—Louise actually was smitten by Amelia Brent, a photojournalist from Arkansas. Whether it was confusion or compliance, and though still enamored of Amelia, Louise eloped—as Joan had done—with a Memphis boyfriend. She quickly realized the marriage was a mistake and her father had it annulled. That close brush seemingly allowed her to move forward with Amelia. They eventually shared a Greenwich Village apartment and other women would follow. Joan recalled that more than a few of Louise's romantic interests "just lived off her money."

* * *

One day a friend of Louise's asked Joan if she could photograph Faulkner. It was a rather spontaneous arrangement during which the photographer snapped a number of moody shots of Joan and Faulkner. In one, they stand close, his arm behind her back, gazing downward as they look out a window. They appear somber, almost sad. A certain resignation flickers across Joan's enchanting visage with her carefully applied lipstick. Another shot, with different shadowy angles, captures animated expressions. Joan glances down toward the smiling Faulkner (a great rarity in photographs of him) with a bemused smile of her own. The photographs reflect intimacy and a quiet companionship.

An artist for *The Atlantic* borrowed from the first photograph, focusing only on Faulkner's image, and inserted an equally prominent illustration of Sherwood Anderson. The magazine cover portrait of the two luminaries accompanied Faulkner's article, "Sherwood Anderson: An Appreciation" [June 1953].

Faulkner and Joan were surprised by the enormous bill Faulkner received for the loosely-organized photo shoot. Even more than with the money, Faulkner was alarmed that Joan might mail the photos to Rowan Oak. That April he'd been called home suddenly when Estelle suffered what might have been a fatal hemorrhage. With more than a little urgency, he instructed Joan not to mail the photographs but to keep them until his return. (In 1980, *The Atlantic* used the photograph of the two peering out the window to accompany Joan's essay, "Twenty Will Not Come Again." By then, editors at the magazine were unable to find the photographer for copyright permission or compensation.)

* * *

Brandon Grove, no longer a romantic rival, enjoyed dropping by Joan's place as well. Their shared history, especially Grove's trip to Memphis and the memorable outing on the *Minmagary* with Mrs. Faulkner, drew all three close. One day Grove surprised by showing up with an armload of Faulkner's books and asked him to sign them. This time it wasn't a prickly Faulkner who surfaced but an irate Joan. She thought it was in bad form and an intrusion on their friendship. But Faulkner shrugged it off, saying merely, "That's what people do."

What Faulkner enjoyed about Greenwich Village dissipated when he was upset with Joan. He derided the neighborhood and returned to his theme that most artists living there talked about art rather than creating it. He described Joan's friends as parasites and sophomores who didn't even have to pass their courses to stay in school. "These people you like and live among dont want the responsibility of creating. They go through the motions of art—talking about what they are going to do over drinks, even defacing paper and canvas when necessary, in order to escape the responsibility of living."[15]

* * *

Faulkner had been in New York two and a half months when Estelle's urgent illness called him home. Jill, still in her spring semester at Pine

Manor, met him in the city and the two immediately flew to Memphis. Estelle had suffered either a stomach or esophagus hemorrhage. A second and even more serious hemorrhage occurred after his return that put her life in grave jeopardy. She required nine blood transfusions at the Oxford hospital. Following her discharge and recuperation, more tests followed in Memphis to better determine a diagnosis, though the exact cause remained elusive. It's hard to say if Estelle's life was better or more difficult with him away. She knew he was involved with Joan and surely that was a source of angst. Yet, without the daily reminders of his presence, it may have been easier to cope. But with his absence the many maintenance details of Rowan Oak fell to her. Along with her age—she was now 56—her compromised health and an unsteady marriage had taken a toll.

Strangely enough, and unbeknownst to Estelle, her health crisis figured into Joan's rationalization about Faulkner. "There was a point when they thought Mrs. Faulkner was going to die," she said, "and I thought, if she dies I will marry him, but I never said that to him. I didn't want to be responsible for breaking up that marriage [and] he never freed himself." Faulkner's ill-phrased proposal to Joan, when it came, was "May I tell her [Estelle] we want to get married?" She didn't reply and the question lingered, free floating between them. Over a lunch with Bob Linscott, Joan asked him if he thought she should marry Faulkner. He was the only person she ever confided in about Faulkner's proposal. She recalled Linscott looking at her "rather huffily" and saying, "Well, has he asked you?" When she said yes, he replied, "Well, I would be very tempted to if I were you."

* * *

Meanwhile Faulkner continued writing Joan to fret about their relationship, speculate on when he might return to New York, and declare his love. He even claimed to dislike drinking without Joan and said he was going back to tomato juice. Though restless and eager to flee Rowan Oak, his work on *A Fable* continued, and his letters reflected growing nostalgia. He had been turning over their first sexual encounter, when they found and accepted one another after three years. He tells her nothing a couple ever has afterwards, regardless of ecstasy and passion, replaces the first part of it, the strangeness. In between erotic references and familiar refrains—he is the man who loves her, loves her girl's body, wants to put as much of his own as he can into it—a remarkable paragraph surfaces in an April 29 letter:

> I know now—believe now—that this may be the last major, ambitious work; there will be short things, of course. I know now that I am getting toward the end, the bottom of the barrel. The stuff is still good, but I know now there is not very much more of it, a little trash comes up constantly now, which must be sifted out.... And

now I realise for the first time what an amazing gift I had: uneducated in every formal sense, without even very literate, let alone literary, companions, yet to have made the things I made. I dont know where it came from. I dont know why God or gods or whoever it was, selected me to be the vessel. Believe me, this is not humility, false modesty: it is simply amazement. I wonder if you have ever had that thought about the work and the country man whom you know as Bill Faulkner—what little connection there seemed to be between them.[16]

* * *

Joan was dissatisfied with her job at *Look* and planned to leave the position in July. She considered a cross-country bus trip to gather writing material. Faulkner belittled the idea, which he found as foolish as attending a writers' conference to learn how to write. On occasion he would remind her that he sent out stories for thirteen years before having one accepted. He believed she should have been learning from him but was too concerned he would dominate. She is stymied, he writes, because even though she slept with him she has not surrendered to him. He hopes this breakthrough occurs with him but the important thing is that it eventually occurs. He again cautions her to write from the outside though Joan insists that is not her style, "I've always written from the inside out," she said. Her novel and story haven't come because they're not ready, ripe. Once they're together again he assures her that he can help. The quality of his advice might have resonated if he hadn't referred to her as a poor baby, a phrase she found belittling.

A curious transition follows when he wonders if Hal Smith will make a pass at her. That happened once before when he introduced Smith to a pretty young woman he was seeing and then left town. He imagines Smith thinking if someone as battered as Faulkner can get to second base, he might at least get to first. The push and pull over his involvement with her work was another—albeit less intense—source of conflict. Their stream of April letters reflects a troubled couple with entrenched positions. Joan worries Faulkner will return to New York and pressure her for sex; she tries to bring the conversation back to her writing. Faulkner fantasizes about her body and their future; asks her to take his sheets and towels to a Chinese laundry near Smith's apartment where he'll be staying.

When the Faulkners returned to New York in early May he was delighted to meet some writers he admired. In the Village, he and Joan attended a party with e.e. cummings. Joan remembered Faulkner as eager to meet the poet he had long enjoyed, a sentiment reciprocated by cummings. At the YM-YWHA Poetry Center on May 24, Joan introduced him to Dylan Thomas, and they shared drinks together following his reading. Joan previously met Thomas through a friend and was amused when, rather than shaking her proffered hand, Thomas paddled her palm. She recalled thinking, "I can't be his girlfriend and Faulkner's!"

* * *

The threesome connected six months later when Faulkner and Joan were having dinner at The Colony, considered one of New York's most fashionable restaurants. (Fiercely devoted patrons crowded the restaurant at 30 East 61st Street upon news of its closure in 1971. Truman Capote cried and said he would never eat another plate of spaghetti.) Thomas stopped by their table for hellos and a quick chat. Merely days later, November 9, Thomas was dead from pneumonia brought on by acute alcoholic insult to the brain. That grim cause of death purportedly followed a record-breaking round of whiskies at one of his favorite West Village bars, The White Horse Tavern. Thomas is said to have confided, "I've had my 18th straight whiskey and I think that's the record."[17] Soon after he fell into a coma.

Faulkner might have heeded the warning. Leaving the November 13, 1953, funeral service for the acclaimed Welsh poet, Joan and Faulkner were stopped by a photographer. He asked Joan to step aside, which she did, so he could get a photo of Faulkner. Of the four hundred or more in attendance at St. Luke's Chapel of Trinity Parish in Greenwich Village, there were a number of personalities. *The New York Times* article [11/14/1953] noted, among others, Tennessee Williams; poets Muriel Rukeyser, John Berryman, and e.e. cummings; James Laughlin, Thomas's American publisher at New Directions; and Harvey Breit, a literary critic well known to Faulkner. Breit had been in the cab with Faulkner, Ruth Ford, and Capote when Faulkner upbraided Capote for his criticism of Hemingway.

Though he was only 39 years old, Thomas's haunting poems were infused with ruminations on death. He had captured a substantial and dedicated readership. So many gathered in the small chapel for the Protestant Episcopal service that admirers stood four deep behind the occupied pews. It was a very formal sendoff for the often boisterous poet, including a reading from St. Paul's First Epistle to the Corinthians, considered evocative of Thomas's verse, and the choir singing two motets in Latin by the Elizabethan composer Thomas Morley. Somewhat out of the ordinary was the absence of a casket. Thomas's body already was aboard a liner destined for Laugharne, Wales, for burial. Following the funeral, his widow, Caitlin Macnamara Thomas, returned on the liner as well. A Dylan Thomas Fund was quickly established, but the treasurer, Philip Wittenberg, said despite generous donations funds were still lacking to cover medical bills and funeral expenses. What was more, according to Wittenberg, Mrs. Thomas and her three children were left without any discernible resources.

* * *

The month of May passed quickly and Faulkner's New York stay was too short to suit him. Yet, while the words went unspoken, Joan felt a renewed sense of freedom at his departure. *Look* magazine's location wasn't only close to Random House but also in the same building as *Esquire*. Those in junior positions from both magazines socialized on occasion; and at a one party in June, Faulkner's nagging worry that Joan would meet a young man was a fait accompli. The friend Joan went to the party with introduced her to Ezra Bowen, an Amherst classmate of his. When Joan met Ezra it was a welcome respite from Faulkner's sometimes burdensome presence. In physique and personality, Ezra stood in stark contrast to Joan's more mature suitor. Ezra was tall and athletic, a well-educated Navy veteran who laughed and conversed with ease. Her New York life was once more her own and she found herself open to a new relationship. Faulkner's intuitiveness rarely failed him and it certainly didn't that summer. Joan felt he sensed a withdrawal on her part almost as soon as she met Ezra.

The next six months were a strange and confusing time even for a relationship often in flux. After the nearness and consistency of being a genuine couple in New York, they were back to scrambling for meetings in the Mississippi woods—a beautiful memory but not something that could be recaptured. They agreed they were better than that now even though it was sometimes all they had. Joan's lackluster commitment was even more pronounced. She had a new man in her life, someone with whom she might form a lasting bond. She wanted a family. And though Faulkner railed against her marrying a "champion of the middle class," there was every reason to believe Ezra Bowen was anything but. He was a writer and editor and his mother, Catherine Drinker Bowen, an esteemed biographer.

It was a curious period too because even the new romance didn't mean Joan officially ended things that summer. Instead, she and Faulkner continued to correspond and he continued to dream. He sensed a new seriousness in Joan about her writing, especially since she planned to leave her job at *Look*. Naturally, he acknowledges in a letter, she will be afraid of the uncertain future and money will be a concern. He cautions against fear but especially fear about money, "That is death to an artist."[18] He will find her another job or support her. She means more to him than any mumble a j.p. or priest could ascribe. Something brought them together and held them together even when there was nothing physical, when her hand, as he held it, was as still and unresponsive as a child's.

In closing, he curses the Winchell thing. Walter Winchell, a well-known gossip columnist at *The New York Daily Mirror*, reported that Faulkner and Nora Stone, a friend of Joan's from Bard, took a walking tour of Ireland. Faulkner and Joan surmise that Winchell has confused Nora for Joan even though there was never a trip to Ireland. Faulkner plans to correct the fabrication for Nora and Joan's sake. While it was clearly a matter of misinformation, Faulkner calls Winchell unscrupulous and worries the matter might harm both women.

This same period elicits some of his most candid writing advice:

> Where you didn't work hard enough was in using the time I was with you to learn from me the best point of view to approach a story from, to milk it dry. Not style: I dont want you to learn my style anymore than you want to, nor do I want to help you with criticism forever anymore than you want me to. I just want you to learn, in the simplest and quickest way, to save yourself from the nervous wear and tear and emotional exhaustion of doing work that is not quite right, how to approach a story to tell it in the manner that will be closest to right that you can. Once you learn that, you wont need me or anybody.
>
> I learned to write from other writers. Why should you refuse? ... The putting of a story down on paper, the telling it, is a craft. How else can a young carpenter learn to build a house, except by helping an experienced carpenter build one? He cant learn it just by looking at finished houses. If that were so, anyone could be a carpenter, a writer.[19]

* * *

At home the predictable stresses surfaced and were intensified by his loneliness. Faulkner's letters are filled with desire and impatience. By the outset of June, he is floundering, sending letters asking her where she is. He guesses she's still in New York but admits he doesn't know. The anxious letters continue. A June 16 letter wonders if she received his telegram from Athens, Pennsylvania. (The Faulkners had been East for Jill's graduation from Pine Manor College and Faulkner's speech was later published in *The Atlantic*.) The note acknowledges the silence and distance between them. He tells her it hurts as he knew it would. For him, their love was for keeps.

As crushing as losing Joan was, so too was losing the mental and emotional escape of a love affair. These intrigues were essential for navigating his personal existence. Without the imaginative release they offered, life seemed dreary and duty bound. The big book, he tells Joan, is stymied without her presence to encourage him. There is no one at Rowan Oak to write for, to help him celebrate when the writing is going well; nothing to work toward except money. Every night for two terrible weeks in July he destroyed what he'd written that day. Miserable, he longed for a postcard from her asking him to return though his better sense told him not to imagine such happiness. His better sense, however, didn't stop him from floating ideas for possible rendezvous—from Paris to Vermont to Mexico. Ideas that seemed to fall on deaf ears.

If Faulkner was miserable, so too was Estelle. Perhaps even more so. By the end of July, she wrote her dear friends the Comminses about her plans to go to Mexico with Jill, who would attend the University of Mexico, and the swirling innuendos:

The summer has been hot and most trying—however, I've persevered and restocked our pantry with jellies, jams, preserves etc—more to be busy I dare say than from necessity—Bill has done a prodigious amount of work on his book, despite interruptions of all sorts that I've been unable to prevent—But, even at that—he is frightfully unhappy here, and Jill and I will be relieved and glad when he decides to "take off" again—

Lately though, Joan has come South—I've heard, so perhaps Jill and I will leave first after all—...Unfortunately, a man in Bill's position is an object of envy—and an awful lot of malice—A friend? of mine from Shanghai days delights in sending me accounts that could be disturbing—.[20]

* * *

Estelle's sources were correct, Joan was in Memphis, and Faulkner quickly sent a formal letter of greeting. The mid-July heat even has Faulkner complaining and he admits he's ready to be transported to a place that isn't 95 degrees. (Estelle's pleas for air conditioning at Rowan Oak went unanswered.) Rather than the usual notes of affection and sexual desire, he is anxious to hear about Joan's last story and suggests a phone call or a lunch date. In closing, he asks to be remembered to her parents. Perplexed, Joan questions the tone of the letter and he assures her it was composed to be read by her parents without raising eyebrows. They both realize Joan's mother especially is concerned about her seeing him.

The six weeks they've been apart are six years to him! A day later his letter describes her as a pretty falcon—a girl hawk—middle sized and azure colored. Her lover is a peregrine, which means distance, freedom and speed. He assures Joan that her novel is ripe. It is starting to nag and worry her, asking her to write, to make it stand up and breathe. Because she is pretty and charming and has many qualities other people want, she'll have to fight against forces asking her to choose a conventional path over her art. If she can prevail and write her novel, she will have everything. A meeting is arranged for Holly Springs where their tryst, according to Faulkner, led to a breakthrough on *A Fable*.

The sexualized language is back and he tries to lure her with a promise of an arranged meeting with Eudora Welty in Jackson, Mississippi, which doesn't come to pass. As Estelle and Jill's end of August departure date approaches, he admits he has probably overanticipated the prospect of his freedom. Such declarations raise the familiar question: why didn't he ever take the necessary steps to truly free himself?

* * *

The final phase of their affair is almost painful to consider. The slightest encouragement offered him false hope and the slightest disappointment sent him spiraling. He began to fixate on his wife's absence and Joan staying at Rowan Oak without recognizing the awkward accommodations. When Joan casually mentioned subletting her Greenwich Village apartment for the month of August, he raced ahead with all kinds of impractical and unfulfilled fantasies. Perhaps to cool things down, Joan planned a trip to the beach; and the one night she spent at Rowan Oak on her way to Florida was surreal.

As their evening together waned, Faulkner excused himself, and a bit later walked down the stairs in his RAF uniform. He was quite proud and pleased that it still fit. (Joan remembered him as very small and conscious of staying in shape and trim.) The next day he drove her to the Birmingham, Alabama, airport to catch a flight for Pensacola Beach. Another uncomfortable moment occurred when an airport employee mistook Faulkner for Joan's father.

A deflated Faulkner returned to his empty home still hoping Joan would make time for him on her return. Their meeting at a café on the square in Holly Springs as she and a female friend returned to Memphis fit his definition of "crumbs and subterfuge." His anger spilled in a letter he wrote that very evening, noted as 6:30, just home again.

> One of the nicest conveniences a woman can have is someone she can pick up when she needs him or wants him; then when she doesn't, she can drop him and know that he will be right there when she does need or want him again. Only she should remember this. Sometimes when she drops him, he might break. Sometimes, when she reaches down for him, he might not be there.

The tone doesn't soften when he tells her he still has the capacity to believe that she will do what she says she will. He maintains hope that on her return to Memphis Tuesday he'll drive up there and bring her back to Oxford with him. The pressure she dreaded reasserts when he tells her she let him down; he's needed her and his work has suffered, "I love you. Dont lie to me. I dont know which breaks my heart the most: for you to believe that you need to lie to me, or to think that you can." In a postscript he adds that he needs "help," though it was more likely companionship. He tells her he plans to visit Greenville and will call her Tuesday.[21]

The characteristic pattern was in place for a full-fledged breakdown.

Faulkner was overwrought and his plans with Joan were dashed. What happened next was eerily similar to the completion of *Absalom, Absalom!* when he took the manuscript to a friend's hunting lodge in Louisiana and forgot it. The decade-long work on *A Fable* was semi-complete and he wanted to share the manuscript and celebrate. With that in mind, he drove about 135 miles to Ben Wasson's home in Greenville, Mississippi, in the Mississippi Delta, an area that has been called "the most southern place on earth," and nicknamed "the heart and soul of the Delta."

As was his custom, Faulkner didn't phone ahead. Faulkner entered the Wasson home with his well-worn satchel. Inside the bag, as he quickly told Wasson, was the fruit of many years' labor, "Here's the manuscript of my new novel, *A Fable*. I want you to be the first to read it. I know it's my finest." After visiting Wasson's mother in her room, Faulkner continued telling his friend about the new book, "I've put everything I have into that one. It sure took it out of me, but I found out the sap's still in me even if it surges slower and more painfully now. I do want your opinion."[22]

Perhaps because Wasson himself had embraced sobriety, he missed the cues that Faulkner's mood was too elevated and trouble was around the corner. After his customary visit with Wasson's mother, Faulkner asked, "Haven't you got something in the house to drink—and not a Coca-Cola?"[23] He took the offered beer and asked his friend for help with a couple of matters. A young Black worker from Rowan Oak had driven Faulkner to Greenville. He needed to find him accommodations, and he needed to find some real liquor. This was a very special occasion after all! Faulkner's "yard boy" turned chauffeur appeared to be about 20 years old to Wasson. They left him at the El Morooco (the sign drew a chuckle from Faulkner) on Nelson Street. The hotel was for Blacks as it was pre-integration, and Nelson Street was a mini version of Beale Street in Memphis. Faulkner cautioned him not to get into any mischief; Wasson thought the young man looked "lost."

Their second errand was a little more complicated since Mississippi was still a dry state. The drive took them past plentiful Delta cotton fields and plantation tenant cabins to a liquor store selling illegal bourbon. Faulkner ribbed Wasson about not drinking—"Sorry you've gone teetotal on me, Bud"[24]—and Wasson now observed Faulkner's agitated state.

Back at the Wasson home, Ben's sister, Mary, and his brother-in-law, Charles Wilkinson, joined Faulkner for cocktails. The men had a spirited discussion about art with Faulkner trumpeting da Vinci as the all-time greatest artist and Charles citing Michelangelo. There was a dinner party that night at the Greenville county club and Faulkner readily accepted his latecomer invitation, another cue he was not quite himself. At dinner his animated state continued and Wasson now anticipated a prolonged drinking episode. The spirited dinner ended around midnight and the evening's hostess, a society doyenne of Greenville, suggested after-dinner cordials at her house.

Fearing what might occur in her beautiful and stately home, Wasson asked another couple, Bern and Franke Keating, to move the group to their house. Bern Keating, a writer-photographer, was originally from Canada, and like Faulkner, a Francophile. Once there, the after party kicked into high gear and Faulkner was in no mood to go home with Wasson. Instead, he announced he would get a motel room, and suggested to Wasson that they drive down to Biloxi on the Mississippi Gulf Coast the next day. Out of naïveté and kindness, the Keatings invited Faulkner to spend the night, a second invitation he readily accepted. Full of misgivings, Wasson said good evening.

About three a.m., the Keatings' houseguest, apparently in search of a bathroom, fell in the kitchen and cut his head. The crash alerted the couple and they did their best to stanch the bleeding with ice. Faulkner's blood-spattered tie hung on a kitchen towel rack as testimony to the nocturnal mishap. The next morning the Keatings along with Wasson transported Faulkner, who kept insisting they "go to the coast," to Oxford. Trouble appeared to also have found Faulkner's young chauffeur whom he had cautioned not to get in any scrapes. When they went by the El Morooco so he could follow them to Rowan Oak, he appeared in torn clothes with a black eye.

Hopes that Faulkner would sleep through the drive were soon dashed by intermittent requests for whiskey (which they provided), his insistence that they go to Biloxi, and continued flirtations with Franke while "beaming foolishly" at her. The two men also helped him to the side of the road off and on for nature breaks. "Bern or I [Wasson] would lead him from the car and to a sheltered place along the highway. He would get back into the car, leer at Franke and say, 'You sure are pretty,' and go to sleep, then wake up and demand that we go to the Mississippi Gulf Coast."[25]

At Rowan Oak, a miraculously revived Faulkner ushered them inside expressing his regret that Estelle wasn't there to greet them, and, appearing sober, suggested they tour the Square. At the drugstore, Faulkner's old friend, Mac Reed, asked Wasson if Faulkner was drinking. "I thought so," Reed replied.[26] The seemingly "sober" Faulkner didn't fool his friend. The group returned for a tour of the house and were amazed to witness the outline of *A Fable* on Faulkner's study wall. With Faulkner's permission, Bern took a photo that eventually appeared in *Life* magazine.

Faulkner insisted on wine to accompany Franke's dinner. Wasson noticed the display and great care he took with the inexpensive wine from California and the flourish with which he mixed the dressing and tossed the salad. Afterward, a "jovial" and flirtatious Faulkner showed his guests upstairs to their dimly lit bedrooms. With no breeze of any sort, mosquitoes buzzing, and Faulkner endlessly traipsing up and down the stairs, no one got much sleep.

Franke came to the rescue in the morning with coffee and a hot breakfast. Wasson called Faulkner's stepson, Malcolm, and filled him in on Faulkner's visit to Greenville. Malcolm showed little surprise at his stepfather's condition and promised Wasson he'd look after him. Malcolm attributed this latest binge to Faulkner being lonesome for his wife and daughter and the emotional upheaval of finishing his novel. No one knew the real source of Faulkner's despair was his failed plans with Joan and his belief that she was slipping away.

Where many people would have gladly relinquished their drunken guest, the goodhearted Keatings couldn't shake their concern. Franke asked Wasson to return to Rowan Oak with her the very next day. Wasson spent the night between trips reading *A Fable*, as Faulkner had asked, and wondered how to frame his comments. To him, the disappointing novel was uneven with parts of it "magnificent" and other parts "badly organized." He anticipated most readers finding it "too obscure and lethargic."[27]

Wasson fretted in vain because the Faulkner they found at Rowan Oak was in no condition to hear a critique. The author, back on Seconal and liquor, was passed out on the couch in his study surrounded by empty bottles, a yellow hue to his skin and dark pouches under his eyes. Franke especially was distraught that the help at Rowan Oak who were supposed to be caring for Faulkner delivered the liquor he requested. Her fresh set of eyes differed radically from the household's familiarity with such episodes. Malcolm was hoping to turn the tide with raw eggs and vitamin shots. Wasson's nagging feelings followed him to Greenville and the next day he was once again at Rowan Oak.

This time Faulkner's condition was even more deteriorated. Rather than passed out on the couch, he'd apparently tumbled off and lay in an unwashed heap beside it. Faulkner's complexion had gone from yellowish to ashen, and to Wasson, his face looked "mask-like." While he attempted to clean up his friend, a call came in from Joan for Faulkner. When Wasson relayed her simple message that she had called, he roused, "God. Godamighty," he said, before drifting off to sleep again. A second call followed from Howard Hawks' people inviting Faulkner to work on a film in Egypt, *Land of the Pharaohs*. Later, with some sobriety, Faulkner would address that request.

Wasson and Malcolm agreed the situation was out of hand and Malcolm said the sanitarium in Byhalia would be their best option. As Malcolm made the necessary arrangements, Wasson spent a few reflective moments in Faulkner's study where Faulkner remained asleep on the floor. He pondered what happened to the young man full of promise in Maud Falkner's portrait on the wall. The fame, money, and honors had done little to soothe his torment. Deeply touched by the anguish he saw in Faulkner's "tragic face,"[28] Wasson retreated.

* * *

The two friends picked up correspondence again when Wasson wrote Faulkner suggesting Bern photograph Jill's wedding. Her intended was

Paul Summers, a West Point graduate and Korean War veteran she met in the spring of 1954. Summers was unaware he was dating a literary legend's daughter—he didn't know the first thing about William Faulkner—and that revelation cinched Jill's already favorable impression. Wedding plans were soon in motion including an interview of sorts between Bern and Jill. Happily, an almost instant rapport was evident. Prior to Faulkner's arrival home, they spent the afternoon dancing to Jill's record collection. Faulkner handled the business arrangement and Bern was hired for the August 21, 1954, wedding and reception.

Like a number of other out-of-town guests, Wasson and Bern lodged at the Alumni House on the Ole Miss campus. Wasson particularly was glad to see Saxe and Dorothy Commins make the trip from New York. With its convenient location to Rowan Oak, the Alumni House, newly constructed in 1951, was the perfect site for Friday night's rehearsal dinner and party. (Paul's groomsmen, no doubt in high spirits after the rehearsal festivities, attempted a late-night serenade for Jill. They gathered below an open second-floor window at Rowan Oak and sang romantic songs familiar to West Point cadets. Instead of reaching the soon-to-be bride, the young men heard Faulkner's cough through the open window.)

The carefully arranged weekend included a prewedding luncheon Saturday, also at the Alumni House. Wasson and Bern missed the earlier two events but arrived for preceremony photographs. After an outfit change, the two men were at Rowan Oak in time to help Faulkner into his tux. Faulkner made sure to announce it was rented, "I rented this outfit, in Memphis. Just like I rented that fancy dress get-up I wore in Sweden." During a private moment between Faulkner and Wasson, Faulkner gave him an inscribed copy of *A Fable*—"To Ben: much love, much long time"—and told him he hoped the edited novel was more to his liking than the manuscript, "Saxe worked really hard with me on it. He tells me critics don't like it much, some saying it's 'muddied.' I still believe in it. I don't write for critics. Never have. And it's too late for me to start trying to please them."

He was stationed in his office while Jill and Estelle dressed upstairs. Author Shelby Foote wandered in for hellos and a waiter stopped by to announce that Estelle and Jill were ready. The reception waitstaff worked at the Peabody in Memphis and wore the hotel's traditional red coats. Wasson described the temperature that day as "torrid."[29]

Bern was delighted with his role as family photographer. The Faulkner he encountered August 21 was a far cry from the man he met in Greenville. Faulkner was composed as he, Estelle, and Jill made their way down the stairs. Estelle wore a blue gown from New York and Jill a lace-trimmed satin gown with a sheer veil flowing from her bridal cap. At the bottom,

Faulkner kissed his wife and daughter. It was a tender moment for the family to relish. The three then paused for a champagne toast and photographs. Estelle demurred on the toast but Faulkner insisted. (That one drink proved her undoing as the evening progressed.)

From the home place, the wedding party traveled to St. Peter's Episcopal Church for the ceremony. Vicki was maid of honor to a radiant Jill, and cousin Dean, a bridesmaid. Naturally attention shifted toward the bride, and where one might expect compliments on her beauty, Faulkner's aside to Shelby Foote—"Isn't Jill the perfect virgin?"[30]—puzzled. Most fathers would steer clear of commenting on their daughter's virginity. In his case, given all the attention Faulkner paid to Joan's modesty and inexperience, and especially the dominant theme of virginity in *The Sound and the Fury*, it was even more curious.

* * *

Faulkner and Estelle worked the wedding reception like pros. They seemed genuinely to be enjoying their guests and the nature of the occasion. The intimate church ceremony, with carefully selected and arranged flowers and candles, was followed by the gathering in Estelle's rose garden. Estelle's talents with decorating and social finesse were evident throughout the ambitious celebration. Champagne was offered until gone and then white wine was provided. A burst of tossed rice accompanied Jill and Paul's exit. Besides her abundant happiness with the groom, Jill undoubtedly felt exhilarated by the promise of a new life.

The couple planned to live in Charlottesville where Paul would attend law school at University of Virginia. She of course worried about her mother and secured a much-needed promise from Faulkner. He would finally open a checking account for Estelle so she had funds and independence during his frequent absences. Her father felt relief as well. Jill, he determined, was more Faulkner than Oldham, banishing his worry that the opposite might be true. "The Oldhams are very unstable people," he once confided in Jimmy. "I've been watching Jill carefully for a long time now, and she hasn't got any of the Oldham characteristics."[31]

The distance from Oxford meant Jill would no longer endure the day-to-day stress of her parents' rollercoaster life. The unpredictability of their drinking and arguing haunted her since childhood. Relatives like Sallie Murry Williams understood Jill's plight. "You would never know if you went down there," she said, "what kind of fix things would be in."[32] Sallie told Faulkner she feared for his health if he didn't stop drinking. His reply confirmed the hopelessness of that outcome: "If I can't lead a normal life," he said, "I'd just as soon be dead."[33] Now, for their daughter at least, stability seemed at hand, commencing with her honeymoon in Mexico. The trip allowed her to escape a classic meltdown that sent her father and mother to Wright's.

After the couple's lively sendoff, observers noted that her parents appeared dejected. "I saw that Bill, for a moment caught off-guard, looked downcast," Wasson recalled. "He and Estelle stood together, with wine-glasses in their hands, watching the automobile drive away from Rowan Oak." The warm family embrace they recently had shared made the moment bittersweet. By the time Saxe and Dorothy retired for the evening, Faulkner and Estelle were in their cups. Faulkner was now drinking whiskey and Estelle wasn't holding back either. The Comminses would have chuckled had they known that earlier in the evening Faulkner asked Wasson's assistance in removing an unruly reception guest. He wanted it quietly handled. "Too much drinking," Faulkner said, "was inexcusable and very bad-mannered."[34]

The situation hadn't improved the next day when the Comminses came for lunch and to say their goodbyes. Faulkner was wandering around without clothes swearing someone took $50 out of his trousers. Estelle looked forlorn, and after an unfortunate fall from her chair at lunch, went to bed. Faulkner likewise followed. The loss of Jill had fully registered with her parents. It fell to Vicki, a new driver without even a license, to care for her grandparents. For days Vicki tried to at least keep the beds clean. Her grandmother she described as "blotto," drinking to pass out with no memory of the preceding days. Her grandfather was on a drunken rant calling for Malcolm to take him to Byhalia.

Even in his debilitated state, Faulkner realized Vicki was in over her head. She couldn't drive with any real confidence, and she certainly couldn't drive to the bootleggers for the liquor Faulkner wanted. Once again Malcolm came through and safely deposited Faulkner at Wright's where he stayed from August 29 until September 1. When Vicki returned one afternoon from her careful drive to town for groceries, Faulkner was sitting on the front porch. Having "dried out" he was in a good mood, and laughingly told Vicki he knew she was in for trouble with her unruly grandparents. Unfortunately, the trouble persisted with Estelle. It's possible she was never completely sober after Jill's wedding until after her five-day stay at Wright's, September 15–19. Yet, it was a turning point of sorts. Estelle made her last visit to Wright's on July 10, 1955, staying five days, with a discharge card that read "alcoholism, acute."[35] It would be her last visit to Wright's before fully embracing sobriety. Vicki marveled at her grandmother's accomplishment. Faulkner likewise was quite proud of his wife though he kept a watchful eye on her for years thinking she would backslide. Estelle had done it, Vicki said, "Without too damn much help from him, either."[36]

* * *

In the fall of 1953, as the world continued to close in on him, he was hardly up to the challenge of the *Life* feature, "The Private World of William Faulkner." *Life* ran the two-part article September 28 and October 2, 1953. Since late spring 1951, the article's possibility swarmed around him like gnats, and he was dead set against it, writing Robert Haas, "I have deliberately buried myself in this little lost almost illiterate town, to keep out of the way so that news people wont notice and remember me. If in spite of that, this sort of thing comes down here, I not only wont co-operate, I will probably do whatever I can to impede and frustrate it."[37] Random House welcomed the publicity; and what was more, Robert Coughlan was a friend of Harrison Smith. All of which did nothing to budge their recalcitrant author.

When Coughlan showed up on the porch of Rowan Oak August 16, 1951, to introduce himself, Estelle looked "startled and horrified."[38] Faulkner asked him to leave but then softened, perhaps realizing his harsh behavior was at odds with the civility and hospitality he liked Rowan Oak to project. He offered the reporter a beer and they talked a bit after he made it clear personal questions were off limits. He even offered to show him some locations that were composites for fictional settings. That outing didn't come to pass. Word reached Faulkner that the questions Coughlan was asking were of a personal nature. For nine excruciating days as Coughlan collected interviews in Oxford, Faulkner felt his world invaded. One day the two men passed each other on the street and Faulkner didn't speak. The article was far from inflammatory. The piece was a full, engaging look at the Faulkner family, Oxford, and the southern milieu dictating Faulkner's themes. It did, however, address Faulkner's drinking, describing him as "an alcoholic refugee, self-pursued."[39]

Faulkner's uncle, J.W.T. II, added color, telling the reporter his nephew "never was nothin' but a writer" and that "He just wouldn't work." A fellow classmate remembers Faulkner's ready response when he was very young and asked about a grownup occupation. "I want to be a writer," Faulkner invariably replied, "like my great-granddaddy."[40] Coughlan surmised Oxford residents simply explained away Faulkner's peculiarities:

> The town was used to expecting the unexpected from the Faulkner family, who were famous for a self-assurance that made them oblivious to the opinions of others. The common explanation of William's behavior was, "It's the Faulkner in him." On the other hand, the Faulkners were proud, aristocratic and considered snobbish.[41]

The reporter chose not to include unflattering and disparaging remarks from Phil Stone about Faulkner's inability to handle success, and that the complexity of his prose actually reflected his inability to spell, punctuate, or grasp basic grammatical principles.

Despite the article's adversarial subject, the writer captured Faulkner's essence. Blotner proclaimed Coughlan's "description of the man himself [the] best ever written."[42] Coughlan wrote:

> His is not a split personality, but rather a fragmented one, loosely held together by some strong inner force, the pieces often askew and sometimes painfully in friction. It is to ease these pains, one can guess, that he escapes periodically and sometimes for periods of weeks in alcoholism, until his drinking has become legendary in the town and in his profession, and hospitalizations and injections have on occasion been necessary to save his life.[43]

So it was that those professional interventions would soon be necessary.

* * *

Though he had almost two years to stew and fume about the *Life* article, Faulkner was still unprepared for its reality. He might have harbored a fear his indiscretions would surface—an alarming threat! Already absorbed with worry of losing Joan, and confronted with the attention generated by the article, he turned to the usual toxic combination of drink and Seconal. On September 26, Joan's 25th birthday, and just one day shy of Faulkner's 56th birthday, he checked in to Wright's for a two-week stay. Earlier in the month he had insisted on a premature discharge after a mere two days. Those false recoveries were part of his cycle.

His medical charts now skirted back pain and cited treatment for his alcoholism, "an acute and chronic alchoholic." The Old Country Club no doubt calmed his state of mind and nourished his body, but made no pretense of helping him conquer his drug and alcohol abuse. His condition was noted merely as "improved" on October 4 when he left Wright's with a hefty sanatorium bill.[44]

Faulkner's anger likely hampered a full return to vitality from his weakened condition. Upon his discharge from Wright's he fired off a spirited letter to Phil Mullen, one of Coughlan's interview subjects. Sweden awarded him the Nobel Prize, France the Légion d'Honneur, while his native land invaded his privacy over his emphatic wishes to the contrary: "No wonder people in the rest of the world dont like us, since we seem to have neither taste nor courtesy, and know and believe in nothing but money and it doesn't matter how you get it."[45]

Oxford simply had become intolerable and he reached out to Joan for help. Given her usual ambivalence, he must have been surprised when she agreed to fly from New York City and drive back to New York with him. It was a convoluted and puzzling travel solution. Instead of flying to New York himself he met Joan's incoming flight at the Memphis airport where he immediately was recognized. Red flags were going off but dismissed in his eagerness to get out of town.

They drove east in his old, gray station wagon with the first day of driving left to Joan. At one point she missed a curve and ran off the road, badly scaring them both. As he began to feel stronger, Faulkner helped with the driving. For Joan, the long drive was compounded by guilt. She hadn't told her family she was even in Memphis—albeit briefly. This haunted her because her mother was in the hospital having her tonsils removed, a serious operation for someone her age. Whether or not Faulkner appreciated her family conflict isn't clear. His hope that her cooperation signaled a fresh start loomed large.

* * *

The promise of their clandestine departure from Memphis carried them through part of October. Joan was still in her small Greenwich Village apartment on Horatio Street and Faulkner settled at One Fifth Avenue, a residential hotel adjoining Washington Square not far from the Village. His accommodations included a sitting area and bedroom. Besides his writing area in the suite, Faulkner provided Joan a card table and typewriter where she worked most mornings. He encouraged her to write an epistolary novel about their good fortune as "soul mates to spin round in orbit together a while."[46]

Faulkner would walk forty blocks to Random House as progress continued on *A Fable*. Saxe Commins was out recovering from a heart attack and Faulkner worked in his office. He credited Joan's diligence with helping him finish his novel, and upon its 1957 release, she received a copy with his inscription, "This should have been the first copy off the press since if you had not been working hard then so that I had to work to keep up with you, I never would have taken myself in hand and finished it."[47]

Seemingly, they had picked up where they left off in May. There were dinners, theater, and social events. An especially poignant date was seeing Edmond Rostand's *Cyrano de Bergerac*. Faulkner rarely gave Joan gifts but for her birthday he had given her a small bell from Tiffany's. It was a sentimental gift meant to echo lines from Rostand's play—Roxane's name is in Cyrano's heart like a bell; should he tremble thinking of her the bell shakes and rings. The small necklace with the tiny bell attached became part of Faulkner and Joan's courtship. Experiencing the play together no doubt triggered a host of emotions.

Their relationship was in a limbo of sorts in which the age and sexual tensions would recede only to come to the fore. Yet they might have gone on had it not been for a blustery October afternoon when Joan bumped into Ezra as he made his way to the employment office. He was the victim

Twelve. I Wont Stop In: 1953

of a layoff at *Esquire*. With little fanfare, he was back in her life and she saw both men. Unlike the fitful starts and stops she and Faulkner knew, there was an intensity to dating Ezra. Two months after his wind-bound reappearance, Ezra met Joan's parents in Memphis at Christmas.

If Faulkner sensed a rival when Joan first met Ezra that summer he was morosely confident one existed by fall. Joan's manner of parting from him was a gradual drifting away. And while he might have anticipated a younger man coming into her life, that didn't stop the raw passions from surfacing. He sent her an angry letter acknowledging things had changed between them:

> I wont stop in. If this is the end, and I suppose, assume it is, I think the two people drawn together as we were and held together for four years by whatever it was we had, knew—love, sympathy, understanding, trust, belief—deserve a better period than a cup of coffee—not to end like two high school sweethearts breaking up over coca cola in the corner drugstore.[48]

In November, even with the discomfort of their estrangement, Faulkner and Joan spent Thanksgiving at the Comminses' Princeton home. The holiday included work as well as festivities. At long last it was time to organize *A Fable*'s manuscript pages. Faulkner was delighted to have Joan's help with the carelessly collected but fortunately numbered pages. The nearly decade-long work was complete and Faulkner noted on page 654, the manuscript's conclusion—"Oxford, December 1944 / New York and Princeton, November 1953."

* * *

The end for the couple wasn't as clear and orderly. This relationship operated on intimation and nuance. Rarely did they speak directly and there were no decisive steps toward a shared future. Angry outbursts generally were limited to letters. As Joan became more unavailable, Faulkner eventually resigned himself. The quagmire had to be resolved. When he told her he was leaving she didn't protest. Yet his practical nature was troubled by the groceries in his One Fifth Avenue apartment and he wanted her to have them. He told her he would bring them to her apartment. Joan recalled:

> And it was very early in the morning, and I was asleep and I heard this rattling outside the door and there was just this one moment when I sat and thought about it and thought I don't want this to end like this. And in that moment of indecision while I was lying there listening to the rattling of his putting the packages down outside the door it was all it took. Because by the time I got to the door. I ran out to the street. And he was gone. And so I can only think that he had a taxicab waiting for him because there was no way he could have

walked off that quickly. And I thought about that a lot. If I hadn't—just that one moment's hesitation what, how it might have changed things if I'd said, opened the door and said, "Oh, well don't leave."[49]

* * *

The affair that had consumed his imagination and fueled his desire was over. Almost consecutively his opus concluded. For both driving forces of his life to end at once was devastating. That sizeable letdown increased when the new novel failed to find a readership. Worse, Faulkner himself was far from pleased with it. Vicki felt the disappointment cast a lingering shadow. Jill agreed her father "was dissatisfied with it when it was finished.... The theme is religious, so this was to be a great work. But it wasn't. I think he knew it all along. He knew that he was out of his element ... he made this big play about dedicating it ... but he never mentioned it again."[50]

When he tried to turn to new projects, they didn't excite him as they once had. Life without an intrigue seemed unfathomable, as did life without his twin remedies of liquor and Seconal. Within a month of parting from Joan, he tried to recreate a similar, age-disparate affair, with a 19-year-old American student. Jean Stein was studying at the Sorbonne in Paris and met Faulkner at a party in St. Moritz, Switzerland, hosted by Howard Hawks. There was little to sustain the affair and the end wasn't a crushing blow like losing Joan. Faulkner wrote as much in a letter when he admitted his heart wasn't in it, telling Joan that what remained to him of this in his life, he had already given to her. Even Estelle had had enough of him. Her letter to Commins in the spring of 1954 makes that very clear:

> For the past two springs I felt physically unable to do much, and as Bill was away most of the time, Rowan oak has suffered from neglect.... I was just on the verge of writing Bill that I was suing for divorce—I still believe it the only wise thing to do.... Bill has been home very little the past four years, and a good bit of that time spent here, has been a nightmare of drunkenness—he must be very unhappy—so the only cure I know of is to help him get free—legally—Heaven only knows he has been free in every other sense.[51]

(Apparently Commins advised against dissolving her 25-year marriage. Three years later, however, Estelle offered Faulkner his freedom. He declined.)

The years that followed were a circuitous journey through familiar patterns—overdrinking, domestic unrest, and deepening mental and emotional issues. Particular low-water mark years were 1955 and 1956 with six hospitalizations, four occurring at Wright's. His two-week sojourn in Nagano City, Japan, in 1955, as a lecturer on American literature to an audience of Japanese professors, was a disturbing if entertaining debacle. The byline under his photograph in the August 15, 1955, *Time* magazine read: "Tourist Faulkner. Gin for all." The article went on to explain Faulkner's absence from Tokyo's Foreign Correspondents Club appearance, "Attended by a doctor and nurse, Tourist Faulkner was bedded down at International House laid low by the heat, lack of nourishment (he abstained from food during his entire transpacific flight), and too many toasts of welcome."[52]

Grasping for solid ground, he adopted a number of inauthentic incarnations. Though Faulkner had cut personal ties with him without Bezzerides ever having a clue as to why, Buzz followed the last years of his once close friend, even working on a documentary script about Faulkner's life.

> Stories were told to me about how he was always drunk, always had a bottle of wine or whiskey during his stay at the University of Virginia, made a ritual of drinking there. To me, Bill seemed to have become a victim of his own legend and was living a part that seemed totally false: the esteemed writer, the Nobel winner. The man who had written these great things bore no relationship to the young man who had written these wonderful things he had written when he was a struggling writer trying to make a scratch, trying to earn a living, writing things he was impelled to write, not written deliberately, but impelled to write because they came out of his subconscious.... He was living a role that seemed fraudulent to me. It seemed sad.... I think in the end it got to him that he was living the kind of life that he was living. I feel strongly he must have been aware of the fraudulency of what he was doing.[53]

Without ever finding a way out of the morass of addictions, all paths led to the old country club.

Thirteen

Mississippi Ghosts: 1962

The last two arrivals at Wright's Sanatorium on Thursday, July 5, 1962, included a subdued Faulkner and a rowdy female latecomer from Greenville, Mississippi. Both were assigned rooms on the main floor near the nurses' station. Nurse Moore took over Faulkner's care when Nurse Burrow's shift ended at 11 p.m. The transition to restfulness Estelle and Jimmy hoped for him seemed to occur. The order to summon Dr. Wright if Faulkner was not asleep by midnight was apparently unnecessary. Nothing indicates Dr. Wright was called. However, at 12:40 a.m. Faulkner was in abdominal distress. Presumably his personal attendant alerted the nurse. His symptoms were treated with a combined dose of Paregoric and Kalpec to ease intestinal cramping. But something was still agitating him.

Faulkner was wide awake and uncomfortable; the brief respite vanished. There are various versions of what happened next. Jimmy's recollection, detailed in a *Southern Living* article almost thirty years after his uncle's death, describes his conversation with Dr. Wright around 2 a.m. after Estelle had been notified, "The nurse was in Brother Will's room shortly after midnight. He sat up while she gave him a shot. Then he put his right hand over his heart, groaned, and lay back down." Dr. Wright was on the scene in five minutes but was unable to resuscitate. "He worked with Brother Will for nearly an hour," Jimmy said, "but he couldn't bring him back."[1] In an interview with Sally Wolff published in 1996, Jimmy's account is somewhat different:

> At 1:30 a.m. the phone rang. Nan, my wife, picked it up. I was told that Brother Will had just died. "He had a heart attack," they [Wright's staff] later said to me. Before he died, he sat up on the side of the bed; the nurse gave him a shot to quiet him down; he groaned and lay back down; and then he died. Brother Will had never had any sign of heart trouble.[2]

More disturbing yet is the scenario a nurse from Wright's recounted to Joan Williams. The nurse told Joan that Faulkner received an injection and ran outside of the sanatorium in his pajamas where he collapsed.

Then, there is Dr. Wright's account provided four years after Faulkner's death in an interview with Blotner. Faulkner was awake and sitting on the side of the bed. It was around 1:30 when he groaned and fell over. Dr. Wright was summoned from his on-site premises and within moments was at the patient's side where he was unable to find a pulse or heartbeat. Despite life-saving measures of the time period, cardiopulmonary resuscitation and mouth-to-mouth breathing, a miracle was not at hand.

Faulkner's handwritten patient card records his strange and sudden passing under "Condition on Discharge." Here the card reads "Expired 1:30 p.m." (the p.m. being in error). For "Final Diagnosis" the card states, "Acute Pulmonary Edema, Probable Cardiac Origin."[3] The diagnosis of acute pulmonary edema, a buildup of fluid in the lungs, would not have been expected given the thorough cardiac exam he'd undergone just six months previous at Tucker Neurological and Psychiatric Hospital in Richmond, Virginia. The cardiologist, Dr. Paul Camp, determined his heart was not enlarged and his blood pressure normal. Likewise, the electrocardiogram results revealed normal rhythm and good tracing for a man in his mid-sixties.

If Faulkner received an injection it was not recorded, either because of the commotion surrounding the doctor and staff's emergency response or because it was deemed best omitted. There are no notations in the doctor's order book indicating an injection; and the sanatorium drug book, a handwritten record of patients who received controlled substances and the dosage, does not include Faulkner on July 5 or 6. The day orders that existed for July 6 listed alcohol and Betalin (a multi-vitamin injection). Those instructions, no longer relevant, had a red strike-through.[4]

What happened in the cloistered environs of Wright's when they realized William Faulkner was dead? They got him out of there as quickly and efficiently as they knew how and he wasn't the first patient dispatched forthwith. Sanatorium expense records show two separate payments of $20 for ambulance fees to Brantley Funeral Home in Olive Branch, Mississippi, located about ten miles from Byhalia. The patients involved were transported September 3, 1956, and November 12, 1956. Brantley Funeral Home also received a $15 payment for flowers on October 6, 1956.[5]

During their phone call in the very early morning hours of July 6, Jimmy told Dr. Wright he would like his uncle's body returned to Oxford. Dr. Wright assured him that was underway, telling him "We've already sent him home."[6] Faulkner was most likely in a Brantley Funeral Home ambulance by the time the conversation occurred. Dr. Wright also would have signed the medical certification portion of the death certificate establishing time and cause of death, a document available only to immediate family members. No autopsy was performed. Even as they dealt with their shock and grief, Estelle and Jimmy were committed to keeping the location of Faulkner's death quiet. The last thing they wanted was a headline revealing the Nobel laureate had died in a sanatorium or "drying out place."

The dizzying sequence of events—from Faulkner's last breath at 1:30 a.m. to his private funeral service the next day—was astounding. Once the news from Byhalia reached Jimmy and his father, Johncy, Faulkner's brother, they went straight to Rowan Oak to check on Estelle. Jimmy had immediately called the family physician, Chester McLarty, to see about her. Dr. McLarty gave her a sedative, but for some time Estelle, hands clasped, continued to pace her bedroom floor. "I can't believe it," she said, "I can't believe it. He's not gone. He's not gone."[7]

Father and son decided it best for Jimmy to remain at Rowan Oak and handle details while Johncy headed to the Douglass Funeral Home located just off the edge of the Square. He arrived before the ambulance from Byhalia and sat on the steps outside thinking about not only Bill, but also his other brother, Dean, who had been gone now 27 years. "I realized suddenly that I was living, for the moment, in memories. I realized too that that was where Bill would be from now on," Johncy said. "I think it was then, as I sat there in the soft summer night, that I first accepted the fact that Bill was gone."[8]

Soon enough he heard the ambulance arrive and Faulkner's stretcher, placed on a dolly, was rolled to the embalming room. Johncy waited at the funeral home until they were finished with Faulkner about 8 a.m., leaving only once to place a call to Phil Stone. Another important detail he took care of was securing the family's privacy. He asked the owner of Douglass Funeral Home, who also was the mayor of Oxford, to station a guard at the gate of Rowan Oak as long as Faulkner's body was in the home. His request was granted and a policeman was in place by the time the hearse passed through that morning.

There was one bit of clarity amid the fast-moving preparations. Faulkner's wishes regarding his service were well known to Estelle and Jimmy. He wanted it just like his mother's, Maud Falkner, who passed October 16, 1960. Maud was unambiguous in her requests: an inexpensive funeral—no flowers—no embalming—and a simple coffin. "I want to get back to earth as fast as I can," she told Jimmy. For her service, she stipulated family only. Jimmy was with Faulkner when he selected Maud's coffin. Thus, Jimmy was confident when he decided on a gray, felt-covered wooden coffin like his grandmother's. He also delivered Faulkner's clothes to the funeral home. Meanwhile, family members were arriving, Jill and her husband, Paul Summers, from Virginia; Estelle's daughter, Victoria, and her husband Bill Fielding, from Caracas; Estelle's son, Malcolm, from South Carolina; and Murry "Jack" Faulkner, the other remaining brother, from Mobile, Alabama.

It was early morning on July 6 when Faulkner's body was returned to Rowan Oak. His coffin, on a wheeled funeral bier, was placed in the parlor in front of the fireplace. Yet the solemnity of the moment was quickly dashed. Estelle's sister, Dorothy, took one look at the austere coffin and decided it needed to be returned. When Douglass Funeral home retrieved the coffin, they took its occupant with it. Jimmy was speechless when he came down stairs and saw the empty space. His Uncle Jack advised him to let it be. "Bill's up there laughing like hell right now over the trouble he's causing at his own funeral," Jack said.[9] Jimmy was later able to see the humor in the coffin caper, though he described the replacement as an "atrocious damn thing."[10]

Dorothy had chosen a coffin made of "cypress wood, covered with a darker grey all-wool felt. The hardware was larger, heavy plated silver. It had a plain tailored interior. There was a cypress box in the ground which went around it."[11] Keeping strictly in line with Faulkner's wishes, once the coffin was closed it was not to be opened again, the only exception being an old southern tradition which allowed for a viewing by the family's domestics. And indeed, some of the Rowan Oak help as well as some of Faulkner's Black friends asked to see him. Estelle naturally agreed. The funeral director remained in the parlor with the group, opened the coffin for them, and then closed it for the last time.

Estelle made allowances for a few close local friends like Ben Wasson to attend the service, and others like fellow authors William Styron and Shelby Foote and Random House executives Donald Klopfer and Bennet Cerf from New York. Before leaving his Westchester County home for Oxford, Cerf told reporters he was "terribly shocked. I saw him a few weeks ago and he was bursting with health and happier than he had seemed to be in many years."[12] (Cerf had been a favorite of Estelle's at Random House; but after Faulkner's funeral service and before he returned to the Peabody in Memphis where he was staying, he asked Estelle if there were any manuscripts in the house. The timing of his question struck her as untoward and she was not very receptive to him afterward.)

"Besides being one of the greatest authors of our times," Cerf said, "he was about as fine a gentleman as I have ever met in my whole life.... His literary impact was simply enormous. He has the respect of every type of author. Every other author in America looks upon Bill Faulkner as one of our all-time greats."[13]

Random House executives provided Faulkner's comprehensive book sales to *The New York Times*, citing about 10,000,000 copies sold in hardcover and paperback editions. Other spin-off publications of paperback Faulkner works included Vintage series, Signet series, and Dell Publishing Company that brought out one novel, *Mosquitoes* (original hardcover publication date 1927 by Boni and Liveright). Dell reported sales of around a half-million.

A flurry of cables and messages poured in from around the world including a tribute from President John F. Kennedy released just hours after Faulkner's death, "It can be said with assurance of few men, in any area of human activity, that their work will long endure. William Faulkner was one of those men. Since Henry James, no writer has left behind such a vast and enduring monument to the strength of American literature."[14] (Three months earlier, Faulkner regretted the President and Mrs. Kennedy's invitation to dine at the White House, explaining that "Why that's a 1000 miles away. That a long way to go just to eat."[15])

Other outsiders were not so welcome. Worries about the press bedeviled Estelle and Jimmy from the outset of the unwelcome news. When they conferred early morning July 6, Jimmy suggested they tell reporters that Faulkner died of a heart attack in his sleep at Rowan Oak. Estelle agreed but assured him the truth would come out. Jimmy hoped to stall the press until his uncle's death was "back-page news."[16]

They started getting phone calls from the press about 7:30 a.m., July 6, and other reporters tried to approach the house but were turned away by the guard. In an effort to mollify, Jack and Jimmy, a retired Marine lieutenant colonel, met with a group of the press in a back area of Aubrey Seay's Mansion restaurant, a favorite of Faulkner and Estelle's. Jack was the perfect envoy for the meeting; a well-mannered southern gentleman who was also an FBI special agent, he was gracious but stern. Polite handshakes went around when Seay introduced the press to the Faulkners. Hughes Rudd was among the group gathered.

Rudd's *Saturday Evening Post* article published a year later would explore the nebulous details surrounding Faulkner's death. Jack related that the family "wanted to make certain there would be no unpleasant scene, no disturbance at the funeral."[17] Of utmost concern was preserving decorum and dignity. The audacious request to take a photograph of "Bill in his coffin and Estelle in her grief"[18] was denied. Jack and Jimmy once again confirmed Faulkner's wishes. He wanted to belong to his family "until the hearse passed out of his gate on the way to the cemetery. After that moment he belonged to the public, the world."[19]

Public word was indeed spreading by way of newspapers and it was front-page news. Major newspapers related the same statements, that William Faulkner, 64 years old, died in the Oxford, Mississippi, hospital at 2:30 a.m. on July 6. *The New York Times* added that his wife, Estelle, was by his side. Various headlines conveyed Faulkner's prominence: *The Memphis Press-Scimitar*, an afternoon paper (July 6, 1962): "William Faulkner, Literary Giant, Dies in Oxford: Death Stills Pen of Nobel and Pulitzer Prize

Winner"; *The [Memphis] Commercial Appeal* (July 7, 1962): "Faulkner Rites Will Be Today at Family Home"; and *The New York Times* (July 7, 1962): "William Faulkner Is Dead in Mississippi Home Town."

The Commercial Appeal's Mississippi edition (July 7, 1962)—"Writer Believed Man Immortal: Faulkner Described Works as 'Agony and Sweat of Human Spirit'"—dedicated almost the entire front page to Faulkner. The edition included the text of his Nobel speech, the sweeping array of tributes from dignitaries and literary luminaries, and a summary of his numerous letters to the editor regarding integration: "His letters usually brought a cascade of responses—praising and damning Mr. Faulkner and his position."

The New York Times carried extensive coverage, reprinting Faulkner's Yoknapatawpha map of his fictional kingdom; interviewing fellow authors Irving Stone, Robert Frost, John Dos Passos, British novelist Charles Snow, and Pearl Buck (whom Faulkner disparagingly referred to as Mrs. Chinahand Buck). Fellow Mississippian Eudora Welty offered the most illuminating assessment to The Associated Press:

> William Faulkner saw all the world in his fictional county where we can see it now—where he made it live. His work is a triumphant vision. This vision, like life itself, has its light and dark, its time and place, and love and battle.... What is great and phony, what is tragic and uproarious about us in all our own dogged lives everywhere, is a living life itself on any page of his.[20]

The formality of the tributes surely would have amused Faulkner, who loved a good laugh as well as anyone. Seay related to Rudd a story he'd heard from Faulkner not long before his death:

> One of his favorites the last time I saw him was about the farmer who was down plowing in the field when his little chap came running up to him. "Daddy," says the little chap, "They's a preacher up to the house and Mama says for you to come up right away." Well, the farmer studies awhile, and then he says to the boy, "You run on back to the house, and if it's an Episcopal preacher, you tell your Ma to give him a cup of coffee. If it's a Methodist preacher, tell her to start frying up chicken. But if it's a Baptist preacher, you set in your Ma's lap till I gets to the house."[21]

* * *

The various newspapers ran also an array of sidebar stories. One such by Paul Flowers, a friend of Jimmy Faulkner's, focused on Oxford's reaction. "Storied Oxford Unruffled at 'Curious Bill's' Passing," predicted that his death would be of more significance in New York, London, Paris and Tokyo, because Oxford

> was where they knew 'Bill' Faulkner as a man, and in the ancient tradition of the Old South, they let him go his own (to them peculiar) way as he let them

go theirs.... Few people in [Oxford] had read Faulkner's score of books, novels and collections of short stories, but they were familiar with the man, slight of stature with a neat mustache, who lived by moods.[22]

Locally there were numerous comments on Faulkner's seeming aloofness, how he might cordially greet an individual one day and the next time look straight through them. "Everything from [Faulkner's] novels is in Oxford," Rudd determined:

> either present or remembered.... And perhaps for those who live in Oxford reading the books would seem merely repetition, the events part of the town's shared experience and recollection, experience and recollection immediately familiar to the Southerner no matter where he may be; always strange, Gothic, bizarre and melodramatic to those outside the South. And even now, in this death, there was something strange, and the reporters knew it.[23]

It is remarkable that with the league of journalists and correspondents in Oxford—five alone from *Life* magazine, three from the Columbia Broadcasting System, as well as *Time* magazine, the National Broadcasting Company, *The New York Times*, both Memphis newspapers, United Press International and Associated Press—the site of Faulkner's death went unchallenged. Rudd's article, "The Death of William Faulkner," links Faulkner's unknowability to his puzzling death, "All his life he remained an enigma to the little town his novels had made famous. Even his death, a year ago this month, was attended by an atmosphere of mystery."

Rudd, part of the press brigade at the time of Faulkner's death, wrote, "The first wire-service stories said William Faulkner has died in Oxford, and we came to Oxford believing it. But soon, in guarded conversations, in looks, in smiles, we were not quite told the truth but pointed toward it."[24] Facts could not be confirmed. No one could say which hospital he died in or if he died at home. Reporters had no access to Rowan Oak or the family outside of their brief meeting with Jimmy and Jack at the Mansion restaurant. Incrementally, details emerged about Byhalia and the "alcoholic clinic there."

The word around Oxford was that Faulkner died at the clinic, "some said in a convulsion, some said in a fall downstairs. Mrs. Faulkner was with him when he died, everyone said. As for proof, there was none. The superintendent of the clinic [Wright's] wouldn't talk, and the death certificate gave Oxford as the place of death. The family wanted it that way, everyone said."

Amazingly, the visiting reporters gathered in a room at the Ole Miss motel and "agreed to forget Byhalia." It couldn't be proved and what difference would it make? "We were there because a great man was dead, not because a man had died in an alcoholic clinic."[25] When they had an opportunity at the Mansion meeting, no one asked the Faulkner representatives about Wright's Sanatorium and the swirling rumors.

* * *

Timing was such that Joan was still visiting her parents in Memphis. She was stunned to read of Faulkner's death in the morning paper. During her current visit, she'd met Edwin Howard, a former Southwest College classmate and current *Press-Scimitar* reporter, at a friend's barbeque. Howard had reviewed her first novel, *The Morning and the Evening*, and they'd talked a good deal at the party about Faulkner. They agreed that *The Sound and the Fury* topped their best-novel list and that his newly released book, *The Reivers*, was a charming departure.

Joan called Howard to see if he was going to Faulkner's funeral and asked if she might ride with him. By 8 a.m. Saturday the pair was in Oxford. On the drive down, Joan told Howard she'd just visited Faulkner last Sunday at Rowan Oak. She had spoken with Mrs. Faulkner and her sister, Dorothy, as well, and then they left her and Faulkner alone on the front porch. "He said he was not writing another book, that he never writes in the summer. Oh, I just can't believe it."[26]

Howard, who was covering the author's service for his newspaper, felt a hush over the Oxford courthouse square as they rolled into town. His first stop was the Douglass Funeral Home where he received a less-than-cordial greeting from the exhausted manager Richard Patton. "I oughtn't to tell you," Patton said, "I been up all night on this Faulkner funeral. Folks from all over wantin' to know about it."[27] Howard felt his next stop as a journalist should be Rowan Oak, but Joan convinced him not to intrude. Instead they drove to the cemetery where the labors of the gravediggers forced a reckoning with reality. As the two men toiled with red clay earth Joan wept. Faulkner's singularity followed him even in death: his resting spot was in the new section and a good distance from the three generations of Falkners who preceded him.

From the cemetery, Joan and Howard made their way to a place Faulkner always felt welcome, the Rexall drug store, formerly the Gathright-Reed Drug Store, that doubled as a lending library and social hub. There they found Shelby Foote and William Styron. Over coffee they talked of Faulkner's legacy. "I'll just miss knowing he's here," Joan said, "it's so hard to realize that there'll be no more books from him. And yet he has left us a great body of work. I think his stature will grow."

Foote was even bolder in his pronouncements. "It's a curious thing," he said, "but a man's death seems to give shape to his whole life. The four great writers of our time—Faulkner, Fitzgerald, Wolfe and Hemingway—are gone now, and I don't think there is any question that Faulkner stands above them all, both for the volume and quality of his work." Foote applauded also Faulkner's willingness to experiment: "He always reached beyond himself. He was not always successful, but his work was greater because of the things he was willing to try." Howard championed Faulkner's success, noting he couldn't think of another southern author of his stature. Of that there was little to dispute. It even drew a chuckle from Foote who quoted Flannery O'Connor, "When you hear the Dixie Special coming down the line," she had said, "you better get off the track."[28]

Howard mistakenly believed the home service was open to the press but now understood that was not the case. He decided to spend the free time researching the truth and fiction of *The Reivers*. That quest took him a few miles out of town to a small shack on State Highway 6 where Earl Worthham, Faulkner's blacksmith, worked.

> I been shoein' horses for Mr. Bill ten or fifteen years, I reckon, I knowed him since I was a little boy.... He was fine little boy, but he was always different. They had a nurse for him and the other children they called "Nanny." I remember she used to walk 'em downtown and all the children would walk on the board sidewalk 'cept little Bill. She'd say, "Get up here on this sidewalk, Billy," and he'd say, "I aint gonna do it," and he wouldn't. I don't know why but he liked to walk in the dust of the road.

Wortham, like others, was trying to grasp Faulkner's passing.

> Lately, I been gettin' on him—a man his age ridin' and jumpin' the way he did! Sometimes one of them horses would come out from under him. I reckon it was about two weeks ago one of them throwed him, and he didn't look like he felt like hisself since.... Mr. Bill was the finest kind of man to work for. I never did see him get mad once. We shore are goin' to miss him.[29]

* * *

With the replaced coffin situated in front of the parlor hearth, Faulkner's brothers, Johncy and Jack, and Faulkner's two nephews, Jimmy and Murry "Chooky" Cuthbert II, kept an around-the-clock vigil. Meanwhile, work at the cemetery for what many considered a hastily arranged burial was ongoing. There was sadly no room in the old Falkner family section of St. Peter's Cemetery. There, elaborate headstones are situated among the boxwoods, cedars, crepe myrtles and magnolias. Faulkner, however, was interred in a rather forlorn section under two white oak trees.

The plot was situated on a downward slanting bank bridging the old and new cemetery sections. Even in the morning hours of July 7, the weather was sweltering as two brothers, Elbert and Will Houston, dug the grave with long-handled shovels. Along with rumors of Byhalia, local gossip about the sparse arrangements and speedy funeral circulated. Many were puzzled by a man of such prominence being buried so quickly. There was scarce travel time for some who might have wished to come. The haste seemed at odds with southern tradition, as did the family's private service with no viewing of the deceased and their request of no flowers (many of which were delivered regardless).

The Rev. Duncan Gray, Jr., of St. Peter's Episcopal Church conducted the service at Rowan Oak and graveside although admittedly, Faulkner was far from a faithful parishioner, and Estelle a rather infrequent visitor. Jill, who was married at St. Peter's, was more attentive to the church. She and Johncy's wife, Lucille, as well as Jimmy and Chooky were members of the congregation. As requested, the rector's service in the parlor was brief.

The family stood close by Faulkner's casket while his friends gathered in the nearby dining room, then Faulkner's brothers and nephews moved his casket from the hearth to the black Cadillac hearse. The finality of his departure from the home he'd loved and restored to the cemetery was deeply emotional, especially for Estelle. Phil Stone, who often had criticized her, softened when he witnessed her despair. "Estelle Faulkner's emotional upheaval as she left the house was not Oldham dramatics: 'Stelle and Bill loved one another in spite of their difficulties their whole lives.'"[30]

Outside the gate of Rowan Oak the world intruded. Photographers gathered beside curious onlookers who Johncy believed merely wanted to witness "Bill's last ride."[31] The last ride included a drive around the Square, the site of Faulkner's many walks to the post office and drugstore. *The Oxford Eagle* distributed flyers that were posted on storefronts, "In Memory of William Faulkner, This Business Will Be Closed From 2:00 to 2:15 P.M. Today, July 7, 1962,"[32] a striking bit of ephemera that Phil Stone made sure to collect for his son and daughter.

The cortege made its way past the courthouse with its flag lowered to half-staff, and the Confederate soldier, who from his elevated perch seemed an omniscient recorder. William Styron rode in a limousine with Shelby Foote. Foote commented on the size of the crowd lining the processional, "This is okay, but if this was the head of the Elks or Rotarians, you'd have 25 times more people." Styron noted that "He was not despised but ... he was a literary man, and being a literary man was not that important.... It took some time for his influence to sink in."[33]

Outside the Cadillac's window, Johncy saw photographers scrambling for opportunities, some running next to the hearse as others settled on balconies and even the tops of buildings. Rudd recalled the Square as very quiet and the heat as "violent, beyond belief."[34]

At the cemetery, the press found an assigned area removed from the folding chairs and tent prepared for the family. Joan and Howard likewise stood at a distance. Later that day, Howard set up his portable typewriter in Joan's aunt's backyard. Regina and her husband, John Reed Holley, first

Estelle and Jill Faulkner with two male relatives leaving Faulkner's graveside service the afternoon of July 7, 1962. On the one-year anniversary of Faulkner's funeral and burial the day after he died, the influential *Saturday Evening Post* published "The Death of William Faulkner" by Hughes Rudd. "All his life he remained an enigma to the little town his novels had made famous. Even his death, a year ago this month, was attended by an atmosphere of mystery" (Martin J. Dain Collection, Archives and Special Collections, J.D. Williams Library, the University of Mississippi).

introduced Joan to Faulkner and there was a certain symmetry to Howard writing his story there. In order to make the afternoon edition, he phoned in the article, then he and Joan drove back Memphis, "mostly in silence."[35]

During the early days of their courtship when they often met in the woods, a butterfly landed on Faulkner's beer can. His words stayed with Joan and she recorded them in her novel, *The Wintering*. "It would be nice," he said, "to be a butterfly. Come out and fly about and die in a few days. They have no knowledge of death and can't fear it then. Since it wouldn't harm anything, they have no reason to suspect harm."[36] Fourteen years later during a visit to Rowan Oak, a butterfly was flitting around Joan and her group. "Maybe, maybe" she said, "it is Bill reincarnated. Maybe he's back at Rowan Oak free and without hassle any time any more. And Rowan Oak is so beautiful and peaceful. It would be the sort of place where he would want to be if he could come back. Maybe that's the way things work out."[37]

The small contingency made their way to the open grave. Phil Stone and Mac Reed, serving as honorary pallbearers, walked ahead of the casket followed by Estelle, Jill, family and friends. Estelle's black straw hat kept her face out of view. Once seated, seeking comfort and strength, she held Malcolm's hand. A deep quiet descended and the relentless heat was unabated. At the lonesome spot in the new area, the Reverend Gray briefly read from *The Book of Common Prayer*. In rapid succession, the casket was lowered, covered with dirt; and on top, an abundant floral display marked the fresh grave. Except for the forbidden flowers and ornate casket, the service went according to Faulkner's wishes. The lush silence would have pleased him and the presence of those near and dear: his family, friends, protectors, advocates, and lost love.

Chapter Notes

Introduction

1. Joseph Blotner, *Faulkner: A Biography* (New York: Vintage, 1984), 568.
2. *Ibid.*, 561.
3. Audiotape of lecture by William Faulkner for Joseph Blotner's Novel and Frederick Gwynn's American Fiction Classes at the University of Virginia, Tape: T-114, 13 April 1957.
4. Audiotape of lecture by William Faulkner for Joseph Blotner's Types of Literature and Frederick Gwynn's Graduate Class in American Literature Classes at the University of Virginia, Tape: T-144c, 8 May 1958.
5. *Ibid.*
6. Blotner, *Faulkner: A Biography*, 453.
7. Karen S. and James C. Castleberry, Castleberry Collection, Byhalia, MS.
8. Jack D. Elliott, Jr., and Sidney Bondurant, "Death on a Summer Night: Faulkner at Byhalia," *The Journal of Mississippi History* 79, nos. 3–4 (Fall/Winter 2017): 109.
9. Castleberry Collection.
10. Blotner, *Faulkner: A Biography*, 559. This signature line occurs in *The Wild Palms* [If I Forget Thee, Jerusalem] (1939; New York: Vintage, 1995), 273, and in letters to Meta Carpenter and Joan Williams.
11. Blotner, *Faulkner: A Biography*, 478
12. Elliott and Bondurant, 111.
13. Blotner, *Faulkner: A Biography*, 671.

Chapter One

1. Larry Levinger, "Faulkner's Gift," *GEO*, January 1983, 43.
2. *Ibid.*
3. Joseph Blotner, *Faulkner: A Biography, Vol. 2* (New York: Random House, 1974), 1831.
4. Jospeh Blotner Papers, 27 November 1965, Louis Daniel Brodsky Collection of William Faulkner Materials, Special Collections and Archives, Southeast Missouri State University.
5. Blotner, *Faulkner: A Biography*, 709.
6. *Ibid.*, 708.
7. *Ibid.*, 709.
8. *Ibid.*, 710
9. Joan Williams, interview about William Faulkner, Mississippi Educational Television, 1976.
10. Victoria Fielden Johnson, "White Beaches," in *William Faulkner Life Glimpses*, ed. Louis Daniel Brodsky (Austin: University of Texas Press, 1990), 173.
11. *Ibid.*
12. *Ibid.*, 171.
13. *Ibid.*, 173.
14. Susan Snell, *Phil Stone of Oxford: A Vicarious Life* (Athens: University of Georgia Press, 1991), 320.
15. Levinger, 51.
16. Jim Faulkner, "Brother Will's Passing," *Southern Living*, March 1992, 108.
17. Blotner, *Faulkner: A Biography*, 713.
18. Sue Waton, "Loyal Respected Employee Retires," *Pigeon Roost News*, Holly Springs, MS, 7 January 2004, 1.
19. Elliott and Bondurant, 121.
20. Blotner, *Faulkner: A Biography*, 713.
21. Elliott and Bondurant, 122.
22. *Ibid.*
23. Jim Faulkner, 109.
24. Castleberry Collection.
25. Watson, p. 1.

Chapter Two

1. Advertisement for Wright's Sanatorium, *Texas State Journal of Medicine*, August 1956.
2. Levinger, 43.
3. Johnson, 169.
4. William D. Fitts, III, interview by the author, Byhalia, MS, 21 April 2015.
5. Fitts, interview.
6. Ibid.
7. "The Peabody Hotel ... and the Famous Ducks in Historic-Memphis," Historic Memphis website.
8. Fitts, interview.
9. Castleberry Collection.
10. Johnson, 169.
11. Judith L. Sensibar, *Faulkner and Love: The Women Who Shaped His Art* (New Haven: Yale University Press, 2009), 397.
12. Johnson, 169.
13. Louis Daniel Brodsky and Robert W. Hamblin, eds., *Faulkner: A Comprehensive Guide to the Brodsky Collection, Vol. II: The Letters* (Jackson: University Press of Mississippi, 1984), 94.
14. Fitts, interview.
15. Adolphus Shipp, interview by the author, Byhalia, MS, 5 August 2015.
16. Blotner, *Faulkner: A Biography*, Vol. 2, 1755–1756.
17. Blotner Papers re 17 November 1966 visit to Wright's Sanatorium and interview with Dr. Wright, Louis Daniel Brodsky Collection of William Faulkner Materials, Special Collections and Archives, Southeast Missouri State University.
18. Shipp, interview.
19. Ibid.
20. Blotner Papers re 17 November 1966 Special Collections and Archives, Southeast Missouri State University.
21. Castleberry Collection.
22. Shipp, interview.
23. Elliott and Bondurant, 122.
24. Shipp, interview.
25. Fitts, interview.
26. Shipp, interview.
27. Ibid.
28. Fitts, interview.
29. Watson, 1.

Chapter Three

1. Joseph Blotner, *Faulkner: A Biography, Vol. 1* (New York: Random House, 1974), 630.
2. Joel Williamson, *William Faulkner and Southern History* (New York: Oxford University Press, 1993), 128.
3. Andrew Marion, "Jacob Thompson's 1848 Vision for the New College," University of Mississippi Slavery Research Group, 13 February 2017.
4. "April 27, 1864: Jacob Thompson," Almost Chosen People: A Blog about American History, and the Development of a Great Nation, 27 April 2023.
5. Ben Wasson, *Count No 'Count: Flashbacks to Faulkner* (Jackson: University Press of Mississippi, 1983), 81.
6. Malcolm A. Franklin, *Bitterweeds: Life with William Faulkner at Rowan Oak* (Irving, TX: The Society for the Study of Traditional Culture, 1977), 22.
7. Blotner, *Faulkner: A Biography*, 285–286.
8. Ibid., 286.
9. Ibid.
10. Ibid.
11. Ibid., 289.
12. Ibid., 291–292.
13. Franklin, 74–75.

Chapter Four

1. William Faulkner, *Absalom, Absalom!* (New York: Vintage, 1986), 194.
2. Blotner, *Faulkner: A Biography*, 276.
3. Ibid.
4. Levinger, 51.
5. Blotner, *Faulkner: A Biography*, 310.
6. Ibid., 353.
7. James Campbell, "Mississippi's Talebearer," *Wall Street Journal*, Saturday/Sunday, 18–19 November 2023, C17.
8. Blotner, *Faulkner: A Biography*, 371.
9. Meta Wilde Carpenter and Orin Borsten, *A Loving Gentleman: The Love Story of William Faulkner and Meta Carpenter* (New York: Simon & Schuster, 1976), 79.
10. Snell, 101.
11. Ibid., 226–227.
12. Ibid., 302.
13. Blotner, *Faulkner: A Biography*, 365.
14. Wasson, 147.
15. Ibid., 149.

Chapter Five

1. Blotner Papers re 29 April 1968 Special

Collections and Archives, Southeast Missouri State University.
2. Lisa C. Hickman, "William Faulkner: Dealing with His Demons," *Memphis Magazine*, September 1993, 91.
3. Franklin, 75–76.
4. Hickman, "William Faulkner," 93.
5. William Faulkner, "Uncle Willy," in *Collected Stories of William Faulkner* (New York: Random House, 1950), 227.
6. *Ibid.*, 225.
7. *Ibid.*, 226–227.
8. *Ibid.*, 228.
9. *Ibid.*, 232.
10. *Ibid.*, 233.
11. Hickman, "William Faulkner," 85.
12. Albert I. Bezzerides, "Bill and Buzz: Fellow Scenarists," in *William Faulkner Life Glimpses*, ed. Louis Daniel Brodsky (Austin: University of Texas Press, 1990), 81.
13. Carpenter and Borsten, 143.
14. Blotner, *Faulkner: A Biography, Vol. 2*, 955.
15. Blotner, *Faulkner: A Biography*, 180.
16. Sherwood Anderson to Laura Copenhaver (November 11, 1937), in *Sherwood Anderson, Selected Letters*, ed. Charles E. Modlin (Knoxville: University of Tennessee Press, 1984) 213–214.
17. Carpenter and Borsten, 230.
18. *Ibid.*

Chapter Six

1. Snell, 253.
2. Blotner, *Faulkner: A Biography*, 413.
3. Snell, 198.
4. Blotner, *Faulkner: A Biography*, 376.
5. *Ibid.*, 375.
6. Snell, 309.
7. William Faulkner, "Wash," in *Collected Stories of William Faulkner* (New York: Random House, 1950), 539.
8. *Ibid.*, 539–542.
9. *Ibid.*, 537.
10. *Ibid.*, 535.
11. *Ibid.*, 547.
12. Bezzerides, 60.
13. *Ibid.*, 65.
14. *Ibid.*, 165.
15. Carpenter, 305.
16. Blotner, *Faulkner: A Biography*, 467.
17. Williamson, 268.
18. Carpenter, 312.
19. Levinger, 112.
20. Dean Faulkner Wells, *Every Day by the Sun: A Memoir of the Faulkners of Mississippi* (New York: Crown, 2011), 173–174.
21. Mike Donahue, "The Day Faulkner Died," *Memphis Press-Scimitar*, Tuesday, 13 July 1982, Section B.
22. Bezzerides, 66.
23. *Ibid.*, 68.
24. *Ibid.*

Chapter Seven

1. Author's note. Unless otherwise indicated, Joan Williams' quotations are attributable to my book, *William Faulkner and Joan Williams: The Romance of Two Writers*, numerous articles, or our extensive interviews spanning a decade.
2. Audiotape of lecture by William Faulkner for Undergraduate Contemporary American Literature, Undergraduate Writing, Graduate Class in American Fiction at the University of Virginia, 3 May 1958.
3. Billy Swift, "Bridge Suicide Is Believed to Be Kenneth Orgill, Jr.," *The* [Memphis] *Commercial Appeal*, Monday Morning, 1 February 1960, Final p. 1.
4. "Man Who Jumped Off Bridge Believed to Be Kenneth Orgill, Jr.," *Memphis Press-Scimitar*, Monday, 1 February 1960, p. 4.
5. Swift, "Bridge Suicide."
6. *Ibid.*
7. "Man Who Jumped Off Bridge."
8. *Ibid.*
9. Keith Coulbourn, "Fatal Leap Turns Practice into Real Rescue Operation," *The* [Memphis] *Commercial Appeal*, Monday Morning, 1 February 1960, p. 17.
10. Swift, "Bridge Suicide."
11. Charles Edmundson, "Couple Report They Saw Leap," *The* [Memphis] *Commercial Appeal*, Saturday Morning, 13 February 1960, p. 1.
12. "Did She Follow Husband into River? Widow Is Believed Suicide," *Memphis Press-Scimitar*, 12 February 1960.
13. Les Brumfield, "Widow of Kenneth Orgill, Jr. Believed to Be Bridge Suicide," *The* [Memphis] *Commercial Appeal*, Friday Morning, 12 February 1960, Final p.1.
14. "Session Twelve," 27 April 1957, in *Faulkner in the University*, eds. Frederick

L. Gwynn and Joseph L. Blotner (Charlottesville: University Press of Virginia, 1959, 1995), 95.
15. Audiotape of lecture by William Faulkner for Undergraduate Class in Contemporary American Literature, Undergraduate Class in Writing, Graduate Class in American Fiction at the University of Virginia, 2 May 1958.
16. William Faulkner, *The Sound and the Fury* (New York: Jonathan Cape & Harrison Smith, 1929; New York: Vintage, 1984), 174.
17. *Ibid.*, 44.
18. *Ibid.*, 101.
19. *Ibid.*, 100.
20. *Ibid.*, 174.
21. *Ibid.*, 179.
22. Hickman, *Faulkner and Williams*, 40.
23. *Ibid.*, 19–20.
24. Williamson, 289.

Chapter Eight

1. Blotner, *Faulkner: A Biography, Vol. 2*, 1254.
2. *Ibid.*, 1255.
3. Blotner, *Faulkner: A Biography*, 494.
4. Blotner, *Faulkner: A Biography, Vol. 2*, 1260.
5. Blotner, *Faulkner: A Biography*, 472.
6. *The Portable Faulkner*, ed. Malcolm Cowley (New York: The Viking Press, 1946), 1–2.
7. Blotner, *Faulkner: A Biography*, 475.
8. Blotner, *Faulkner: A Biography, Vol. 2*, 1264–1265.
9. *Ibid.*, 1265.
10. Melissa Kravitz Hoeffner, "Why the 21 Club in a Hugely Important Part of NYC History," Thrillist, 9 December 2016 (Group Nine Media, Inc.).
11. Blotner, *Faulkner: A Biography, Vol. 2*, 1266.
12. Blotner, *Faulkner: A Biography*, 502.
13. John Beifuss, "Stars of Yesteryear to Appear at Midsouth Nostalgia Festival," *The* [Memphis] *Commercial Appeal*, 10 June 2022, Go Memphis section.
14. *Ibid.*
15. Johnson, 159.
16. Blotner, *Faulkner: A Biography*, 509.
17. *Ibid.*, 159.
18. Blotner, *Faulkner: A Biography, Vol. 2*, 1297.
19. Johnson, 159.
20. *Ibid.*, 162.
21. Blotner, *Faulkner: A Biography, Vol. 2*, 1291.
22. Johnson, 164.
23. *Ibid.*
24. Blotner, *Faulkner: A Biography*, 618.
25. *Ibid.*
26. Johnson, 163.
27. Blotner, *Faulkner: A Biography, Vol. 2*, 1263.
28. Faulkner, *Absalom*, 303.
29. Blotner, *Faulkner: A Biography*, 511.

Chapter Nine

1. Hickman, *Faulkner and Williams*, 79, 75, 76, 117.
2. *Ibid.*, 20, 22, 39, 42.
3. Blotner, *Faulkner: A Biography*, 513.
4. Hickman, 75.
5. Blotner, *Faulkner: A Biography*, 514.
6. Hickman, 45.
7. Blotner, *Faulkner: A Biography*, 517.
8. John Faulkner, *My Brother Bill* (New York: Trident Press, 1963), 177.
9. Hickman, *Faulkner and Williams*, 60.
10. *Ibid.*, 57–58.
11. Sensibar, 245.
12. Wells, 191.
13. Hickman, 70, 72.
14. Castleberry Collection.
15. *Ibid.*, 78.
16. Levinger, 113.
17. Blotner, *Faulkner: A Biography, Vol. 1*, 888.
18. Blotner, *Faulkner: A Biography, Vol. 2*, 980.
19. *Ibid.*, 1343.
20. *Ibid.*, 1343–1344.
21. Blotner, *Faulkner: A Biography*, 529.
22. Blotner, *Faulkner: A Biography, Vol. 2*, 1351.
23. Williams, Mississippi Educational Television, 1976.
24. Hickman, *Faulkner and Williams*, 81.
25. Blotner, *Faulkner: A Biography, Vol. 2*, 1356.
26. *Ibid.*, 1357.
27. Levinger, 113.
28. Paul Gray, "Mister Faulkner Goes to Stockholm," *Smithsonian*, October 2001, 60.

29. Blotner, *Faulkner: A Biography*, Vol. 2, 1359.
30. *Ibid.*, 1207.
31. *Ibid.*, 1362.
32. *Ibid.*, 1364.
33. Snell, 276.
34. Blotner, *Faulkner: A Biography*, 562.
35. *Ibid.*, 1367.
36. *Ibid.*, 1369.

Chapter Ten

1. Hickman, *Faulkner and Williams*, 89–90.
2. Blotner, *Faulkner: A Biography*, Vol. 2, 1379.
3. Blotner, *Faulkner: A Biography*, Vol. 2, 1311.
4. Kirkus Reviews, *Requiem for a Nun*, Kirkus Media LLC, 1 September 1951.
5. Blotner, *Faulkner: A Biography*, Vol. 2, 1319.
6. Johnson, 166–167.
7. Blotner, *Faulkner: A Biography*, Vol. 2, 1388.
8. Hickman, *Faulkner and Williams*, 100, 104.
9. Johnson, 166.
10. Blotner, *Faulkner: A Biography*, 548.
11. Blotner, *Faulkner: A Biography*, Vol. 2, 1406.

Chapter Eleven

1. Blotner, *Faulkner: A Biography*, 368.
2. Wilde and Borsten, 322–324.
3. *Ibid.*, 329.
4. Blotner, *Faulkner: A Biography*, Vol. 2, 1222.
5. Blotner, *Faulkner: A Biography*, 227.
6. Wasson, 175.
7. The Delta, A Bicentennial History of Mississippi, 304.
8. Blotner, *Faulkner: A Biography*, Vol. 2, 1417.
9. Hickman, *Faulkner and Williams*, 115.
10. Blotner, *Faulkner: A Biography*, 555.
11. Wilde and Borsten, 321.
12. Williamson, 283.
13. Williams, Mississippi Educational Television, 1976
14. Joan Williams, *The Wintering* (New York: Harcourt Brace Jovanovich, 1971), 172.
15. *Ibid.*
16. Hickman, *Faulkner and Williams*, 122.
17. *Ibid.*, 123.
18. *Ibid.*, 117.
19. Castleberry Collection.
20. Hickman, *Faulkner and Williams*, 124.
21. Johnson, 166.
22. Hickman, *Faulkner and Williams*, 131.
23. Brodsky and Hamblin, *Vol. II: The Letters*, 89–90.
24. *Ibid.*, 90–91.
25. Faulkner to Williams, Gartly-Ramsay Hospital stationery, 18 September 1952 [Williams, Mississippi Educational Television].
26. Hickman, *Faulkner and Williams*, 135.
27. *Ibid.*
28. Brodsky and Hamblin, *Vol. II: The Letters*, 93.
29. Wells, 187.
30. *Ibid.*, 190.
31. Brodsky and Hamblin, *Vol. II: The Letters*, 94.
32. Williams, Mississippi Educational Television.
33. Johnson, 167.
34. Wasson, 166.
35. Williams, Mississippi Educational Television.
36. Blotner, *Faulkner: A Biography*, 567.
37. Bezzerides, 78.
38. Hickman, *Faulkner and Williams*, 148.
39. Faulkner to Williams, 31 December 1952.

Chapter Twelve

1. John Faulkner, 235.
2. Blotner, *Faulkner: A Biography*, 699.
3. Hickman, *Faulkner and Williams*, 152.
4. *Ibid.*, 154.
5. *Ibid.*, 173.
6. Williams, Mississippi Education Television.
7. Blotner, *Faulkner: A Biography*, 700.
8. Hickman, *Faulkner and Williams*, 154.
9. Williams, Mississippi Educational Television.

10. *Ibid.*
11. Williams, *The Wintering*, 244.
12. Blotner, *Faulkner: A Biography*, 567.
13. Bezzerides, 78–79.
14. Blotner, *Faulkner: A Biography, Vol. 2*, 1455.
15. Hickman, *Faulkner and Williams*, 180.
16. Hickman, *Faulkner and Williams*, 157.
17. Tina Jordan, "New York's Legendary Literary Hangouts," *The New York Times*, 26 August 2021.
18. Hickman, *Faulkner and Williams*, 160.
19. *Ibid.*, 162.
20. Brodsky and Hamblin, *Vol. II: The Letters*, 116–117.
21. Hickman, *Faulkner and Williams*, 174–175.
22. Wasson, 177–178.
23. *Ibid.*, 178.
24. *Ibid.*, 179.
25. *Ibid.*, 183.
26. *Ibid.*, 184.
27. *Ibid.*, 187.
28. *Ibid.*, 188–189.
29. *Ibid.*, 190–191.
30. Blotner, 1984, 591.
31. *Ibid.*, 577.
32. Williamson, 295.
33. Blotner, *Faulkner: A Biography*, 579.
34. Wasson, 193.
35. Castleberry Collection.
36. Johnson, 171.
37. Hickman, *Faulkner and Williams*, 103.
38. Blotner, *Faulkner: A Biography*, 543.
39. Robert Coughlan, "The Man Behind the Faulkner Myth, Part I," *Life*, 28 September 1953, 127.
40. *Ibid.*, 133.
41. Robert Coughlan, "The Man Behind the Faulkner Myth, Part II," *Life*, 5 October 1958, 58.
42. Blotner, *Faulkner: A Biography*, 575.
43. Coughlan, "Part I," 127.
44. Castleberry Collection.
45. Blotner, *Faulkner: A Biography*, 575.
46. Hickman, *Faulkner and Williams*, 151.
47. Faulkner inscription.
48. Hickman, *Faulkner and Williams*, 181.
49. Williams, Mississippi Educational Television.
50. Blotner, *Faulkner: A Biography*, 589.
51. Brodsky and Hamblin, *Vol. II: The Letters*, 134.
52. *Time*, "People," 15 August 1955, 26.
53. Bezzerides, 77.

Chapter Thirteen

1. Jim Faulkner, 109.
2. Sally Wolff with Floyd C. Watkins, *Talking About William Faulkner: Interviews with Jimmy Faulkner and Others* (Baton Rouge: Louisiana State University Press, 1996), 177.
3. Castleberry Collection.
4. *Ibid.*
5. *Ibid.*
6. Wolff, 177.
7. John Faulkner, 3.
8. *Ibid.*, 5.
9. Jim Faulkner, 109.
10. Wolff, 178.
11. Blotner Papers re 23 March 1965 Special Collections and Archives, Southeast Missouri State University.
12. Carl Crawford, "Literary World Shocked by Death," *The* [Memphis] *Commercial Appeal*, Saturday Morning, 7 July 1962.
13. "Faulkner Hailed by Cerf and Snow: Author Ranked by President as the Most Important Since Henry James," *The New York Times*, Saturday, 7 July 1962.
14. *Ibid.*
15. Clark Porteous, "Death Still Pen of Nobel and Pulitzer Prize Winner," *Memphis Press-Scimitar*, Friday, 6 July 1962.
16. Jim Faulkner, 109.
17. Hughes Rudd, "The Death of William Faulkner," *The Saturday Evening Post*, July 13–20, 34.
18. John Faulkner, 7.
19. *Ibid.*, 8.
20. "Faulkner Hailed," *The New York Times*.
21. Rudd, 34.
22. Paul Flowers, "Storied Oxford Unruffled at 'Curious Bill's' Passing," *The* [Memphis] *Commercial Appeal*, Saturday Morning, 7 July 1962.
23. Rudd, 34.
24. *Ibid.*
25. *Ibid.*
26. "She Is Shocked by His Death," *Memphis Press-Scimitar*, Friday, 6 July 1962.

27. Edwin Howard, "Oak Trees Will Shade Great Author's Grave," *Memphis Press-Scimitar*, Saturday, 7 July 1962.
28. *Ibid.*
29. *Ibid.*
30. Snell, 321.
31. John Faulkner, 8.
32. Wells, 247.
33. *Ibid.*
34. Rudd, 37.
35. Edwin Howard, "Burying 'Mr. Bill': Faulkner 'Liked to Walk the Dust of the Road,'" *Memphis Business Journal*, 22–26 September 1997.
36. Williams, *The Wintering*, 145.
37. Williams, Mississippi Educational Television.

Bibliography

Advertisement for Wright's Sanatorium. *The Mississippi Doctor*, June 1948.
———. *Texas State Journal of Medicine*, August 1956.
Beifuss, John. "Stars of Yesteryear to Appear at Midsouth Nostalgia Festival." *The* [Memphis] *Commercial Appeal*, 10 June 2022, Go Memphis section.
Bezzerides, Albert I. "Bill and Buzz: Fellow Scenarists." In *William Faulkner, Life Glimpses*, edited by Louis Daniel Brodsky, 132–178. Austin: University of Texas Press, 1990.
Blotner, Joseph. *Faulkner: A Biography*. New York: Random House, 1984.
———. *Faulkner: A Biography, Vol. 1*. New York: Random House, 1974.
———. *Faulkner: A Biography, Vol. 2*. New York: Random House, 1974.
———. Papers. Louis Daniel Brodsky Collection of William Faulkner Materials, Special Collections and Archives, Southeast Missouri State University.
———, ed. *Selected Letters of William Faulkner*. New York: Random House, 1977.
Brodsky, Louis Daniel. *William Faulkner, Life Glimpses*. Austin: University of Texas Press, 1990.
Brodsky, Louis Daniel, and Robert W. Hamblin, eds. *Faulkner: A Comprehensive Guide to the Brodsky Collection, Vol. II: The Letters*. Jackson: University Press of Mississippi, 1984.
Brody, Leslie. *Sometimes You Have to Lie: The Life and Times of Louise Fitzhugh, Renegade Author of Harriet the Spy*. New York: Basic Books, 2020.
Brumfield, Les. "Widow of Kenneth Orgill, Jr. Believed to Be Bridge Suicide." *The* [Memphis] *Commercial Appeal*, 12 February 1960, final edition, 1.
Campbell, James. "Mississippi's Talebearer." *The Wall Street Journal*, Saturday/Sunday, 18–19 November 2023.
Castleberry, Karen S., and James C. Castleberry. Castleberry Collection. Byhalia, MS.
Coughlan, Robert. "The Man Behind the Faulkner Myth." *Life* (5 October 1953): 55–68.
———. "The Private World of William Faulkner." *Life* (28 September 1953): 118–136.
Coulbourn, Keith. "Fatal Leap Turns Practice into Real Rescue Operation." *The* [Memphis] *Commercial Appeal*, 1 February 1960, final edition.
Crawford, Carl. "Literary World Shocked by Death." *The* [Memphis] *Commercial Appeal*, 7 July 1962.
Dardis, Tom. *The Thirsty Muse*. New York: Ticknor and Fields, 1989.
Donahue, Michael. "The Day Faulkner Died." *Memphis Press-Scimitar*, 13 July 1982, sec. B, 1–2.
Edmundson, Charles. "Couple Report They Saw Leap." *The* [Memphis] *Commercial Appeal*, Saturday Morning, 13 February 1960, 1.
Elliott, Jack D., Jr., and Sidney W. Bondurant. "Death on a Summer Night: Faulkner at Byhalia." *The Journal of Mississippi History* 79, nos. 3–4 (Fall/Winter 2017): 101–135.
Faulkner, Jim. "Brother Will's Passing." *Southern Living* (March 1992): 108–109.
Faulkner, John. *My Brother Bill: An Affectionate Reminiscence*. New York: Trident Press, 1963.
Faulkner, William. *Absalom, Absalom!* New York: Random House, 1936; New York: Vintage, 1990.

_____. *Collected Stories of William Faulkner*. New York: Random House, 1950.
_____. *The Sound and the Fury*. New York: Jonathan Cape & Harrison Smith, 1929; New York: Vintage, 1984.
Fitts, Elizabeth "Lis." Interview by the author. Byhalia, MS, 21 August 2015.
Fitts, William D., III. Interview by the author. Byhalia, MS, 21 August 2015.
Flowers, Paul. "Storied Oxford Unruffled at 'Curious Bill's' Passing." *The* [Memphis] *Commercial Appeal*, Saturday Morning, 7 July 1962.
Franklin, Malcolm A. *Bitterweeds: Life with William Faulkner at Rowan Oak*. Irving, TX: The Society for the Study of Traditional Culture, 1977.
Gauch, Patricia Lee. "Faulkner and Beyond: A Biography of Joan Williams." Ph.D. dissertation, Drew University, 1988.
Gray, Paul. "Mister Faulkner Goes to Stockholm." *Smithsonian* (October 2001): 56–60.
Gresset, Michel. *A Faulkner Chronology*. Jackson: University of Mississippi Press, 1985.
Gwynn, Frederick L., and Joseph L. Blotner, eds. *Faulkner in the University*. Charlottesville: University Press of Virginia, 1959, 1995.
"Harvey Breit, 58, Writer, Is Dead." *The New York Times*, 10 April 1968.
Hickman, Lisa C. *William Faulkner and Joan Williams: The Romance of Two Writers*. Jefferson, NC: McFarland, 2006.
_____. "William Faulkner: Dealing with his Demons." *Memphis Magazine*, 1993.
Hoeffner, Melissa Kravitz. "Why the 21 Club is a Hugely Important Part of NYC History." *Thrillist*. 9 December 2016. (Group Nine Media, Inc.).
Howard, Edwin. "Burying 'Mr. Bill': Faulkner Liked to Walk in the Dust of the Road." *Memphis Business Journal*, 22–26 September 1997.
_____. "Oak Trees Will Shade Great Author's Grave." *Memphis Press-Scimitar*, 7 July 1962.
_____. "Tho Renowned Now, His Stature Will Increase as More Discover His Message of Hope." *Memphis Press-Scimitar*, 6 July 1962.
Howell, Elmo. *Mississippi Scenes: Notes on Literature and History*. Memphis: Elmo Howell, 1992.
Johnson, Victoria [Vicki] Fielden. "White Beaches." In *William Faulkner, Life Glimpses*, edited by Louis Daniel Brodsky, 132–178. Austin: University of Texas Press, 1990.
Johnston, Laurie. "Colony Restaurant Closes Amid Tears." *The New York Times*, 6 December 1971.
Jordan, Tina. "New York's Legendary Literary Hangouts." *The New York Times*, 26 August 2021.
Lambert, Bruce. "Albert R. Erskine, 81, an Editor for Faulkner and Other Authors." *The New York Times*, 5 February 1993.
Lawrence, John, and Dan Hise. *Faulkner's Rowan Oak*. Jackson: University Press of Mississippi, 1993.
Levinger, Larry. "Faulkner's Gift." *GEO* (January 1983): 40–53, 112–114.
"Man Who Jumped Off Bridge Believed to Be Kenneth Orgill, Jr." *Memphis Press- Scimitar*, 1 February 1960.
Marion, Andrew. "Jacob Thompson's 1848 Vision for the New College." University of Mississippi Slavery Research Group, 13 February 2017.
Meares, Hadley. "Off the Boulevard of Broken Dreams: The Knickerbocker Hotel's Haunted History." *Lost Landmarks*, 19 June 2015. KCET.org (Public Media Group of Southern California).
"Memorial Is Today for K.W. Orgill Jr." *The* [Memphis] *Commercial Appeal*, 2 February 1960.
Michael, Thomas. "Faulkner Rites Will Be Today at Family Home." *The* [Memphis] *Commercial Appeal*, 7 July 1962.
Modlin, Charles E. ed. *Sherwood Anderson, Selected Letters*. Knoxville: University of Tennessee Press, 1984.
"Mrs. Nancy Orgill Is Buried Quietly." *The* [Memphis] *Commercial Appeal*, 14 April 1960.
Parini, Jay. *One Matchless Time*. New York: HarperCollins, 2004.
"Poets Attend Rites for Dylan Thomas." *The New York Times*, 14 November 1953.
Porteous, Clark. "Death Stills Pen of Nobel and Pulitzer Prize Winner." *Memphis Press-Scimitar*, 6 July 1962.

Prescott, Orville. "A Literary Personality." *The New York Times*, 7 July 1962.
Railton, Stephen. Faulkner at Virginia: An Audio Archive. University of Virginia Library. 1957 and 1958.
Rudd, Hughes. "The Death of William Faulkner." *The Saturday Evening Post* (July 13–20, 1963): 32–37.
Sensibar, Judith L. *Faulkner and Love: The Women Who Shaped His Art*. New Haven: Yale University Press, 2009.
Shipp, Adolphus. Interview by the author. Byhalia, MS, 5 August 2015.
Smith, Ted L., Sr. "Attorney Reveals Connection with 1962 Death of Nobel Prize Winner." *The Panolian* (Batesville, MS), 4 September 2007.
Snell, Susan. *Phil Stone of Oxford: A Vicarious Life*. Athens: University of Georgia Press, 1991.
Swift, Billy. "Bridge Suicide Is Believed to Be Kenneth W. Orgill Jr." *The* [Memphis] *Commercial Appeal*, 1 February 1960, final edition.
Time (15 August 1955): 25–27.
Wasson, Ben. *Count No 'Count: Flashbacks to Faulkner*. Jackson: University Press of Mississippi, 1983.
Watson, Sue. "Loyal, Respected Employee Retires." *Pigeon Roost News* (Byhalia, MS), 7 January 2004.
Wells, Dean Faulkner. *Every Day by the Sun: A Memoir of the Faulkners of Mississippi*. New York: Crown, 2011.
"Widow Is Believed Suicide: Did She Follow Husband into River?" *Memphis Press-Scimitar*, 12 February 1960.
Wilde, Meta Carpenter, and Orin Borsten. *A Loving Gentleman: The Love Story of William Faulkner and Meta Carpenter*. New York: Simon & Schuster, 1976.
"William Faulkner Is Dead in Mississippi Home Town." *The New York Times*, 7 July 1962.
Williams, Joan. Interview about William Faulkner. Mississippi Educational Television, 1976.
———. *The Wintering*. New York: Harcourt, Brace & World, 1971.
Williamson, Joel. *William Faulkner and Southern History*. New York: Oxford University Press, 1993.
Wolff, Sally, with Floyd C. Watkins. *Talking About William Faulkner: Interviews with Jimmy Faulkner and Others*. Baton Rouge: Louisiana State University Press, 1996.

Index

Abernethy, Wilbur 155
Adler, Justin H 70
Adler, Michael 70
Adler, Susan 70
Adolf, Gustav 129
Algonquin Hotel 73, 128
Anderson, Claude 38
Anderson, Sherwood 45, 73, 116, 162
Aria da Capo 161
Ayers, Lemuel 134

Bacall, Lauren 8, 49, 82
Bailey, Ellen C. 36
Bailey, John M. 36
Baker, Kate 120
Balzac, Honoré de 61
Barnett, Ned "Uncle Ned" 42–43
Barr, Caroline "Mammy Callie" 42, 43, 75, 97, 125
Berns, Charlie 106
Berryman, John 165
Bezzerides, Albert "Buzz" 56, 65, 71, 78–90, 152, 160, 181
Bezzerides, Peter 82
Bezzerides, Yvonne 82, 83, 87, 90
Bezzerides, Zoe 82–83
The Big Sleep 84
Biltmore Hotel 115, 134
Blotner, Joseph 7, 25–28, 66–67, 125, 142, 177, 183
Bogart, Humphrey 8, 49, 82, 84, 131
Bonnier, Kaj 128
Bonnier, Tor 128
Bonnier, Ulla 128
Booth, John Wilkes 37
Bouguereau, William Adolphe 153
Bowen, Ezra Drinker 13, 166, 178–179
Bramlett, Eugene 68
Breit, Harvey 115, 165
Brennan, Walter 82
Brent, Amelia 161

Brown, Clarence 107–108
Brown, Maggie 103
Brown, Ross 102
Bryant, Sallie 36–37
Bryant, W.C. 36–37
Buck, Pearl S. 121, 187
Burrow, Jean 18, 33, 182
Burrow, Lillian 20
Burrow, Myra Herring 20
Burrow, Thomas "Tom" D. 19
Butterworth, Walton 123, 127–130
Button, Geoffrey 127, 129–130
Byrnes, James F. 140

Camp, Paul 183
Campbell, Essie 23
Campbell, James 52
Campbell Clinic 13, 148
Camus, Albert 8. 112
Cape, Jonathan 76
Capote, Truman 8, 115, 136, 165
Carmichael, Hoagy 82
Carpenter, Billy 57
Carpenter, Meta Wilde Dougherty 8, 20, 57–64, 70–74, 76–77, 79, 81–86, 102, 118–119, 131–132, 139, 141, 146, 148, 152–153
Carter, Katrina 61
Castleberry, James 1, 7
Castleberry, Karen 1, 7
Cather, Willa 51
Cavenor, Rex 96
Cavenor, Mrs. Rex 96
Cedars of Lebanon Hospital 8, 65, 83–84
Cerf, Bennett 46, 76, 105–107 124, 126, 147, 185
Cerf, Phyllis 105, 124, 126
Chandler, Raymond 84
Charles P. Townes Hospital 159
Clinique Remy de Gourmont 142
Cofield, J.R. 108
Colbert, Claudette 8, 56

Index

Collins, Carvel 103
Commins, Dorothy 21, 125, 147, 149–150, 167, 173, 175, 179
Commins, Saxe 21, 24, 111, 115, 147–150, 152, 167, 173, 175, 178–180
Cooper, Gary 85
Copenhaver, Eleanor 73
Cotton, Joseph 138
Coughlan, Robert 176–177
Cowley, Malcolm 7, 103–107, 111–112
Cowley, Muriel 105, 107
Les Croix de bois 55
Crown, John 59
Culley, John 66–68, 78
Culley, Nina 67
cummings, e.e. 164–165
Cyrano de Bergerac 178

Davies, Julie 72
Devine, Jim 73, 105
Diamond, "Legs" 106
DiMaggio, Joe 55
Doctors Hospital 160
Dorgelès, Roland 55
Doxey, Wall 77
Dreiser, Theodore 45, 116
Dulles, John Foster 123

Eliot, T.S. 61
Elliott, Jack Jr. 1, 7
Ellison, Ralph 142
Erskine, Albert 142, 159
Evans, Hugh 102–103
Evans, Mary 103

Falkner, Alabama Leroy "Aunt Bama" 44, 108–109
Falkner, John Wesley Thompson "The Young Colonel" 42
Falkner, Maud Butler 50–51, 53–54, 109, 172, 184
Falkner, Murry Cuthbert 37, 50–51, 53
Falkner, William "The Old Colonel" Clark 12, 18, 42–44
Farley, Bob 139–140
Farmer, Frances 55
Faulkner, Alabama 4, 44, 46, 52, 54, 67
Faulkner, Dean Swift 4, 9, 44, 50–55, 67, 105, 184
Faulkner, Estelle Oldham 4, 17–18, 34–47, 49, 58, 61–63, 67, 74, 87, 117, 122, 132, 153, 155, 162–163, 168, 174, 185, 191–192; alcoholism 5, 8, 10, 15, 21, 23, 31, 59, 63, 145–146, 175; first marriage 4, 35, 39; marital difficulties 8, 9, 24, 46, 72, 90, 118–120, 131, 148–149, 180

Faulkner, James Murry "Jimmy" 11–12, 16–18, 32, 146, 156, 174, 182–188, 190–191
Faulkner, Jill 21, 24, 47, 58–59, 63, 70, 72, 77, 83, 85–87, 90, 108–110, 115, 118–119, 121, 123–132, 135, 150, 152, 162, 167–168, 172–175, 180, 184, 191–193
Faulkner, John Wesley Thompson III ("Johncy") 25, 52, 116–117, 122, 155, 184, 190–191
Faulkner, Lucille 110, 191
Faulkner, Murry Charles, Jr. ("Jack") 52, 137, 184–186, 188, 190
Faulkner, Murry Cuthbert II ("Chooky") 190–191
Faulkner, Nancy "Nan" 12, 182
Faulkner, Suzanne 137
Faulkner, William: *Absalom, Absalom!* 4–5, 8, 48, 52, 54–55, 62, 76, 79, 111, 133, 136, 169; *As I Lay Dying* 4, 44, 52, 76, 78, 133; "Barn Burning" 75; "The Bear" 78; *Collected Stories of William Faulkner* 115, 117, 131; *A Fable* 6, 9, 14, 35, 81, 102, 112–113, 133, 136, 146, 149, 150, 156, 158, 163, 168–173, 178–179; *Go Down, Moses* 75, 78; *A Green Bough* 58; *The Hamlet* 75, 77, 152; *Intruder in the Dust* 102, 104, 111–112, 124; *Intruder in the Dust* (film) 107, 110; *Knight's Gambit* 112; "A Letter to the North" 110; *Light in August* 4, 47, 50–52, 54, 76; *The Mansion* 75, 156; *The Marble Faun* 61; *Mosquitoes* 43, 185; *Pylon* 76, 122; "Red Leaves" 42; *The Reivers* 6, 12, 14–15, 76, 189, 190; *Requiem for a Nun* 9, 112, 132–134; *Sanctuary* 44, 45, 47, 51–52, 75–76, 104, 133; *Sartoris* 43, 52; "Sherwood Anderson: An Appreciation" 162; *Soldiers' Pay* 43; *The Sound and the Fury* 4, 41, 43, 52, 76, 94, 97, 98, 143, 174, 189; "That Evening Sun" 134; *These 13* 44; *The Town* 75, 152, 156; "Uncle Willy" 68; "Wash" 79, 133; *The Wild Palms* 7, 74–75, 146; *The Wishing-Tree* 77
Fielding, Bill 184
Fieldstone Sanitarium 106
Fitts, Elizabeth "Lis" 22
Fitts, William D., Jr. 21
Fitts, William "Bill" D. III 1, 21–25, 33
Fitzgerald, F. Scott 49, 189
Fitzhugh, Louise 91–92, 161
Fitzhugh, Mary Louise 161
Fitzhugh, Millsaps 161
Fleisher, Wilfrid 127–129
Flowers, Paul 187
Foote, Shelby 173–174, 185, 189, 190–191

Index

Ford, Ruth 9, 105, 112, 115, 133–134, 165
Frank, Waldo 160
Franklin, Cornell Sidney 35–36, 39–42, 61
Franklin, Malcolm 21, 41, 45. 47, 66, 124, 145, 147, 153, 171–172, 184, 193
Franklin, Victoria "Cho-Cho" 39–41, 45, 184
Frawley, William 55
Frazer, James George 36
Frost, Robert 187
Furthman, Jules 82–83

Gable, Clark 8, 51, 56, 63
Garbo, Greta 49
Gartly-Ramsay Hospital 1, 8, 20, 62, 66, 68, 70, 146, 148–149
Gathright-Reed Drug Store 87
Gibbons, Irene 55
Gilbert, Benjamin "Dr. Broadway" 158–159
Glasgow, Ellen 45
Goldman, Morton 52
Good Samaritan Hospital 8, 73, 84
Gordon, Caroline 104
Gray, Duncan, Jr. 191, 193
Gray, Paul 126
Greenfield Farm 116–117
Griffith, D.W. 55
Grove, Brandon 57, 118, 120, 162

Haas, Merle 105, 115, 124–126, 160
Haas, Robert "Bob" 76, 103, 105, 115, 124–126, 147, 160, 176
Hairston, Mamie Franklin 40
Hammett, Dashiell 56
Harkins, Bob 77
Hawks, Howard 8–9, 50–52, 54–55, 57, 60, 65, 71–73, 82, 84, 131, 172, 180
Healy, George 137
Hellström, Gustaf 127
Hemingway, Ernest 8, 51, 82, 84, 104–106, 112, 115, 136, 152, 165, 189
Hempstead, Dave 52
Henning, Donald G. 95
Hernández, Juana 8, 107–108
Holley, John Reed 13, 100, 192
Holley, Regina Moore 13, 100, 192
Hotel Monteleone 136–137
Houdini, Bess 55
Houdini, Harry 55
Housman, A.E. 61, 118
Houston, Elbert 190
Houston, Will 190
Howard, Edwin 189–192
Howe, Russell W. 111
Humphrey, William 99

James, Henry 186
Jamison, Willie 16
Jarman, Claude, Jr. 107, 108, 110
Jenkins, Mary 67
Johnson, Victoria "Vicki" Fielden 15, 21, 23, 24, 108–111, 119, 121, 134–135, 146, 149–150, 174, 180
Jonsson, Else 9, 15, 128, 130, 131, 133, 137, 138, 142, 143, 152, 161
Jonsson, Thorsten 128, 161

Keating, Bern 170–173
Keating, Franke 170–172
Keats, John 61
Keeley Institute 68–69
Kennedy, Jacqueline 186
Kennedy, John F. 186
Klopfer, Don 106, 115, 185
Knickerbocker Hotel 54–55, 57
Kriendler, Jack 106

Land of the Pharaohs 172
Laughlin, James 165
Lee, Robert E. 23, 111
Legion of Honor, Légion d'Honneur 131, 136, 177
Leonard Wright Sanatorium 1, 7, 8, 10, 16, 19, 23, 25, 62, 66, 120, 145, 182, 189
Lewis, Sinclair "Red" 45, 105, 116, 121
Linder, Felix 13, 77
Linscott, Robert "Bob" 6, 135, 153, 158, 163
Little, Ashford 102
Little, Minnie Ruth 103
Longfellow, Henry Wadsworth 6, 135
Lowry, Malcolm 142
Lucy, Autherine 110–111
Lyman, Guy 61, 136–137
Lyman, Helen 61, 136

Mademoiselle magazine 99–100
Malone, Roy 95
Malraux, André 141
Mann, Thomas 51
The Mansion 15, 108, 188–189
Marre, Albert 136, 141
Martin, Henriette 85
Massey, Linton R. 15
Mayer, Louis B. 60
McCarthy, Cormac 142
McCool, D.C. 66–68, 70
McEwen, Narcissus 63
McLarty, Chester 13, 66–67, 184
McQueen, Steve 14
Meeks, Elma 35
Melchionna, Robert 160
Mencken, H.L. 45–46

Index

Metro-Goldwyn-Mayer 49, 60
Michener, James A. 142
Millay, Edna St. Vincent 161
Minmagary 103, 115, 117, 120, 162
Monroe, Marilyn 55
Moore, Arvenia 99
Moore, Ethel 101
Moore, Nurse 182
Mosse, Eric P. 151–152
Moran, Mae 23
Morley, Thomas 165
Mullen, Curtis 121
Mullen, Faye 122
Mullen, Phillip "Moon" 121–122, 128, 177

National Book Award 131, 159
National Institute of Arts and Letters 14
New Weston Hotel 142, 152–153, 157
Nielsen, Mr. 82
Nobel Prize 2, 5, 9, 19, 105, 112, 116, 121–126, 128–133, 140, 142, 177, 181, 184, 186–187

O. Henry Memorial Award 75
Ober, Harold 6, 77, 110, 126, 146
O'Connor, Flannery 190
O'Hara, John 8, 56, 126, 142
The Old Country Club 1, 19, 29, 177, 181
Oldham, Dorothy 40, 185, 189
Oldham, Lemuel E. 35, 39–41, 43, 63, 100, 174
Oldham, Lida 35, 39–41, 43, 100, 174
Oldham, Ned "Little Major" 67
Oliver, Jack 63
One Fifth Avenue 178–179
O'Neill, Eugene 121
Orgill, Edmund 95
Orgill, Elizabeth 96
Orgill, Kenneth W., Jr. 94–97, 99–100
Orgill, Kenneth W. III 95
Orgill, Nancy Wilson 96–97
Österling, Anders 127

Parker, Dorothy 8, 46, 49, 56
Passos, John Dos 51, 187
Pasternak, Boris 112
Patton, Richard 189
Peabody Hotel 23, 119, 120, 173, 185
Pitts, ZaSu 56
Porter, Katherine Anne 142
Prall, Elizabeth 73
Presley, Elvis 55
"The Private World of William Faulkner" 176
Pulitzer Prize 156, 186

Rebner, Wolfgang 8, 59–60, 70–74, 132
Red Acres 15
Reed, William M. "Mac" 87–89, 171, 193
Richards, Sally 59
Rivers, Amelie 45
The Road to Glory 55–57
Rosenthal, Sylvia 83
Rostand, Edmond 178
Rowan Oak 3–4, 8, 13, 15, 34–36, 41–44, 47–49, 51, 54, 59, 62, 68, 77, 86–87, 90, 95, 100–101, 103–104, 107–109, 113–114, 120–123, 127, 131–132, 135, 138–139, 142, 147, 149–150, 153, 155–157, 159, 162–163, 167–173, 175–176, 180, 184–186, 188–189, 191–192
Rudd, Hughes 186–188, 191–192
Rukeyser, Muriel 165
Russell, Bertrand 112, 129

Salomon, Monique 133
Sardi, Vincent, Sr. 158
Sayre, Joel 56
Seay, Aubrey 186–187
Sheegog, Judith 36–37
Sheegog, Robert B. 35–38
Sherman, William 37
Shipp, Adolphus 1, 22, 25, 27–29, 33
Shipp, JoAnn 27
Smith, Harrison "Hal" 76, 105, 156–159, 164, 176
Snow, Charles 187
Southern Baptist Hospital 137
Stanley Rose's Bookshop 56–57
Stein, Jean 9, 180
Steinbeck, John 112
Stone, Araminta 77
Stone, Emily 15, 77
Stone, Irving 187
Stone, Phil 15, 39, 59, 61, 75–77, 87, 122–123, 129–130, 150, 176, 184, 191, 193
Stone, Philip Alston 77
Styron, William 185, 189, 191
Summers, Joseph 99
Summers, Paul 173, 184
Swinburne, Algernon Charles 61

Taylor, Elizabeth 85
Taylor, Peter 91–92
Thomas, Caitlin 165
Thomas, Dylan 8, 164–165
Thompson, Jacob 37
Thompson, Ralph 106
Thurber, Helen Muriel Wismer 8, 60
To Have and Have Not 82
Turner, William 35

Index

Wadsworth, W.L. 95
Wadsworth, Mrs. W.L. 95
Warner, Jack 79, 81, 84–85
Warner Brothers 78–79, 82–83, 105
Warren, Robert Penn 142
Wasson, Ben 39–40, 56, 63, 90, 118, 140, 169–173, 175, 185
Wayside Inn 6, 135–136
Wellman, Paul 85
Wells, Dean Faulkner 52–54, 77, 87, 109, 119, 149, 174
Welty, Eudora 14, 142, 168, 187
West, Nathanael 8, 56
Westhill Sanitarium 151–153
White, Dorothy Orgill 96
White, Hugh 140
White, Thomas 96
Whitfield, Mississippi State Hospital 61, 153
Wilder, Thornton 136
Wilkinson, Charles 170
Wilkinson, Mary 170
William Dean Howells Medal 116
Williams, Bob 107–108
Williams, Ethel 93
Williams, Joan: "The Morning and the Evening" 146, 156; *The Morning and the Evening* 189; *Old Powder Man* 93; *Pariah and Other Stories* 100; "Rain Later" 99–100; "Twenty Will Not Come Again" 162; *The Wintering* 99, 144, 158, 192
Williams, Maude 91–94, 99, 119
Williams, P.H. "Priestly" 91–93, 99
Williams, Sallie Murry 51, 102, 107–108, 174
Williams, Sydney Howard 93
Williams, Tennessee 136, 165
Wilson, Gilbert 96
Winchell, Walter 166–167
Wittenberg, Philip 165
Wolfe, Thomas 106
Wolff, Sally 182
Wortham, Earl 190
Wortis, Bernard S. 160
Wright, Ida 21
Wright, Leonard, Jr. 21–22
Wright, Leonard Davidson, Sr. 1, 16–22, 24–29, 32–33, 146, 182–183; see also Leonard Wright Sanatorium
Wright, Teresa 138

Yeats, William Butler 61
Yoknapatawpha County 4, 54, 79, 104, 133, 187
Young, Stark 73

Zanuck, Darryl 60

www.ingramcontent.com/pod-product-compliance
Lightning Source LLC
Chambersburg PA
CBHW032043300426
44117CB00009B/1167